f**P**

LAST DANCE
in HAVANA

The Final Days of Fidel and the Start of the New Cuban Revolution

Eugene Robinson

Free Press

New York   London   Toronto   Sydney

*f*P

FREE PRESS
A Division of Simon & Schuster, Inc.
1230 Avenue of the Americas
New York, NY 10020

FREE PRESS and colophon are trademarks of Simon & Schuster, Inc.

For information regarding special discounts for bulk purchases,
please contact Simon & Schuster Special Sales at 1-800-456-6798
or business@simonandschuster.com

Designed by Karolna Harris

Manufactured in the United States of America

10   9   8   7   6   5   4   3   2   1

Library of Congress Cataloging-in-Publication Data
Robinson, Eugene, 1954–
Last dance in Havana : the final days of Fidel and the start of the new Cuban
Revolution / Eugene Robinson.
p.   cm.
Includes index.
1. Cuba—Description and travel. 2. Popular music—Cuba—History and criticism.
3. Cuba—Social life and customs. 4. Cuba—Social conditions—1959–
5. Communism—Cuba—History. 6. Robinson, Eugene, 1954– I. Title.
F1765.3.R63 2004
917.291—dc22
2004046957
ISBN 0-7432-4622-5

The photographs in this book are by Dudley M. Brooks
and are reproduced by permission.

For my sons, Aaron and Lowell,
with love and pride.

CONTENTS

INTRODUCTION: DRUM ROLL

In 1997, a Cuban musical phenomenon called Buena Vista Social Club was born. The album was the unlikeliest of hits—a bunch of aging, forgotten crooners singing songs few had ever heard of in a language most Americans don't even understand. Despite all that, it was wildly successful. The *music* was the thing. It was music that compelled you to move, compelled you to dance. Gently sexual and savory-sweet, the album's sounds and singers came from Cuba's musical golden age—a time before revolution, before communism, before the missile crisis and the Mariel boat lift and the Helms-Burton Act. A time even before anyone had ever heard of a tall, ambitious, socially awkward rich kid from the sticks named Fidel Castro.

Today in Cuba, those sweet Buena Vista songs are played around the clock in tourist bars, expensive restaurants, and five-star hotel lobbies, but hardly anywhere else. The rest of Cuba dances to more urgent sounds.

After forty-four years Fidel is still in firm control of Cuba. He faces no serious challenge; the dissident movement is tiny, largely ineffectual, and was recently shown to be riddled with government spies. More than a decade after the Soviet bloc collapsed and international Marxism died, Cuba remains a defiantly communist state; long after nominally communist China embraced the free market, Cuba still does not allow its citizens to buy and sell property, establish private companies, or even purchase a car for private use without permission. It would be easy to conclude that amid a swirling, transforming world, nothing much is happening in Cuba.

But that easy conclusion is wrong. The sudden cutoff of lavish Soviet subsidies created massive economic and social dislocation, plunging the average Cuban citizen into poverty—cultured, well-educated poverty with good health care, to be sure, but poverty nonetheless. So that his people might eat, Fidel was forced to allow limited exercises in free enterprise. He had to let two highly suspect influences—foreign tourism and remittances from Cuban exiles—become the twin pillars of the economy. In what must have been a galling move, he had to legalize the holding and spending of U.S. dollars, and then watch as the currency of his imperialist enemy captured ground from his own battered peso. He turned a blind eye as Cubans invented their own ways to get by. When asked about the thousands of young women who had flocked to the cities to tease love and money out of visiting Spaniards and Italians, he remarked that at least they would be the healthiest and best-educated prostitutes in the world.

All this happened, and also something else: Fidel got old.

When he passed seventy-five, the unthinkable suddenly became the inevitable. Someday, not long from now, there will be no Fidel. Most Cubans have known no other leader, no other system. His brother Raúl, the designated successor, is just five years younger and has none of Fidel's magnetism, cleverness, or eloquence. What on earth will happen then?

Cubans worry about the future. Meanwhile, they do the best they can, scraping and scrambling to get through the day, through the month.

And whenever they can, they go out and dance.

Two generalizations about the Buena Vista era hold true today: Cuba is a land of music, a thick stew of African and European elements that is astoundingly rich and influential to have come from such a tiny island. And Cuban music, even more than American music or Brazilian music or any of the other comparable strains, is dance music. Cubans move through their complicated lives the way they move on the dance floor, dashing and darting and spinning on a dime, seducing joy and fulfillment and next week's supply of food out of a broken system. Then at night they take to the real dance floors and invent new steps.

Today's dance-floor sounds are harder-edged: a furious brand of salsa called *timba,* a brassy update of the traditional Cuban *son,* a still-nascent native brand of hip-hop whose lyrics take up topics like racism and police harassment, subjects that couldn't have been addressed from a stage a decade ago.

There's a national newscast on Cuban television every night at eight, but it's slow and stilted, and everyone knows it's far from complete. The *music* of Cuba is the real news. Those who make the music are the real journalists, analysts, social commentators. To understand what's happening in Cuba, you have to meet the musicians and listen to their fabulous music.

Then you have to go out and dance.

LAST DANCE
in HAVANA

1. "THESE PEOPLE DANCE"

Like most nights in Havana, this one started late. First came a long cab ride across the city, not in one of those huge, chrome-dipped Chryslers from before the Triumph of the Revolution, but in a tiny red Kia that was still under warranty. The backseat was somebody's idea of a joke. I had to sit up front, beside the driver, and even then my knees dented the dashboard and my head brushed the roof. Every pothole was pain.

It was hot—it's always hot in Cuba in the spring—but there was a godsend breeze that cut the humidity, or at least moved it around, drawing a lacy scrim of cirrus over the moon and stars. We sped past gloomy courtyard tenements, glimpsed through narrow doorways that were like the mouths of caves; past the faded high-rise that had been the brand-new Havana Hilton before Fidel Castro rode into town and christened it the Habana Libre, the "Free Havana"; past midcentury cabarets and cinemas with neon signs in jewellike colors, script written in rubies and emeralds. We skirted the Colón cemetery, Havana's walled necropolis, with its rococo crypts and tombs where the Triumph of the Revolution had never been announced and the rich were eternally rich. We crossed the little Almendares River, high above its narrow gorge, and careened into the genteel, shabby sprawl of a desirable neighborhood called Buenavista, whose state of decline said a lot about the nature of desire in contemporary Cuba. It was a fast trip down empty boulevards—few Cubans have the government's permission to own cars, much less the money to buy them, and gasoline is too expensive to burn on short trips around town. Even at night people wait for the bus, and when the bus doesn't come they try to thumb rides, and when all else fails they give up and walk, half-seen figures making their way along sidewalks and medians. The night is dark in Havana, much darker than first-world night. Streetlights are anemic and few, homes sparingly lit and often shuttered. Nobody seems to sleep so there are always focal points that blaze with light and motion, but to move from one to another is to speed through a ghostly void, an emptiness peopled by shadows.

"We're going to the Tropical," the driver said as we crossed the bridge.

"Correct."

"Not the Tropicana."

"Correct."

"The Tropi-*cal*, right?"

"That's right."

He looked to be in his fifties, white enough to be called *blanco*, gray-haired, trim, no-nonsense in the way he worked. Up north in *la Yuma*, as Cubans call the United States—the reference is from *3:10 to Yuma*, a 1957 Glenn Ford Western, and no one in Cuba can explain why—he might have been a midlevel insurance executive in a suburban office park. These would be his peak earning years at Wonderful Life, the time to really sock it away for the condo in Florida he had his eye on, a lovely unit off the eighth fairway in a non-sea-view development with a Seinfeldian name like Del Boca Vista. Instead he was driving halfway across Havana in the middle of the night for six or seven bucks, with practically no hope of a return fare.

If I'd said "Tropi-*cana*," that would have been a different story. The Tropicana was one of the most famous nightclubs in the world, the crystal Xanadu where perfect cinnamon showgirls paraded down the aisles wearing chandeliers on their heads and very little anywhere else, where Meyer Lansky and Santo Trafficante and other mobsters of renown had once commandeered the very best tables, and where tour buses now nightly deposited loads of earnest Canadians and randy Italians prepared to pay the seventy-dollar cover charge and sip *mojito* after overpriced *mojito* without complaint. There were always foreigners with pockets full of dollars coming and going from the Tropicana. My driver wouldn't have had to hang around long to find some work. But I was going to the Tropical, which was mostly patronized by Cubans—black Cubans, at that—and Cubans weren't supposed to take cabs like this one, which were reserved for tourists. *Turi-taxis,* they called them. He'd end up going all the way back downtown empty.

The driver didn't complain, though, because in turn-of-the-century Cuba his was a success story. He probably lived in a nice house, supported his wife's parents, and had enough left over to keep a mistress or two. To an average José, a run-of-the-mill patriotic worker trying to support his family on a state salary in pesos, the six or seven dollars I'd pay for this ride was half a month's pay. Even after settling up with the cab company for use of the car and the gas he burned, he could still claim membership in the elite class of this classless society: the dollar class.

We pulled into a smallish parking lot where a few dozen Cubans were lined up at a ticket booth. Behind the booth was a high wall, and there was just enough light to see that it was painted a violent pink.

"The Tropical," the driver said.

The cover was ten dollars. I bought my ticket, gave it to the man at the gate, and was swept with the crowd down a walkway, emerging into the concrete splendor of what might just be the best dance hall in the world.

"Hall" isn't quite right because the Tropical is open-air, fully exposed to the heavens. To my left was an array of tables, and behind the tables a long bar. Ahead there was a railing—I had entered on the upper level, I now realized, and was on a balcony—and a set of stairs on the right that led down. That was where the crowd went, so I followed. At the bottom it was clear just how vast the place was, maybe a third the size of a football field. On the left and right were rows of tables, and at the far end a big stage, trimmed in pink, bearing the legend Salón Rosado Beny Moré—the Beny Moré Pink Room. In the middle of the space was the biggest dance floor I had ever seen.

The Tropical had been the place black Cubans went for relaxation and release back in the day, before the Triumph of the Revolution, when the Tropicana, the Montmartre, and the Sans Souci had special sections reserved for blacks—the stage and the kitchen. Of course, President Fulgencio Batista and a few other brown-skinned officials of the republic were most welcome, but Batista preferred to curl up in his official residence or his mansion in Florida and spend the evening counting his money. Great black musicians like Chano Pozo, Israel "Cachao" López, Celia Cruz, and even Beny Moré—Beny Moré, the genius of rhythm, the Cuban equivalent of Charlie Parker and Frank Sinatra and Chuck Berry, and Elvis Presley too, all rolled into one—would finish their sets at the fancy clubs and then come to the Tropical and jam until dawn. The beer was ice cold and the atmosphere as hot and funky as a Mississippi juke joint. Rare was the night back then without at least one knife fight, at least one other-woman slapdown with intent to kill, and at least a handful of patrons deposited in a corner to sleep it off. Since Castro and his moralizing rebels arrived, nights at the Tropical offered less drama. But there was still something raffish and wonderful about the place, still an electric charge of possibility in the air.

The tables were almost all full, and this was a different crowd than at the other music halls around Havana, where sometimes there were more tourists than locals. The Tropical crowd was mostly black and practically all Cuban. Recorded music was playing over the sound system, recent hits by the great Cuban salsa bands. I sipped beer and watched the two couples at the table across the dance floor from me. One of the men, overweight and dressed in a light-green polo shirt and faded jeans, was already quite drunk and kept getting up to dance alone in a wobbly, meandering little three-step. He kept perfect time, but always a consistent fraction of a second behind the beat. Every once in a while he would lean so far off the vertical that I was sure he would fall, but he always caught himself, barely, as if his internal gyroscope had just enough spin left to snap him upright one last time. At that point his wife would roll her eyes, get up, dance with him for a moment, and then lead him back to the table, where he would pour another drink from a fast-dwindling bottle of three-year-old Havana Club rum.

The music stopped, the lights went down, and an announcer with the deep voice, toothy smile, and perfect hair of a game-show host came out to launch the preliminaries.

First, believe it or not, was a fashion show. After forty years of socialism, economic embargo, and principled rejection of bourgeois comforts, nobody should go to Cuba for the fashion. The clothes on display at the Tropical looked unexceptional and the fabrics were cheap, clinging where they should have draped and draping where they should have clung. Women in the audience paid rapt attention, though, and clapped warmly at the end, proving that all fashion is local.

Next came a comic who spoke so fast and used so much slang that I missed every single one of his punch lines. I did make out that part of his act was a long nostalgic bit about the old days, when Cuba was a mighty weapon in the Cold War and Havana was full of clumsy hayseed Russian sailors. The crowd found this material hilarious, proving that all humor is local too.

Finally the announcer came back to bring on the headline act: Bamboleo, one of the hottest salsa *orquestas* in Havana. The lights dimmed. The musicians came out, a dozen shadow-men taking their stations, quietly preparing for battle. There was a pause, and then a male voice said, *"Un', dos, un', dos, tres . . ."*

Kaboom.

The horns played a fanfare, the bass answered with a bluesy lick, the four percussionists set up a mighty clatter. Four singers bounded onstage, two men and two women. For a moment I don't think I was able to breathe.

The two female singers were the focus of the show and the cause of my asphyxia. Both were lithe and brown skinned, both were surpassingly beautiful, and both had their hair cut very short, mannishly short, which is a rare look in Cuba. They weren't quite a matched set—one, whom I later learned was named Vannia, was tall and leggy; the other, Yordamis, was petite and pixieish. Vannia had taken the further step of straightening her hair and dyeing it a rich and shocking blond, while Yordamis kept hers in a short dark afro, but they wore identical slinky silver gowns that sparkled in the stage lights, and they moved in perfect tandem. They seemed unreal, idealized, as if they were avatars or sirens instead of real women. They were transfixing.

I looked around and realized that the Tropical, in that instant, had exploded in sound and movement. The band was playing with power, filling the open sky with music so loud it made ripples in a glass of beer at twenty-five paces. The crowd screamed as if for life itself. Scores of young people had rushed the stage and were already standing four deep, moving to the music, singing along with the tune. And the endless dance floor had magically filled, giving itself over to some powerful enchantment.

Enchantment, witchcraft, magic, Santería—these were the only possible explanations for what I was witnessing. Across the extent of this huge space, filling it to capacity and beyond, couples were dancing. But "dancing" does not begin to tell what they were doing. They were whipping, they were twirling. They were circling, diving beneath locked arms, embracing. They were bumping, grinding, releasing, spinning, caressing, all but making love. They were doing all these things in a dense crowd, somehow coordinating their moves so that whenever a man swung his partner toward a given point on the floor, the man or woman in the neighboring couple who was occupying that space somehow moved out of the way just in time, gracefully shifting into another space that a millisecond earlier had likewise been magically vacated. At first it looked to me as if some higher intelligence were guiding the movements of each of these hundreds of people. But then, as I continued to watch, a new metaphor took over: This was an exercise in massively parallel computation, many minds each solving its own bit of an otherwise unsolvable problem. No one genius could have attended to so many vital details so perfectly. This group movement was decentralized but coordinated, almost like flocking or schooling but not at all instinctive, not in the least unconscious. It was brilliantly human and clever and aware, both spontaneous and purposeful, and it was one of the most stirring and beautiful sights I have ever seen.

Individual couples were no less amazing. All good dance partners look as if they're reading each other's minds, but this was speed reading. These people were channeling Evelyn Wood. A man would spin his partner, and while she was spinning he would circle to the left or the right, and when she came out of the spin she'd know just where he was, know that he had gone left and not right, or right and not left. And then without pause he'd spin her the other way, only this time he wouldn't move at all, but she'd anticipate that too and know where to find him. Then they'd cross hands and start circling each other, at the same time rotating so that sometimes they faced the same direction and other times in opposite directions, passing their locked arms above their heads and across their shoulders and behind their backs, managing to go around and around, back and forth, always to the beat, without ever breaking their gentle grasp. They'd separate, riff for a while, then rejoin. They'd hear a particular rhythm from one of the drummers and it would suggest an appropriate dance step, and they'd ease into it simultaneously, seamlessly, before flowing on to the next. This was not just about moving to the beat, or even about looking graceful in motion. Event followed event followed event in this dancing. Each couple was writing its own private narrative, a tropical saga told in a language that an outsider like me could appreciate, even begin to understand, but never really learn to speak.

They say that great salsa dancers are made, not born. Feeling the rhythm is hardly even a beginning; there is an enormous amount of technique to learn, a huge vocabulary of moves and a complicated syntax for stringing them together. Application counts more than talent. But as with gymnastics or tennis, you have to start young. It was obvious that anyone who hadn't learned this language from birth could drag his bones across dance floors night after night until the end of time and never learn to do it like the crowd at the Tropical.

Bamboleo would have blown the roof off the joint, if it had had one. The band was tight and disciplined, instantly responsive to nods and gestures from the keyboard player, a stocky chestnut-skinned man wearing red pants, a red vest over a white T-shirt, and a bright red do-rag on his head. These clearly were fabulous musicians, with the kind of technique that comes from years of scales and finger exercises. But this show was as much about dance as music. Vannia and Yordamis had a signature move, a kind of exaggerated, undulating, dirty-dancing grind that made men desire, women aspire, and chiropractors see dollar signs. Most of the youngsters in the crowd could do it too, and there were moments that night when the Tropical was like a waving field of sea grass, washed by a powerful current that pulsed to a three-two Latin beat.

The energy level actually rose as the morning rolled on. When Vannia sang the opening bars of Bamboleo's biggest hit, a hit-the-road-Jack revenge anthem called "Ya No Hace Falta" ("No Longer Needed"), the kids up near the stage, hundreds of them by now, crowded in so tightly that someone could have been trampled. They knew every word of the song, and they caterwauled along so loudly that Vannia finally gave up and held the mike out over their heads, giving them their glory.

The show ended at half past three.

After the finale, as patrons filed out and waiters collected empties, the members of the band began to assemble at a big table in the back. They looked happy and pumped, chattering about the show as they mopped their faces with towels and guzzled bottles of water. I walked over, introduced myself, and got a phone number from the bandleader, whose name was Lázaro Valdés and whom the others called "Lazarito." There was no point in trying to talk to him tonight, after a show that must have left him and the band completely drained, so I went out to the parking lot, flagged down a cab, and took the long, dark ride back to the hotel.

The next morning, looking over my fragmentary notes, I found a page where I had written just three words:

"These people dance."

Yes, they do. They always did.

Cuba has spent the past hundred years whipping, twirling, spinning, swinging wildly between extremes. It began the twentieth century as an American protectorate, for all intents and purposes an American colony, and ended it as one of the few nations in the world with which the U.S. State Department refuses to have full diplomatic relations. It spent decades under the sway of an authoritarian leader as devoted to private enterprise as any leader could be, and then decades under the sway of an authoritarian leader who so abhors private enterprise that to this day he does not allow Cubans to incorporate a business, purchase a car without permission, or even buy and sell real estate. It went from being one of the richest countries in Latin America to one of the most lacking in all kinds of material goods, from electronics to underwear; from having one of the widest chasms between rich and poor in the region to having no gap at all; from an agrarian society with a largely ignorant peasantry to an urbanized nation acclaimed as one of the better-educated nations on Earth. It saw an effective takeover by the Italian mob, followed by a literal takeover by the Marxist mob; it saw, amid its timeless fields of tobacco and sugarcane, the construction of state-of-the-art missile batteries that brought the world to the brink of a nuclear holocaust. It went from being a playground of sun, sin, and sex for American tourists to a forbidden zone that Americans cannot legally visit—but that now hosts many thousands of Europeans, Canadians, and Mexicans each year, most of whom come for the sun, the sin, or the sex.

Through all these bipolar lurches, two things have been constant: music and dance. From decade to decade, from decadence to communism to communist decadence, Cuba has been a land of music and Cubans have danced as if their lives depended on it. Now, at the dawn of a bleak new century, the music is faster and harder-edged, and the dancing more frenetic and unceasing. Standing still is no option at all, not during the day, when Cubans scramble madly to assemble the bare necessities of life, not at night, when cold beer and incandescent rhythms bring joyous, blessed relief.

Today all of Cuba dances to live; today all of Cuba lives to dance.

* * *

The Hotel Nacional is a grand old pile that sticks out on the low-rise Havana skyline, a huge Italianate palace built the way one of Florida's robber barons would have built it. The approach is down an allée of towering royal palms toward a structure that looks stolid yet also whimsical, with useless balustrades and twin Florentine bell towers that house no bells. The lobby is half a city block long, appointed with handmade tiles and a grove's worth of *caoba*, or Cuban mahogany. The huge swimming pool once was ringed by private *cabañas* where big-time mobsters spent long afternoons cheating each other at poker while their bored, beautiful molls lazed in the sun and did their nails. That was in the '40s and '50s, when the Mafia was one of the big players in Havana, along with the Catholic Church, the sugar aristocracy, the U.S. embassy, and the clever, corrupt strongman Fulgencio Batista. The mob felt comfortable enough in Havana to choose the Nacional to stage one of its bloody-minded summits, the one depicted in the movie *The Godfather, Part II*. The assembled Bosses of All Bosses met on the mezzanine, with its sumptuous meeting rooms and its glorious views of the Florida Strait. Even today, in the kitchens and storerooms of the Nacional, there are still a few employees who remember those heady days, or claim to.

One magical January evening in 1956, a lithe, young Eartha Kitt slinked and purred her way across the cabaret stage at the Nacional. Before her was a packed house that included the cream of Havana society, a smattering of international jet-setters, hordes of American tourists on holiday, a few professional and many nonprofessional gamblers, rich men with mistresses, rich women with gigolos, plainclothes cops, a government spy or two, and a discreet and well-behaved handful of the century's leading criminals.

Kitt was a kitten then, not yet the lioness she would become. But she already knew how to use her claws. She wore a strapless gold lamé dress that somehow stayed put, at least above the waist. Below, there were thigh-high slits up the sides that fell open with each step, revealing her long legs and the five-inch mules on which she managed to dance and prance with feline grace. She had the confidence of young fame, and it was justified; *tout* Havana, by then used to seeing stars of the first magnitude, was enthralled. Before she even sang a note she had them in her palm, in her little paw, and was toying with them.

It was a special night: the opening of Wilbur Clark's International Casino, just off the Nacional's soaring lobby. This was meant to be an event of significance not only in Cuba but also in the United States, which would supply most of the casino's paying customers, so the owners—the real owners, who chose not to have their names on any paperwork—had arranged a junket. They flew more than fifty journalists down to Havana, including editors from the Florida papers, columnists from all over the East Coast, wire-service hacks, and assorted others who had managed to acquire a press card and an appreciation for the sporting life. Also scattered at tables across the big, elegant room were travel agents and airline company officials, also traveling at the owners' expense. The owners had arranged for these guests to be accompanied by beautiful Cuban "hostesses" who seemed in endless supply. If a guy wasn't hitting it off with tall-and-dark, well then, short-and-fair would materialize before he could say *"Rum-and-Coke!"*

Seated at the head table that night were the actress Terry Moore, Howard Hughes's longtime paramour, and her mother from Florida; a smattering of wealthy locals; a couple of American expatriate stalwarts, for respectability's sake; and of course Mr. Wilbur Clark himself, the premier front man of his time, accompanied by his lovely wife.

Wilbur Clark must have been sent by central casting. He had an open Midwestern face, crowned by a thinning silver pompadour. Usually he wore casual clothes, light-colored knit shirts and light-weight Sansabelt slacks, but tonight, naturally, he was elegant in a tux. He looked and sounded like an honest man, but one who was also gloriously ambitious—the very picture of an American arche-type, the heartland entrepreneur whose life was dedicated to hitting it bigger than anyone had ever hit it before. What could be more American than ambition? There was nothing intimidating about Wilbur Clark, nothing alien or occult. People who met him almost always concluded that with a little luck, they too could have had his great success. For years he had managed to convince the Nevada gaming authorities that he, and not certain criminal elements from Cleveland, held the controlling interest in the famed Desert Inn casino in Las Vegas. He was so good at this charade that sometimes he even convinced himself.

He was at the table of honor for the opening of "his" new casino, which he had painstakingly planned and built after long and careful study of Havana's potential as a gambling center. At least that's what he told the newspapers. The truth was that he had set foot in Havana for the first time just a couple of weeks earlier, didn't know a single local, didn't speak a *como-está-usted*'s worth of Spanish, and was set to blow town in a couple of days with no plans to return. His name was on every available surface, down to the gambling chips and the dice—"Wilbur Clark's—Havana." But the real proprietor of the new casino in the Nacional—nowhere in evi-dence, not at the head table or any other table, perhaps watching from behind some curtain—was a much less gregarious and much more dangerous man named Meyer Lansky.

Who *must* have been watching from somewhere at the fringes of the room, out of sight. Meyer Lansky, one of the smartest mob-sters of the century, was known for his steely self-control. But how could he have resisted witnessing the culmination of all his labors? This casino, and the ones that would soon follow, represented per-sonal and professional vindication, proof that he had bet the right horse—that Havana could be, and soon would be, much bigger and better than Vegas, and much more profitable for Lansky and his Sicilian colleagues. It was so obvious: Who, in their right mind, would go out to the middle of the hot, stinking desert to gamble in Nevada, when they could come here, to beautiful Havana? To warm sea breezes and caramel-skinned beauties? To horses, jai alai, and hot jungle-bunny music, less than an hour's flight from Miami?

Lansky must have been somewhere watching, if only because he took care with his investments and had laid out a small fortune for the services of the famous Eartha Kitt. That was one expensive little dame. But was she ever paying off!

After giving the room a big tease, she cued the band and swung into her first number, and the place went crazy. It was one of her signature songs, the one some radio stations back in the States wouldn't even play. They thought it was a little racy.

I wanna be evil, she sang.
I wanna spit tacks,
I wanna be evil
And cheat at jacks . . .

It went on like that, but you could hardly hear her for the cheering. She was mahvelous, outré, larger than life, over the top, just like the whole evening. It was, in fact, the most glamorous evening Havana had ever seen, not just for the delights it offered but those it promised.

The music that night was sweet and savory. Lansky's managers had hired the best Cuban musicians money could buy, a combo as hot as any band Eartha Kitt would ever front. They gave a Latin twist to the music, spicing it with that three-two rhythm that seems to travel direct and unmediated from the bandstand to the hips, causing them to sway.

Of course, there was dancing.

Why not dance the night away? Havana had become the glamorous playground of the Western hemisphere. Lansky must have beamed at his own genius. Maybe, behind the curtain, he even abandoned his reserve and cut the rug a bit. Yeah, baby, things were just heating up. . . .

But it soon became evident that Lansky, famous for his foresight in matters criminal and pecuniary, hadn't paid nearly enough attention to those bearded schoolboys and barefoot peasants up in the hills with their rifles and their dog-eared books of Marxist philosophy. After being booted out of the country by the victorious Fidel Castro, he explained his failure with one of history's more elegant shrugs: "I crapped out."

The Hotel Nacional crapped out too. After the Triumph of the Revolution, the hotel was used as a guesthouse for foreign dignitaries—socialist heads of state, honored Soviet advisers, Black Panthers, and other sons and daughters of revolution who had fled the land of imperialist aggression, often by way of hijacked aircraft. Later, after further decline, the hotel became one of the prizes in the government's incentive system for patriotic workers: Help spur your unit to harvest more sugarcane or produce more asphalt and win a two-week stay, all expenses paid. It was also one of the hotels where newly married couples were given rooms to enjoy their honeymoons, courtesy of the state.

But when tourism became the new national economic strategy, the Nacional was too much of a potential asset to ignore. The hotel was closed and given a superficial renovation, and then another superficial renovation, the final result being to restore its splendor and glory, but only to a depth of about one inch. The rooms look worthy of the hotel's five-star designation, but the plumbing always delivers too much water or too little, the windows don't seal when they close, the phones are balky, the equipment in the "health club" is wobbly, the pattern on the restaurant china has begun to fade. At times these lapses only reinforce the hotel's stately grandeur, and at times they are nothing more than annoying lapses. Like the rest of Cuba's best hotels, the Nacional is reserved exclusively for foreigners. A patriotic worker can still go there for a good meal, but it will cost him a month's pay. The food is mediocre, the service uneven, the elevators antique and distressingly hesitant, and all in all I considered it a fabulous place to stay.

The Nacional sits on a rocky little bluff overlooking the Malecón, Havana's seafront esplanade, and my window happened to overlook a huge empty plaza called the Piragua. And so, one night, I got a jolt at bedtime when I heard a blast of loud music.

The government had scheduled a free concert on the Piragua, and four of Cuba's top bands would perform. The great Herbie Hancock, in town for a jazz festival, was expected to drop by. Downstairs, I fetched myself a *mojito*—a Cuban mint julep, with rum instead of bourbon and a special kind of mint—and found a spot on the well-tended hotel grounds where I could watch and listen. I was looking down from behind the stage, and I could see the musicians, VIPs, and hangers-on all milling around in their roped-off corral.

The Piragua was packed, the music was incredible, Hancock sat in on a couple of tunes, everybody danced, and the concert ended, yes, after three. But what I remember from that evening is not the electricity generated by some of Cuba's finest *orquestas,* or even the spirit of a crowd that numbered in the thousands, but the dancing of one couple.

They were backstage, and they weren't really a couple at all. The woman was middle-aged, somewhere around fifty, and caramel skinned—in the rich and complicated Cuban lexicon for race and skin color, she would have been called a *jaba*. She was rail-thin, with black hair that she wore in a flip. She arrived with a corpulent man, at least in his sixties, who looked unwell. He moved slowly to a chair right behind the stage, sat down heavily, and didn't move the rest of the evening. The woman, by contrast, was pure energy. She sat on the man's lap, but every few minutes she would get up to move to the music. No matter which band was playing, whenever she heard a song she liked she was compelled to jump up and dance. Both she and the fat man seemed to be having a great time. Everyone at the Piragua seemed to be having a great time.

The protean salsa band Los Van Van was the closing act, which was as it should be. If you were to combine the Beatles, the Rolling Stones, and Bruce Springsteen and the E Street Band, you'd have an idea of what Los Van Van have meant to Cuba over the past thirty years. When they started playing, the woman I had noticed, whom I now thought of as the Dancing Woman, could no longer even pretend to control herself. She jumped off the fat man's lap and started dancing in earnest, not just moving her feet in time to the music but *dancing*, shimmying, shaking, and spinning. Every once in a while she threw her head back and laughed with spontaneous joy. The fat man didn't budge but he did bob his head in time to the music, and he watched with apparent pleasure as the Dancing Woman went through her moves.

Then a young guy walked by—much younger than she, probably no older than thirty. He was of medium height and very dark skinned, and he was cooler than ice, with a shaved head, dark sunglasses (it was nearly two in the morning), and a single gold hoop earring. He might have been a musician with another group, or maybe just a member of somebody's posse. At any rate, he was walking past when he saw the Dancing Woman and had to stop.

I could tell from their body language that they didn't know each other, but without a word they started dancing, this supercool young man and this woman who might have been old enough to be his mother.

She wasn't young but, boy, could she dance—and boy, could he dance too. The Dancing Woman and the Dancing Man knew the whole vocabulary and had gotten A's in grammar. They also supplied context for the narrative they were composing: this was her show. The Dancing Man could spin and twirl and bump and grind, all right, but he held his own moves in check and instead partnered the Dancing Woman as if this were classical ballet on amphetamines. He let her lead, let her decide when the spinning phases would begin and end, when to mambo and when to *guaguancó*, when to separate and when to rejoin, when to circle to the right and when left. He even followed her as she invented a step, a kind of head-shaking double-time shuffle that went perfectly with a particular song from the Van Van oeuvre. He let her teach him.

I have no idea who the Dancing Woman was. She could have been somebody's mother, she could have been a bureaucrat in the Ministry of Culture, she could have been a chambermaid at the Nacional. All I know is that for one night only, she was a queen. In socialist Cuba, where "citizen" is a correct form of address, she was a true and noble queen.

They danced for three or four long songs, a little more than half an hour, and I couldn't take my eyes off them. He began to flag before she did. When the Dancing Man finally decided it was time to move on to wherever he had been going in the first place, he stood back, blew a kiss, and applauded the Dancing Woman. He kept applauding until, smiling triumphantly like the prima ballerina that she was, she rewarded him with a bow.

These people dance.

* * *

In earlier trips I had found Cuba absorbing but elusive, and contradictory to the point of madness. It was a foreign language for which I had no dictionary, like the narrative form of dance I'd seen at the Tropical.

Cuba looked like a third-world country, mostly, but Cubans weren't third-world people by miles. They were educated, sharp tongued, worldly, a bit arrogant, as quick to expound and lecture as a freshly minted PhD on his first teaching job. They didn't walk so much as strut, with a chest-first swagger that other Latin Americans found worthy of burlesque. To meet them you'd think they might be a people that once had ruled a great empire, but for much of their history they hadn't even ruled their own little alligator-shaped island.

There was less litter alongside Cuban roads than you'd find in Singapore, unless you counted the cigarette butts, since everyone smoked. The definition of a nonsmoker was someone who didn't light up between courses of a meal. If your smoking caused you to suddenly collapse on the street from a heart attack, however, there was probably no better place on Earth to be stricken, since it was likely that there were two or three doctors within sight. Cuba had such a surplus of doctors that it routinely sent them away at government expense to minister to the wretched of poorer countries halfway around the world, just to give the medical professionals something to do. The doctors were well trained and dedicated, and if they couldn't save you from your smoking-induced heart attack it was only because there was no medicine. Cuba had mastered state-of-the-art biotechnology, had developed an innovative surgical treatment for Parkinson's disease that drew patients to Havana from around the world, but somehow managed to suffer a chronic shortage of basic medicines. First dibs went to the "international" pharmacies that catered to foreigners. One of the nicest gifts you could bestow on a Cuban family was a big bottle of Tylenol.

There were no street kids in Havana. The only children you saw out and about during school hours were being escorted on field trips, dressed in their neat school uniforms, white shirts and maroon shorts or jumpers for the little kids, white shirts and gold pants or skirts for the teens. One afternoon in Old Havana I watched as perfect strangers yelled at a school-age boy for not being in the classroom where he belonged. After school, though, the streets were full of young people. They would play outside as long as they were allowed to, because their homes were scandalously cramped and dilapidated. Buildings that would have been condemned and knocked down in Peru or Bolivia, to name two genuine third-world countries, were jam-packed and teeming with life.

That was all just background, though. More confusing still was the foreground, the moment in Cuba. President and Commander-in-Chief Fidel Castro Ruz, the great mechanic who somehow willed this amazing, inefficient, Rube Goldberg machine to function, was nearly eighty years old, and any reading of the actuarial tables would tell you that he was in his twilight. But who, or what, would be arriving on the dawn? And would this stranger be carrying a beacon or a sword? A torch or a machete?

The future could be chalked up as unknowable, but the present was hardly less obscure. How did these people live, right now? Communists in a capitalist universe, salaried employees of the workers' state at fifteen or twenty or twenty-five dollars a month, curators of a grand al fresco museum of architecture and automotive design, scholars of a broken system, engineers of a fully functioning society—how did they do it? How long could they keep the contraption running? How did they make it through the day?

And how on earth, at the end of the day, did they have the energy to dance?

The answer is that four decades after what all good patriots call "the Triumph of the Revolution," life in Cuba is best understood not as tragedy or comedy or farce, not as an exercise in *marxismo* or *fidelismo* or even geopolitical *machismo,* but simply as a dance. It's all those other things too, but nobody has time to worry about any of that. Everyone is too busy dancing.

The thing is, though, that even while they dance as fast as they can, Cubans know that soon the tune will change. Every Cuban knows it, every Cuban can *feel* it. The master of ceremonies is in his late seventies; the musicians on the bandstand are old and exhausted; the sound system is failing; someone in the wings is flashing the lights on and off, the way chaperones at the senior prom do to announce that this dance, boys and girls, will be the last. And that just begs the question, one that frightens even Cubans who eagerly look forward to the end of the song: What comes next? In a nation capable of the most violent swings of mood, what on earth comes next?

I had always thought that the key to understanding Cuba was one towering, complicated, stubborn old man, Fidel Castro, maker of revolution, torturer of American presidents, icon of the Left, target of exploding cigars, genius, dinosaur, rock star. The single indomitable force that animated Cuba for better or worse, said the conventional wisdom, was Fidel.

So I went in search of him and his country. In the end, the conventional wisdom turned out to be right: Cuba is Fidel, Fidel is

Cuba. The only thing the conventionally wise hadn't told me, perhaps because they didn't know it themselves, was that just like his eleven million compatriots, Fidel spent his days dancing as hard and fast as he could, spinning and twirling to make it through the next day or month or year, sometimes even through the next hour.

Cuba equals dance. Dance equals movement to music. To understand Cuba, you have to understand not only its indispensible Maximum Leader, but also the music—the glorious, indomitable music—that makes the island move.

2. *"LA VIDA ES UN CARNAVAL!"*

Landing after dark at the lugubrious José Martí International Airport is a spooky introduction to the hemisphere's last remaining one-party state. On the plane from Cancún one particular evening, arriving via the most popular third-country outlaw route for Americans who flout the U.S. laws that keep them from Fidel Castro's forbidden island, there was a certain jumpiness among the passengers as we wheeled, punched through the clouds, and touched down on a runway that seemed unusually dark and remote, as if there were no significant city nearby. For that matter there didn't even seem to be a significant airport nearby, just miles of empty runway. Eventually the terminal came into view, modern and gleaming, but well before reaching it the pilot parked and turned off the engines. The door opened and we were herded down a set of creaking metal stairs, with four sullen police officers waiting at the bottom. They put us onto an old airport-transfer bus, which without delay or explanation sped us off, away from the terminal, toward the absolute middle of nowhere. You have just arrived in one of the few places on earth where socialism has not devolved to mere coffeehouse philosophy, nor the Cold War to pre-9/11 ancient history. Welcome to Cuba, *yanquis*.

We skirted the tarmac, speeding past hangars and outbuildings and assorted rusting aircraft that could have been cleaned up and displayed in a museum, heading ever deeper into the gloom. There was no destination in sight. For much of the ride there was nothing at all in sight but the patch of pavement lit by the headlights of the bus, which, from the nameplates and insignia, seemed to have been made in Germany. I was betting *East* Germany. The uniformed driver, a small, age-spotted man with thinning black hair, took occasional drags from the lit cigarette that hung from his lips as if Superglued in place. Eventually we pulled up at an anonymous-looking building that had all the charm of a detention center, with police flanking the one door through which we were required to file. By then the whole thing had come to feel like a scene written by John le Carré, one set in Berlin that ends with accusation, betrayal, and perhaps a short, final burst of machine-gun fire.

The ominous building turned out to be just a smaller terminal, though, one of several in the the sprawling airport complex, and inside was a crew of unsmiling but efficient immigration officers. They were careful to leave no incriminating mark or stamp in American passports for U.S. authorities to discover on the renegade travelers' return, and perhaps use as evidence to levy a punishing fine. This was an act of self-interest on the part of the Cuban government. Tourism had become Cuba's economic Plan B, now that Plan A, eternal solidarity with the brother nations of the Soviet bloc, hadn't worked out so well. American tourists had kept Cuba afloat in the years before the revolution and potentially could do so again, but Americans who got busted, prosecuted, and fined when they got home were hardly likely to tell the neighbors how cold and fruity the daiquiris had been at Hemingway's old bar, the Floridita. The slick move with the passports also felt like a courtesy, though, and it almost seemed as if part of the intent were to forge an instant conspiracy. Imperialist visitor and socialist host immediately had a common purpose—and more important, a secret to share.

I claimed my luggage and went outside into the muggy Havana night to catch a cab. There were billboards along the road from the airport, as in any city in the world, but here they sold Marxism instead of merchandise. One exhorted those who saw it to "Be Like Che!" Another trumpeted that the revolution would last forever. The most succinct said simply: "Free Elián." This was the spring of

2000, and little Elián González was still with the sitcom-ready clan that for all time will be known as the Miami Relatives, being hustled through theme parks and shopping malls as part of his crash course in capitalism.

As we pulled up at the hotel a song was playing on the radio, and it was so catchy that it stuck in my mind. The refrain was hard to forget: *"La vida es un carnaval."* Life is a carnival.

The next morning, that same song spilled out of a window in Old Havana. In the afternoon it thumped out of a boom box in the Parque Central, across the street from the hotel, and at night it rattled the old walls of a dark little discotheque in teeming Centro Habana. I never heard enough to catch much of the lyric, except one bit about there being no need to cry, another bit about how everybody ought to be singing, and the much-repeated chorus. The music fit the theme, a happy, galumphing two-step that sounded like an elephant's walk. *Dum-diddy-dum-dum-dumpiddy-dum.* It was catchy to the point of being infectious. As soon as you managed to make it stop playing through your head, a car drove past and you heard it on the radio and the loop started again, beckoning you to gorge on cheap irony.

For that was what the song offered, a heaping platter of bargain-basement irony. A hanging curveball that an out-of-gas pitcher had left right over the plate. In this beautiful ruin of a city, this achingly picturesque slum, to imagine life as some grand entertainment? Life as a carnival?

It hadn't taken long to recognize Havana's charms. The city was like a former debutante, now of an age and fallen on hard times. She was wrinkled and her clothes were frayed and worn, but she still had her good bones, her noble bearing, and a few pieces of exquisite jewelry that somehow had escaped the pawnbroker. She also had a great laugh: The whole city seemed to laugh all the time, and also shout at the top of its lungs, and argue without giving quarter, and call its children out the window to come to dinner, as if Havava were the site of a giant permanent family reunion. This elegant old broad of a city had lived an interesting life, full of danger and passion. Even now, still proud of her enduring allure, she wouldn't be caught dead without her perfume. If a scent were concocted in Lady Havana's honor it might be called Tropical Intrigue, with ripe undertones of fruit, musk, and romantic decay.

But a carnival? My cab driver from the airport had delivered a bitter soliloquy on all that was wrong with Cuba: the laughably meager state salaries, the isolation from the rest of the world, the struggle for survival, and the inescapable government, which he considered only occasionally a menace but at all other times a huge dead weight that the beleaguered society was forced to bear. Actually, he never used the word *government*. When he wanted to refer to official authority he just put his hand beneath his chin and stroked an imaginary, iconic beard. By the following afternoon, it was true, I had met a number of Cubans with much kinder views of *fidelismo* and the great benefits it had brought, particularly in education and health care. But it was also true that I could hardly step out of my hotel before being swarmed by sharp-dressed hustlers angling to sell me half-price cigars stolen from the factories, or guide me through Havana's famed nightlife, or introduce me to women of any size, shape, or hue—any service at all that might incline me to part with a few of my precious dollars.

The city was gorgeous, but practically every building in town was badly in need of cleaning and a coat of paint. The housing stock was falling down, the streets mined with potholes, the infrastructure so parlous that a tanker truck had to pull up beneath my window every morning to pump the tanks of a five-star hotel full of drinking water. The block-long lines of people waiting at the bus stops looked grim; the few who managed to squeeze aboard the infrequent buses—not really buses at all, but big, swaybacked tractor-trailer rigs with windows, called *camellos*, or camels, and painted an unfortunate shade of pink—looked substantially grimmer. Magical as it was, nobody would have mistaken Havana for a carnival.

So there, that was simple enough: I'd come to Havana to write about music, and in less than a day I'd already found a handy ironic metaphor in that song I kept hearing. I even recognized the voice of the singer, a *salsero* named Issac Delgado whose smoky baritone and refined phrasing brought to mind the young Sinatra. I'd stumbled across one of his CDs at a record store back home in Washington a few weeks earlier and bought it as part of my research for this trip, but this song hadn't been on it. I knew it was Issac, though; his voice is so distinctive that it couldn't be anyone else. All I had to do was hunt down a recording of this song and work out the rest of the lyrics, and I'd have a selection of epigrams that I could italicize and use as subheadings to sprinkle through the newspaper story I would eventually write.

I was at that hallucinatory early stage in my encounter with this new country, the stage at which a perfect descriptive framework emerges, distinct and complete, and all that seems left to do is fill in a few blanks and add a bit of ornament. From that golden and illusion-filled moment, ignorance always increases geometrically. For the next week or month or decade, each day adds a bit of understanding about the place. But if you're paying attention, each day also takes a bit of understanding away.

The glow lasted just long enough to comfort a long, smug afternoon in a little bar in Old Havana. I sipped seven-year-old Cuban rum and nursed a cigar that I had watched being rolled by a woman sitting at a workbench in the corner, a rosewood-dark woman with a gingham headscarf and strong, tobacco-stained fingers. There was a stereo behind the bar, and every fifteen minutes or so the bartender would hit the rewind button so that everyone could enjoy the first song on the tape one more time, which went *dum-diddy-dum-dum-dumpiddy-dum, "La vida es un carnaval!"*

* * *

The force of nature that is Juan de Marcos bounded into the hotel lobby, forty-five minutes late, and lit the place up.

"Hey, man, sorry I'm late," he said in unexpected, unaccented English. "Kids, you know. Had to take my daughter from school to her lesson. Music lesson, what can I say, it runs in the family, right?"

He looked at his watch. "Got to pick her up again in a while, but we've got time to talk. What's happening, man? Good to see you. You're from Washington, man, I love playing Washington. Lisner Auditorium, I was there last year with the All Stars. Cigarette?"

I'd been told by a musician acquaintance in Havana that if I wanted to learn about Cuban music, the first man to look up was Juan de Marcos. All I knew was that he had somehow worked with the American guitarist Ry Cooder on the project that had put Cuban music back on the map, the *Buena Vista Social Club* album and the accompanying film by the German director Wim Wenders. My assumption was that he had been some sort of local contact for these busy international stars, a behind-the-scenes figure who handled the logistics so that the great artists could create their magic. I hadn't realized that this tall, middle-aged Afro-Cuban with skin the color of black coffee, salt-and-pepper dreadlocks, and the winning smile of a million-dollar salesman had been the intellectual and musical author of the whole retro-Cuba movement. I didn't know that without Juan de Marcos there wouldn't have been a Buena Vista Social Club phenomenon at all. I certainly didn't know that he likely had made more money from the project—in fact, more money from Cuban music in general—than anyone else in the world.

He was forty-five years old, not heavy but not in shape, either, with a little potbelly and an overall softness to his body that announced he was a man who made his living with his mind, not his back. His was the physique of a tenured college professor, or perhaps a food critic. His dreadlocks were short but unruly, and his moustache was at the point of open insurrection. His clothes were every bit as unslick and unstudied as his grooming—snap-brim cap, polo shirt, shorts that were *way* too short, navy blue socks, ratty white tennis shoes. All this was dominated by that hundred-watt smile and an effusion of pheromonelike charisma. He had glad-handed his way to my table, stopping to greet the doormen on the sidewalk, the security men inside the door, two waitresses who seemed thrilled to recognize him, and the trio of strolling musicians who wandered through the huge atrium lobby day and night playing nothing but Buena Vista songs. My hotel catered exclusively to foreigners, and any ordinary Cuban would have been challenged at the door. Juan de Marcos, dressed like a peon or a bag person, had sailed right in. I began to understand that even in a society of enforced egalitarianism, some people were Somebodies.

By now, everybody knows the Buena Vista story: Ry Cooder, a musician with great hands but an even better ear, scoured the ruins of Havana to find the forgotten musical stars of the 1950s. He rousted these musicians out of their hovels and shacks and slums, rescued them from their backwaters and dead ends. One had been making a living by shining shoes, another had been playing a beat-up piano for a classroom of nine-year-old ballerinas. Cooder found them and blew from their eyes the dust of age and torpor, using all his formidable powers of persuasion to convince them to turn back the clock, slick back their hair, and make music again. He herded them into an ancient studio where they recorded an album, and against all odds it became a huge best seller, the biggest success in the brief history of what Americans and Europeans chauvinistically call "world" music, as if the "world" consisted only of the lesser places. He turned these suave senior citizens into stars once more, bringing them to New York for a triumphal concert at Carnegie Hall. Set loose in Manhattan, the codgers all but wept at the height of the skyscrapers, the sumptuousness of the streetscape, and the astounding variety of kitsch in the window displays. From start to finish, their ever-present smiles were as warm and sweet as their dulcet voices.

It was a neat, inspirational story, the only problem being that it wasn't exactly true.

"If you want to sell something, you have to create a myth," Juan de Marcos told me, as he lit another in an endless succession of cigarettes. "The story that a white guy came to Cuba to discover these musicians, this music—it's very comfortable, right? But it's a myth. That's all it is, a myth. Man, we don't need any American to come here and discover us."

The truth was that by the time Cooder ever set foot in Cuba, de

Marcos already had the Buena Vista musicians in the studio, ready to record. He was the one who had tracked them down and rounded them up. More important, he was the one who had had the crucial insight that the music of prerevolutionary Cuba would play well, and perhaps even sell well, nearly fifty years later. He had been working on his own retro-Cuba album, which, truth be told, is probably a tad superior.

Enter Ry Cooder, who had come to Cuba for an entirely different, even more exotic project involving a collaboration with some musicians from Mali. For some reason the Malians never arrived, leaving Cooder in Havana with nothing to do. As fate would have it, Cooder and de Marcos had a business contact in common, a British record label owner named Nick Gold. From London, Gold put the two men in touch, and Buena Vista was born.

None of which is to dismiss Cooder's contributions, without which the phenomenon never could have caught fire. He immediately heard the classic midcentury music's possibilities, which someone with a lesser ear would have missed. His influence and participation made the album sweeter, more acoustic, and more folkloric than it otherwise would have been—less urban and brassy, which is the direction de Marcos had intended to lean. And of course he had a name and standing in the American music business that created all kinds of opportunities de Marcos could not have dreamed of. "I've got a new album of great old Cuban music put together by Juan de Marcos" is not a sales pitch to quicken the heartbeat of a buyer for a record-store chain. "I've got a new album of great old Cuban music put together by Ry Cooder" at least gets the man on the phone.

So was de Marcos angry at having been left out of the myth? "No, man, not at all. For me this is like a dream. Like a realized dream."

A few minutes later, though, he was telling how he had found the great Ibrahim Ferrer—the lead singer on many of the *Buena Vista* tracks, with his trademark snap-brim cap and his mellow, patinated voice like a Cuban Nat "King" Cole—in such dire circumstances that he was literally shining shoes for pennies and selling lottery tickets to survive. Now the album and movie had made him an international star, and suddenly, in his seventies, he was the busiest artist in Cuba. His follow-up solo album was doing spectacularly well, he hardly had time to rest his old bones between concert tours of Europe and the United States, and he had become a wealthy man. "We made sure the musicians didn't get screwed," de Marcos said. "They all did well, and that's the thing I'm proudest of. They all have their new cars, their new apartments. But Ferrer especially, because his solo album has done so well. I think it's going to sell a million units, I really do. But already, right now, I can tell you that I'm sure Ferrer is a millionaire. He was shining shoes, man, and now he's a millionaire."

He took a swig of his beer and grinned. "I'll tell you one thing, man. Ibrahim Ferrer is a *whole* lot bigger than Ry Cooder right now."

Letting Cooder receive the credit for the *Buena Vista* album had had nothing to do with ego—even for a black Cuban nationalist like de Marcos, with obvious pride in both his blackness and his *cubanidad*. It had been, simply, a good business decision, one of a series of good business decisions de Marcos had made on his way to becoming Cuba's leading musical impresario.

De Marcos was born in Havana, the son of a musician who "used to play the whole night for a couple of pesos" and was determined that his son would have a different life. His son would be a professional, any kind of professional. "For my father," he told me, "being a musician was not to have a career at all."

These dreams were possible because the Cuban revolution had interrupted Juan's childhood and offered him new options—life choices that weren't previously available to kids with cocoa-colored skin and kinky hair. He did well in school, studied civil engineering, and ended up teaching at the University of Havana, the most prestigious institution of higher learning in Cuba, the school where Fidel Castro had studied and schemed.

Music does run in Cuban families, though, and like an ocean

current it can flow unfelt in the depths and then suddenly surface with irresistible force. De Marcos began to study classical guitar and then became absorbed in midcentury Cuban music. Soon he started his own retro-music band, Sierra Maestra, named after the steep and verdant mountain range in eastern Cuba where Fidel Castro's absurdly small band of revolutionaries had evaded, outmaneuvered, outpropagandized, and finally defeated the huge but uncommitted armies of the Cuban state.

Sierra Maestra's music was, fittingly, rather rural and folk toned, more redolent of Cuba's rootsy eastern provinces. De Marcos then branched out and formed another retro group, which he called the Afro-Cuban All Stars, to play brassy, big-city, Havana-style music from the '40s and '50s, but updated with contemporary orchestrations and production values. It was for an All-Stars album that he had brought Ibrahim Ferrer, Rubén González, Compay Segundo, Omara Portuondo, and the rest of the musicians who would go on to become Buena Vista superstars into the studio.

De Marcos was smart enough to realize that he wasn't a great guitarist, but early on he had two important insights: that Cuban music from the Golden Age of the '40s and '50s played well in the United States and especially Europe, if properly tweaked with a modern sensibility; and that to succeed in these overseas markets, Cuban musicians would have to learn to play, and enjoy playing, some kind of music that did not insist so stridently that listeners get to their feet and dance.

"We tend to make our music too complicated these days," de Marcos said. "It's technically great, but if it's too complicated it just doesn't connect with people, and then it dies, man. And then there's the whole thing about dancing. A lot of bands go up to the States, and they play halls like the one we play when we go to your town, Lisner Auditorium in Washington, and they play all this rocking music, man, and the people just sit there. We've played concerts in Europe where we opened for Los Van Van, the biggest band in Cuba, and in the middle of Van Van's set, everybody started to leave. The Germans just got up and left. The musicians get frustrated, because in Cuba if people don't dance, you're not happening. So they play harder, and it just doesn't work, or else they try to play stuff they really don't know how to play. They end up getting booked in the big dance clubs, but you can't make any money doing that. To succeed on the road in the States you have to play music that works in the concert hall. The old stuff, it works. We've proved it. It works."

De Marcos was looking for a forum to preach his gospel. "I want to have a meeting with the bandleaders to get us back into the international concert hall. If you play in the concert hall, you can't just play loud all the time the way you would in a club. You have to relearn the dynamics. Nothing is going to happen for you in America if you just play in clubs. If you play at Lisner in Washington or Town Hall in New York, you've got three thousand people sitting there who are going to listen to you and buy your albums and tell their friends. *That* can support your band."

Juan de Marcos knew that he was fortunate to be riding "this incredible wave in Cuban music," and he is not the type ever to frown on good fortune. But if there were one thing this race-conscious black Cuban would have changed, in the heady spring of 2000, it would have been to be able to see more black faces among those concert hall audiences in places like New York and Washington. "The audience for Buena Vista is completely middle class and mostly white," he said. "I'm proud that at least you see *some* Afro-American faces. At least a few."

Race is not a factor in the Buena Vista world, and that is perhaps one of the music's most winning attractions. You have this white American, Ry Cooder, sharing the stage with black musicians. When you look closer, you see that not all the musicians are black— the guitarist Eliades Ochoa, for example, looking for all the world like an aging hat-act country star à la Garth Brooks, makes music alongside Ibrahim Ferrer, whose rakish cap and urban style suggest a Motown crooner in his golden years. The visual impression is of a Peaceable Kingdom world in which race does not exist, or at least is not acknowledged, and everybody gets along just the way Rodney

King wishes we all would. But de Marcos, who more than anyone else created this cozy world, kept returning to the subject of race. At one point he quoted the Malcolm X "by any means necessary" dictum. At another, he laid claim on behalf of black Cubans to the whole of Cuban musical culture.

"Get one thing straight, man. Cuban music is Afro-Cuban music. There are no whites in Cuba. There are people who think they are white, but they are all African. The music all comes from Africa."

He was also cold eyed about the current state of the revolution, though he remained committed enough to its principles and his homeland to remain in Cuba—despite having enough money to live anywhere he wanted in the world, and frequent opportunities to leave.

"Yeah, we've got a high level of education in Cuba, but we're losing it," he said. "The younger generation just wants to make money, and the way to make money is to be hustlers. In terms of legitimate activities, music and sports are the only ways to make money here right now."

But he remained a Cuban patriot, one who was worried about the future. "I tell my sons to study hard and prepare themselves. At some point, Cuba is going to be open, and that's when people are going to come to buy Cuba. I tell them that you have to be prepared to fight for your country."

He lit another of his potent, dark Cuban cigarettes. "Anyway, I'm planning to start my own record company. For us. We need to get something going, right here."

So he had decided to stay? He was going to stick it out?

"Sure! Hell, I lived for a year in the States. I know that everything's not perfect over there, not by any means. Not for Cubans. Some people take off, go to America, and after they stay there for a while they come running back—*and join the Party, man.*" Not for the last time, I heard the sardonic laugh of a brilliant, restless, open-eyed, black-and-proud, Cuban-to-the-bone communist millionaire.

* * *

The nightclub called Macumba was a place that didn't belong on any map of Cuba, geographical or mental. It was almost like stepping into some parallel world—leaving the Havana of age, grace, and decay to enter a realm where everything was new, sleek, and wildly expensive. It was a good half-hour drive from downtown, which meant that to get there you either had to own a car or be able to afford a twenty-dollar cab ride. The cover charge was twenty-five dollars, more than a month's salary. A watery *mojito* would set you back six dollars; to have the waitress bring to your table a bottle of good rum, which would have cost no more than seven dollars at the overpriced hotel shops in town, cost an astounding forty-eight dollars, a price beyond all absurdity. A little boutique near the coat-check room sold Cuban cigars at London prices, fifteen dollars for a decent Cohiba. That there were Canadian and European tourists in the audience made sense. But what on earth were all these Cubans doing here?

Macumba was open-air, like the Tropical, but there the similarity ended. It was smaller and roughly circular. The décor was from some lost episode of *Miami Vice*, down to the bleached-white-and-pastel color scheme, the exposed metal struts that supported the stage lights, the neon accents on the walls. Overhead, a huge television screen played music videos; the sound poured through speakers that would have passed muster in any club in South Beach. The tourists in the crowd were middle-aged, as tourists tend to be, but the rest of Macumba's patrons were quite young. They were also disproportionately white and totally buzzed with excitement.

Tonight was a special night at Macumba. I'd been hearing about it for a week: a hot young singer named Paulo F.G., who'd quickly become one of the most popular *salseros* in all of Cuba, was giving his first live performance in months and would be debuting material from his as-yet-unreleased new album. Paulo (the F.G. stood for Fernández Gallo) also would be filming concert footage for use in a music video. His popularity was among the age demographic that cared about music videos, and these were the people who had come out to see his show.

I found a table in the rear, where I could watch the crowd as well as the stage, and ordered a six-dollar *mojito,* and before it was even half-gone I was descended upon by three *jineteras,* one heavy-set, one thin as a waif, and one who betrayed a mouth full of Soviet-style metal dentistry whenever she smiled.

"Do you mind if we sit down?" the heavy one asked, after they had sat down.

Jinetera translates literally as "female jockey," or perhaps more precisely as "female jockeyer." The famed *jineteras* of Havana are women who trade sex for money and entertainment. That's an over-simplification, but good enough for now. These were three of them, and their immediate objective was alcoholic refreshment.

"Would you buy me a drink?" said the one with the metal in her mouth. "And maybe for my sisters?"

I laughed at the audacity of the approach, and at the absurd notion that these three women, who looked nothing alike, could possibly be related. When I didn't respond, the heavy one said, "Come on, just a drink. We won't hurt you. Unless that's what you want."

Before I could say anything, the thin one had already flagged down a waiter and ordered three Cuba Libres, rum-and-Cokes. They introduced themselves; I shook their hands. When the waiter brought the drinks, I paid him and whispered that these were the last—no more orders from *las chicas.* He nodded and smiled.

They tried to initiate a conversation as they sucked down the drinks, but I kept my answers as close to monosyllabic as I could, and eventually they began to look around the room for better prospects.

I looked around at the crowd, too—most of the black people at Macumba that night, like my three swilling graces, were unaccom-panied young women wearing low-cut, thigh-high party dresses, which meant this was a business outing for them. The Cubans who were at Macumba for pleasure—the young couples, the groups of friends—were white. From what I had seen of Cuba thus far, it seemed to me that the rainbow was the rule. I'd been in Havana nearly a week and this was the first time I'd seen a crowd that I could describe as mostly black or mostly white. I formed the obvious hypothesis that this anomaly had to do with the fact that Paulo F.G., the headliner, was himself apparently white. I'd never seen a picture of the guy, but several people, in telling me that he was the flavor of the month in Cuban music, had referred to him as "this little white guy."

But when the lights finally dimmed and the show began, I saw that Paulo F.G. wasn't really that white.

He was whiter than most Cubans, but not white like, say, the drunken Germans at the table down front. I'd spent a lot of time in Brazil, where concepts of race were very different from those in the United States—I'd even written a book about those differences—and so this was hardly a shock. But I was a bit surprised that he wasn't as white as most of the young Cubans who had come to see him. His skin was about the hue and value of a manila envelope, and while his black hair was fairly straight, his features were much more African than European. I wondered just what it was in his relative whiteness that attracted these white kids. And I wondered where these white kids got the money to blow at a place like Macumba.

"Relatives in *la Yuma*," the waiter told me, when he came back to ask if I wanted a refill. He asserted that these young whites and their families were being sent money by their aunts, uncles, and cousins in the United States. Since most of the Cuban Americans in Miami were white, it made sense that most of the relatives they were helping back in the homeland were white as well. I wondered what black Cubans thought of this—whether they thought it was circumstance, luck, or something else.

Paulo F.G. either had an off night or wasn't that good to begin with. I later heard his recordings and they weren't half-bad, so I'm willing to give him the benefit of the doubt, but that night he just wasn't making it happen. The filming of the video didn't help. His whole performance seemed to be focused on the camera that was tracking his every move, and incidentally blocking the view of a good chunk of the audience at any given time. There was no focus, from him or his band, on the music itself, on giving it that incendiary quality that I'd heard from Bamboleo.

Paulo's young white fans either didn't notice or didn't mind. They got up to dance—competently, but without the genius that I'd seen at the Tropical—and they cheered as loudly as if the performance had actually been a good one. If I were Cuban and I'd just spent a quarter of a year's salary on an evening out, I'd be determined to enjoy myself too.

After the concert, my three graces offered to take me home, jointly or severally. I declined, but they persisted—the heavy one locked on to my arm with a grip that meant business, and the one with the bad dental work flashed me the lascivious, glinting smile of a James Bond robo-villainess. Everyone and everything at Macumba was trying much too hard—Paulo F.G. mugging for the video cameras instead of making his music, the club itself with its hyperexaggerated *faux*-Miami sleekness and ridiculous prices, and especially the scary women with their absolute determination not to let a potential payday escape into the night. Escape I did, though; I prised myself loose, bolted, and almost ran for the door.

* * *

The Cuban economy has so little to offer, especially to young people, that one of the few real options is to work the foreigners.

"Whar you frung?" the young man asked as he blocked my path, turning up the wattage on an already incandescent smile.

This was in the Parque Central, in downtown Havana, and I'd heard that question so often in my short time in the city that it hardly even registered—"Where are you from?" shouted in English, with the thick, Ricky Ricardo–esque accent of a Spanish speaker who's done all his language study in the streets. It was the opening line of every Cuban hustler, and this leafy park, ringed by tourist hotels, was full of them night and day.

It was intended as the opening step in a dance, which went like this:

I walked away. The young man followed, matching his pace to mine.

He said, "You're American?" I nodded. He said his name was Marco and asked mine. I told him but kept walking.

He asked where in the States I was from; I said Washington. "The capital," he said. I nodded and said good-bye. He didn't go away.

By then I had reached my destination in the park, as described in my guidebook: the famed *esquina caliente*—the "hot corner"— near the statue of independence hero José Martí, where a crowd gathers every day from morning to night to argue passioniately about the national pastime. That this permanent thorn in the side of Uncle Sam is the most baseball-mad place on earth—that the land of *yanqui*-go-home worships the Yankees—is the kind of easy irony that no first-time visitor to Havana can resist. About thirty men were there, most of them yelling at once in praise or denigration of various players and teams; mostly they were talking about the Cuban leagues, but I heard American Major League franchises and ballplayers mentioned too. I had planned just to linger at the fringe and soak up a little atmosphere, but now I saw the opportunity to lose Marco so I plowed straight into the finger-pointing, chest-thumping mob and out the other side. Once through, I quickly crossed the street in the direction of Old Havana. But by the time I was at the head of Calle Obispo, the pedestrian street lined with shops, restaurants, and bars leading down to the Plaza de Armas and Havana Bay, I sensed a presence at my side and turned to see Marco's inevitable smiling face.

He was in his early twenties, thin and fairly tall, very dark skinned, with just the suggestion of hair on his head, as if he hadn't shaved it in three or four days. He was dressed like an American his age might have dressed a year earlier—baggy jeans that said they were by Kani but probably were knockoffs of a discontinued line; a baggy white T-shirt; over the T-shirt, a yellow Lakers jersey with

Shaquille O'Neal's name and number; and white sneakers that gleamed as brilliantly as his smile. He had on a pair of those yellow-tinted sunglasses that for about five minutes had been terribly chic in circles that thought themselves "downtown."

He asked how long I'd be in Havana. I said I didn't know.

He asked whether I wanted to buy some cigars, "genuine" Montecristos or Cohibas that his uncle could get from the factory and he would sell me for half price. I said no thanks; I'd been warned that there was a good chance they'd be counterfeit or irretrievably stale.

He asked if I wanted to go to a *paladar*, one of the tiny private restaurants that Castro allowed Cubans to open in their homes. I said no, I'd just had breakfast. He said maybe later, okay? I said maybe later, hoping that would be enough to get rid of him. But it wasn't, because if he could get me into a *paladar*, the owner would pay him 40 percent of what I spent. He asked what time I wanted to eat and where we should meet. I spoke of vague appointments I had later that day and the paralyzing uncertainty of my schedule. By this time we were speaking mostly Spanish, his street English having been spent.

He asked if I wanted to go out that night; he, of course, knew all the right people at all the best places. I kept to the story about the unfathomability of my schedule.

He told me he could introduce me to beautiful girls, lots of beautiful girls, and I could take my pick. My schedule, I said; I really didn't know what I would be doing, not from one moment to the next, and in fact I needed to get back to the hotel that instant to meet my friend's friend.

I spun and headed back the way I had come. He matched me stride for stride until we reached the hotel door, where he stopped abruptly. He didn't have Juan de Marcos's cachet; it was as if a force field had blocked his path.

"I'll see you later," he called, as the glass door closed behind me.

The next step in this dance of hustler-hustlee should have been for Marco to jump into my path when I left the hotel for another stroll that evening, but he missed his cue. It was around nine, and the park was as empty as it ever got; maybe the day shift of hustlers had already clocked off, and the night shift hadn't yet arrived. For whatever reason, it was possible to walk through the city in peace.

The lull in the crowds on Obispo made it possible to actually see the place—the age of the buildings, the boarded-up shells next to restored boutiques, the derelict pay phones that no one even tried to use anymore, the charming street signs attached to the corner buildings themselves so that you had to look up to the second floor to see where you were. Most of the shops looked dreary, with only a few items in the windows—two shirts and two pairs of pants in the display at a men's store, a half dozen haphazardly arranged ceramic pieces in a store that sold the work of an artisans' collective. One store's windows were brightly lit, full of random items priced in dollars: Adidas tennis shoes for $70, Sony boom boxes that ranged from $100 to $250, Walkmen, running suits, luggage. Couples stopped and pointed, and I wondered if they were actually debating purchases, perhaps to be made with dollars carefully saved over the weeks and months and years, or just dreaming the impossible. There was an old pharmacy that had been restored to its original state, or maybe kept in that condition all along, and its shelves were lined all the way to the high ceilings with old apothecary jars.

At each intersection stood a police officer. Near Hemingway's old hotel, the Ambos Mundos, a cop had stopped a group of three young black men and demanded that they produce the identity documents that all Cubans are required to carry at all times. The men complied without argument—in Cuba, noncompliance or argument with the police means an automatic trip to jail, with no sense of how long the stay might be. I watched as the policeman, who was white, deliberately dragged out the encounter, using his radio to check out each of the men in turn, standing cockily like a little general as he arbitrarily ordered them to stop talking to one another, stand over here, no I said over there, right here, are you stupid? At times you could read fear on their faces and at times resignation, but there were moments when you saw bitter, bitter resentment, and you glimpsed what might happen if the tables were ever reversed, if ever, just for a moment, the asshole cop were the weak one and those men were the strong.

I walked down to the Plaza de Armas and back, and then stopped for a drink and a cigar in a bar near the Parque Central, a little spot that was ideal for people watching. The night people had begun to emerge, women in high heels and short dresses, men in linen and silks and gold chains, groups of male tourists in their Dockers and polo shirts, predatory packs of *jineteras* stalking them. The bartender whistled and pointed at a woman who was walking alone, a tall *mulata* in a bright red dress. She heard him and rewarded him with a smile, along with a little extra sway in her hips as she came past the bar, turned the corner, and went on her way. "The Lady in Red," I said, but the bartender didn't understand English.

A while later, when I was finally ready to go back to the hotel, I heard music nearby—*Dum-diddy-dum-dum-dumpiddy-dum*—and voices raised in celebration. I followed the sound half a block until I came to its source, a party that had spilled out of a little ground-floor apartment into one of the narrow streets of Old Havana. Some of the revelers were sitting on the hood of a car parked in front of the building. I asked what was going on.

"A wedding party!" one of the men replied, as he handed me a bottle of rum to take a swig.

I lingered for a moment. "Come on in," the man said. "Have some more rum. Come on!"

Inside, the furniture had been moved back along the walls and so many people were dancing that they had to move in unison to move at all. It was nothing but a house party—loud, sweaty, soaked with rum, and suffused with pure joy and pure release.

And there, smack in the middle of the room, was the Lady in Red, locked in a tight embrace with a tall man as black as obsidian, swaying, grinding, moving her hips to the sexy two-step of the beat. She had a glass of rum on one hand, a cigarette in the other, and on her pretty face was a radiant, beatific smile.

Life is a carnival!

3. *FIDEL*-ITY

The Cuban carnival had but one impresario. He was barker, ringmaster, daredevil, lion tamer, roustabout, tightrope walker, but never clown. He decided each night how the show would go—whether it would be a sunny, lighthearted, slightly bawdy revue, or a stark, oppressive performance, painful to sit through, full of nasty surprises and dire consequences. He decided whether the trapeze artists would work with a net, whether the tigers would be fed before their act, whether the clowns would paint their faces into smiles that lit up the arena or sneers that frightened all the children. Part of his power lay in the fact that no one knew how or why he chose the tone for a particular evening. Was he following a pattern that only he could discern? Was he responding to outside events? Was he subtly reading the audience, for whom each and every show was mandatory? Or was he responding to his own moods, the faltering rhythms of an old man's body, the sudden time shifts of an old man's mind? It was an enduring puzzle, but in the end the motivation didn't matter. It was *his* show.

To switch metaphors, Fidel Castro wore the island of Cuba like a mood ring. That first couple of times I visited, the stone would have been blue-green: somewhat relaxed, somewhat happy.

He was on television every night, inspecting new public works or celebrating the achievement of some exemplary group of workers in some provincial hamlet that he had descended upon like a tropical Santa Claus, bearing gifts. After a hurricane scoured a wide swath of farmland (providentially missing the cities, where decrepit homes simply would have been blown down), he arrived to give succor to the *campesinos* even before the sky had cleared. He found frequent occasion to visit government ministries in Havana. For security reasons, he rarely announced his schedule more than a few hours in advance. This was a great frustration to the foreign correspondents based in Havana, but one friend of mine got the jump on the competition by paying close attention to the cityscape: Whenever a ministry, school, hospital, or community center got new landscaping and a coat of paint, it stood out among the general decay and provided a sure signal that Fidel planned to drop by within the next few days.

The television appearances were interesting, but I knew it would be more telling to see him in the flesh. And it was.

I had decided to write a story about boxing, because Cuba had just won its usual slew of boxing gold medals at the Olympics in Sydney. A couple of days of lobbying various officials in the state-run athletic bureaucracy had produced an invitation to sit with the rest of the press at a gala ceremony honoring the hundred greatest Cuban athletes of the century. The cream of the boxing world would be there, so it seemed a good place to start.

The event was held at Ciudad Deportiva, which means "Sports City," a phrase with a distinct Soviet-era ring to it. It turned out that the complex had a Soviet look and feel as well. It was a campus of fields and low-slung cinderblock office buildings, centered on a big flying-saucer sports arena for basketball, volleyball, and other indoor games. There was something *Brave New World*–ish about the place—the utilitarian architecture, the painted slogans touting the benefits of revolutionary sport, the general feeling of the place that said camp more than campus. I soon learned, though, that this powerful vibe was nothing more than an artifact of my own prejudices about Cuba. The arena was actually built under Castro's predecessor, the completely un-Soviet Fulgencio Batista, who was much more satrap than Stalin.

The arena itself was like an early prototype of the modern

sports palace. The size and shape were right, but the materials were all wrong (painted concrete instead of glossier surfaces), the portals of ingress and egress too few and too narrow to satisfy modern theories of crowd flow, the seats too narrow, the pitch of the seating galleries too steep, the spectators dangerously close to the action. Instead of being Oz-like and intimidating, like every arena in every big American city, the place was almost intimate, with the ambiance of a high school gymnasium.

On the way inside I saw some musical instruments piled by the door, including one that I thought I recognized. It was an electric stand-up bass, memorable and all but unmistakable because it was not the usual black but laquered in brightest white.

I turned to the stranger walking beside me, who surely would know.

"Es de Formell, no?" I asked.

"Sí," came the response, with a smile. This would be a better afternoon than any of us had imagined.

When I got to my seat I saw the glory of socialist Cuba arrayed before me, as if in a propaganda film from the 1960s. All that was missing was a soundtrack of East German martial music and perhaps a proud display of the latest tanks and missiles.

The arena was filled to the rafters, not an empty seat in sight, but filled in an improbably organized fashion. Here, to my left, was a bloc of young men and women in uniform, doubtless from some military unit. There, across the way, were teenagers in identical tracksuits, apparently from a school or one of the junior national teams, no clue which sport. Far to my right was a bloc of senior citizens, wizened old men and women who sat waiting with the quiet stoicism of people who have been waiting all their lives. Also to the right was a bloc of seats occupied by men and women who were in unusually good shape for middle age, and I assumed they were the honored athletes. Ringing the floor and clustered near the exits were dozens of police, some in uniform and some in I'm-a-cop plainclothes that didn't fool anyone. A big banner beneath the rafters said: Sports, a Right of the People.

There were groups in which each member held a little Cuban flag, groups organized by age and region and preferred sports, groups of people who obviously had been brought here en masse and whose faces wore looks of duty, as if their volunteering to come today had been less than voluntary. You could look around and for a moment you could convince yourself that you were in some grim, cold land behind the Iron Curtain witnessing some sort of ghastly May Day commemoration.

But only for a moment. A bit of movement in one of the socialist-youth sections caught my eye. The teenagers, bored and restless as nature intended teenagers to be, were batting a balloon back and forth above their heads. It took me a minute to realize that the milky white spheroid wasn't a balloon at all, but an inflated condom.

Quickly, another blown-up condom appeared above another youth section. Then there was another, and another, and soon a dozen distended prophylactics were circulating around the arena, to general delight. The soon-to-be-honored athletes pointed and laughed. To a man, the policemen smiled.

No, this wasn't East Germany.

This was a different place, a place where the socialist state itself, in its corporate imagination, could see a tableau of youth and sex and rambunctiousness and improvisation, and feel nothing more sinister or oppressive than simple joy. Not a simple place, Cuba.

At that point, as if on cue, Fidel came in.

It wasn't much of an entrance. He slipped in silently, without fanfare—a little murmur went through the crowd and suddenly there he was, in a box-seat section just beneath a red-and-black mural of Che Guevara. He was in fatigues and he looked old and tired, moving slowly, supported by solicitous aides at each elbow. Without even acknowledging the crowd, he hugged a few of the men and women in the box, presumably athletes or bureaucrats, and then sat down.

The athletes marched out in groups to receive their crystal loving cups. Special accolades went to Félix Savón, the latest of the great boxing champions, who had chosen this ceremony to announce his retirement. But the warmest applause went to Teófilo Stevenson, the first great athlete produced by Fidel Castro's revolution. Stevenson was arguably the greatest amateur boxer of all time, having won the Olympic gold medal in the heavyweight division in the 1972 games, the 1976 games, and the 1980 games—three Olympics in a row. Boxing promoters around the world salivated over the prospect of a dream-team bout between Stevenson and Muhammad Ali. They waved millions under Stevenson's nose to defect and turn professional, but he turned them all down and stayed in Cuba. This patriotic decision made him a national hero and won Fidel Castro's undying gratitude: Fidel gave him a couple of houses, a couple of cars, and a sinecure in the national sports bureaucracy, where his basic job was simply to be Teófilo Stevenson. It wasn't the millionaire's life he would have had in Miami or Las Vegas, but it was a life of great privilege by Cuban standards and also a life nourished by constant and sincere adulation. Today he looked great in his dark business suit and power tie. He was mostly gone to gray but still tall and handsome, his face still unmarked, his bearing still as regal as in the days when he was lord of the ring. After all these years, no one had been able to lay a glove on him.

After the athletes got their awards there was another not-in-East-Germany moment: Out came Los Van Van, the Rolling Stones of Cuba, led by the owner of the famous white electric bass guitar I had noticed earlier, Juan Formell. They launched into a selection of songs from their latest album, and the crowd did something I hadn't expected: everybody got up and danced.

The honored athletes were dancing. The senior citizens were dancing. The teenagers were dancing in their seats, in the aisles, down on the arena floor. The policemen who were supposed to keep order were tapping their feet and nodding their heads to the beat. Everybody knew the words to all the songs. What had been a stilted ceremony suddenly turned into a pretty good party.

Fidel, near as I could tell, was not dancing, but he did break into a warm smile. It was well known that Los Van Van was one of his favorites, although his affection had nothing to do with music—he was said to prefer classical music, to the extent that music meant anything to him at all. Politically, Juan Formell had been such a stalwart supporter of the revolution over the years that Fidel showed him a level of gratitude usually reserved for old comrades from the Sierra Maestra. Formell's great talents were lauded to the heavens and his minor transgressions quickly forgiven—Fidel pretended not to hear the occasional Van Van lyrics that tweaked the system, found ways to ignore the rumors of drug use within the band. He treated Formell like an artsy, bohemian son who at the end of the day was still family.

The band quit after a few songs, and attention turned to the box seats beneath the Che Guevara mural. Fidel was about to speak.

He stood, unsteadily, and began in a manner that can only be called underwhelming. For me, it was disappointing. This icon of the twentieth century, this legendary orator whose words had moved millions, was mumbling.

He spoke without notes, beginning with a general salutation to the athletes, and the observation that "ninety of the most outstanding one hundred Cuban athletes of the century developed their skills *after* the Triumph of the Revolution." It seemed a hollow achievement, given that the state apparatus of the revolution itself had chosen which athletes would be honored. I figured in any event that he would go on to develop this theme, but he detoured into a peroration on neocolonialism, the U.S. trade embargo (*"el bloqueo"*) and the challenge of the new century. The words seemed perfunctory. Everyone was paying attention, but no one was responding. The attentiveness appeared to come from duty rather than genuine interest. He seemed to have lost the crowd entirely. Perhaps sensing this, he returned abruptly to the theme.

"The athletes of Cuba won six Olympic gold medals before the Triumph of the Revolution," he said. "Since, they have won fifty-one. Fifty-one! And this, without even participating in two Olympiads."

"What a weird scene," I wrote in my notebook. And it was: Fidel, the athletes, the crowd, the police, the mural of Che Guevara. Three pigeons had found their way into the arena and were flitting around, looking for a way out. But gradually something was beginning to happen. Fidel's voice was growing stronger, rising.

"We will have to name not one hundred but *one thousand* greatest athletes of the century that has just begun," he said, "and we would be able to cover this coliseum with gold!" He was no longer speaking now, he was preaching, his voice rising and falling in a singsong cadence that reminded me of a hellfire Baptist minister who had come to his pulpit determined to save some souls today. The audience had begun to respond with cheers and shouts of encouragement. I half expected someone to jump up and shout "Amen!"

"We are showing the rich and powerful!" he said. "We are showing the rich and powerful that there are things in this world better than money!" And he stuck out his jaw like Muhammad Ali, or perhaps more like Teófilo Stevenson.

From that point on, it didn't really matter what he said. He went on for half an hour, and he talked about many things—sport, revolution, the United States, the Olympics, the Cuban spirit. But really, what he communicated was one simple message: "I am Fidel. I am *still* Fidel."

He spoke just long enough to bring all of Sports City to the proper state of rapt attention. That had been his aim, his only aim: to win them utterly. It was something he had always been able to do, and something he did again that day. I looked up at him: the old man who had entered the arena so unimpressively and mumbled through the opening of his speech was gone. In place of Fidel the old man stood Fidel the colossus. "I am *still* Fidel."

He ended as he always ended, with words everyone in the crowd had heard a hundred or a thousand times before, the official benediction of the Church of Fidel: *"Patria o muerte! Venceremos!"*

Fatherland or death. We shall be victorious.

As soon as he had finished, Fidel left the building. Then another group took the stage—a band playing rock, once frowned upon as alien and bourgeois—and everybody got up again to dance.

He was still Fidel. And there was music.

* * *

According to people close to him—men who bring him papers to sign, sit and listen to his lectures in interminable meetings, stand to the side and take photograph after photograph of the great man for posterity—he is still a night owl. Sometimes the bearded old man doesn't leave his office until six or seven in the morning, motorcading past early risers and the dregs of the night to one of his safe houses for a few hours' sleep.

He has no official residence. One of his official photographers, a man who has been taking his picture for more than forty years, since the Triumph of the Revolution itself, told me he has never, ever, been to Fidel's home. Where he lives is in fact a state secret, although many people know the place—a compound in the western part of Havana, palatial by Cuban standards but humble for a Midwestern mayor, to say nothing of a president, and jarringly suburban, as if June and Ward Cleaver had a slightly nicer house and a yard full of palm trees. The *Miami Herald* quoted visitors who described the place as comfortable but not posh—and said that someday, when Fidel's house is seen by all, the Miami Cubans will be shocked at its modesty and the Cuban Cubans shocked at its grandeur. For now, it's not possible even to drive past the house, because the surrounding streets have all been made one-way pointing outward from the compound, making legal entry into the neighborhood impossible. Illegal entry is not recommended.

Only on special occasions does he appear publicly with his brother Raúl, who is his designated successor and the second most powerful man on the island. Those close to the man say that Raúl, five years Fidel's junior, may be the only person in the world he fully trusts. As evidence, they point to the fact that Raúl is the only man he has allowed to command the military, which is the only institution in the country that conceivably could pose a mortal threat to the revolution. Some have suggested that Fidel's reluctance to be seen regularly with his brother is because of Raúl's unpopularity. The more reliable explanation, though, is Fidel's paranoia about security and his desire to have a viable successor in the event of the unthinkable. It's like Bush and Cheney: Fidel prefers to have Raúl ensconced in a secure, undisclosed location.

Raúl lives near Fidel, in a house that is reportedly nicer than Fidel's. He is said to be an exemplary family man, something of a homebody.

Officially, Fidel is a loner. Officially, he has no wife. History records his early marriage, to a beautiful socialite, and the son she gave birth to, Fidelito, and the subsequent divorce. All of Cuba knows of at least some of his other liaisons over the years, including the one with another socialite, Naty Revuelta, that produced a daughter, Alina, who now denounces her father and all he stood for from her home in Florida. But Cuba still does not know, or at least has not been told, what a Spanish newspaper reported a few years ago and other journalists subsequently confirmed: that for thirty years or so he has had a wife. She may be a legal wife, or she may be a common-law wife, nobody knows; her name is Delia Soto del Valle, if you believe the European press, or Dalia, with an *a*, if you believe the *Miami Herald*, the American newspaper that for obvious reasons takes a special interest in all things Fidel. She is generally described as a onetime schoolteacher from the city of Trinidad, on Cuba's southern coast; photographs show a striking woman of perhaps sixty, with good bones and strong eyes. The *Herald* reported that Fidel and Dalia have five grown sons—Angel, Antonio, Alejandro, Alexis, and Alex—several of whom have children of their own. That would mean that the grand old guerrilla now has grandchildren to dangle on his knee. None of this has ever been reported in the Cuban press. When Fidel appears in public, he appears alone. His domestic life is so well hidden from view, it might as well take place in a parallel universe.

In the universe of things seen, Fidel does not know domesticity. He knows only the struggle—himself and his retinue of aging *compañeros* and callow protégés, fighting as if they were still up in the mountains hiding in cane fields and peasant shacks, their lives and their precious revolution in constant peril. Nearly eighty years old, with no serious threat to his person or rule, Fidel now has to man-ufacture the danger that lets him feel alive. He creates crises, unearths conspiracies, mobilizes vast throngs in defense of the fatherland. He excoriates villains and beatifies heroes. He takes spe-cial care to cultivate his enemies, because without enemies he would be invisible, and if he were invisible he could not exist. He knows no repose. He is in constant motion, an intricate choreogra-phy set to steamy boleros, spicy zarzuelas, white-hot rumbas, and some wild, improvisational counterpoint that he alone seems to hear, that must echo constantly through his restless mind.

The hours march, the music plays on, and Fidel Castro dances alone.

There are those who say he's had a stroke or two. See the way he compensates when he walks? The way he swings one leg slightly out and around because he no longer can bring it straight forward? Others swear he's as hale and strong as an old warrior could be. One aide who knows him well says his intensity comes from constant worry about his legacy, about whether history's absolution, once famously given, has finally been snatched away. That same aide also says, with conviction, that he has never met a man so completely innocent of self-doubt.

On the streets of Havana you see ancient, shabby men and women peddling the official newspapers *Granma* and *Trabajadores* for pennies, because they need the pennies for food, and you think that no one should have to work so hard in old age. But do you extend that sympathy to the Maximum Leader? He was already an old man when the system of thought and application to which he had devoted his life suddenly collapsed, eaten away by rot like the sagging, teeming, ruined mansions in Old Havana that occasionally just shudder and fall when a storm blows through. He had to shift, give way, step left and then right and then left again—he had to dance like a youngster again, and by now he must know that he can never rest. He will dance until he dies.

He micromanages, presiding over endless meetings to discuss administrative trivia that should be decided at the level of county clerk, or that should not be matters of public policy at all, such as whether a specific house or apartment should be awarded to a specific athlete or musician or bureaucrat as a reward for some specific achievement or act of loyalty. He has fearsome powers of memory, summoning facts and figures with a precision that intimidates even his brightest young prodigies. Sometimes, though, he forgets. He's an old man; he forgets.

One day he faints. The next, he strides with the gait of a lion.

He still receives visitors from the capitalist enemy to the north, especially "open-minded" visitors, who tend to be the kind that come to communist Cuba. One group will be treated to a learned, witty, razor-sharp tour d'horizon of the international situation, sprinkled with bon mots, delivered with animated gestures and frequent arching of those famous eyebrows. An amazing man, they will say afterwards, wrongheaded but a true giant, a master of statecraft whatever his flaws, quite possibly a genius. The next delegation, summoned to his office at midnight, will suffer through hours of meandering reminiscence about battles in the Sierra Maestra half a century ago, complete with troop rosters, enumeration of weapons, minute description of thrusts and counterthrusts, and a carefully nuanced judgment on which side got the better of each engagement. He's lost it, that group will say later; he lives in the past, the world has passed him by. Sad.

He is nearly eighty years old. He has good days and bad. Sometimes he has good and bad on the same day.

* * *

"He paces," Roberto Salas told me.

Salas wasn't even out of his teens when the revolution swept Fidel into power. His father, Osvaldo, had been a fellow traveler amid the leftist Cuban exiles living in New York, and as soon as he heard the news of Batista's flight on New Year's Eve 1959, he had taken the first plane to Havana, his son in tow. Osvaldo Salas,

Roberto Salas, and two other photographers, Raúl Corrales and Alberto Korda, became the pictorial documentarians of Fidel Castro's revolution. Among them, they took all the iconic pictures of Fidel, Che Guevara, and the rest of the bearded rebels as they transformed Cuba—and as they themselves changed from angry outsiders to the ultimate insiders. Even Fidel, who so many times had risked his life to be an agent of change, finally reached the point where the condition he most valued was not turmoil but stability.

Roberto Salas, a short, silver-haired man with an easy laugh and sympathetic eyes, had drifted away from Fidel's inner circle, but a couple of years ago the inner circle called. They were putting together a retrospective of the work of Korda, the most famous of the four court photographers, and wanted his help.

"Fidel asked me, 'Where have you been? I don't see you anymore.' I told him I had been around. After I saw him, I sent him a copy of the book I had just published."

Salas had moved over the years from photojournalism into fine-art photography, and much of his recent work was of nudes. He hadn't sent Fidel a copy earlier because he hadn't been sure that the commander-in-chief would approve of imagery that was so sensual, so explicit, and that was esthetic rather than political. Fidel's reaction, though, surprised him.

"He yelled at me. He said, 'Why didn't you send it to me? What do you think I am, a priest? A nun?'"

Salas had published some of his early images of Fidel, and he told him he had a mind to do a second book that would document the revolution forty years later. "A week later, I was with him again, inside the inner circle."

He spent hours inside Fidel's office as subordinates and important visitors came and went. "The man is in constant motion, still in constant motion," he told me. "He's always on his feet, always pacing."

One image was taken while Fidel was receiving Oliver Stone, who went on to produce an admiring lion-in-winter documentary.

Stone is not seen in the frame—Salas recalls that he had excused himself to go to the bathroom. Fidel, deep in thought, is pacing in front of his desk, lost in concentrated thought, unaware of the world outside his mind. His brows are knitted and he holds his hands behind his back. His is not the posture of an old man. His is the posture of a man with a long, long list of things to do.

"He *is* old now," Salas said. "He still works sixteen-hour days, eighteen-hour days. He sleeps two hours, three hours, and he's back at work. He's always been that way, ever since I've known him. He never needed sleep like you or me. Some days he's just like he was. But some days, some days, he's old."

* * *

The government prefers to project a different image, however: that Fidel and his revolution are forever young. Just look at the billboards.

The billboards that line Cuba's highways and the murals that grace its crumbling walls are remarkable in several ways. Unlike the billboards along, say, Interstate 95, they advertise ideas instead of outlet malls and cheap fireworks; they encourage communitarian behavior, urge steadfastness in the face of imperialist aggression, proclaim the superiority of Cuba's system of government. Unlike the billboards in other authoritarian, one-party states, they bear no likenesses of the Maximum Leader. The prohibition is not absolute, but Fidel has banned portraits, statues, and other graven images of himself to prevent a "cult of personality" from forming. You almost never see Fidel staring down from the roadside. You see Che Guevara, Camilo Cienfuegos, and other young lions of the revolution instead.

And that may be the most interesting thing: that Che, Camilo, and the others are frozen in their youthful prime. Their images on the billboards are painted from photographs taken by Salas, Korda, and Corrales in the days and weeks after the revolution. The bearded rebels are handsome in their green fatigues, their unlined faces full of joy and unbridled optimism. Four decades after the fact, the

Cuban revolution presents itself as something brand new, as a fresh beginning. True, there could hardly be pictures of a gray-haired Che or a fat, balding Camilo, since both men died young—Che in the Bolivian jungle, Camilo in a mysterious plane crash. But that James Dean quality seems precisely why they were chosen to be the two ubiquitous faces of Fidel's revolution. It's almost possible to forget that this baby-faced government is run by men in their seventies.

This is no Big Lie, though. The image of stopped time is perfectly accurate. Modern Cuba is Fidel Castro's idea, and the last time that idea changed was before most Cubans alive today were born. He saw a Cuba of heroic sacrifice and complete selflessness, a state that came as close as possible to attaining the communist ideal, a land where "bourgeois comforts" were rightly scorned and "private ownership" was a concept consigned to history's dustbin and "constant struggle" was the happiest human condition of all. The Miami Cubans think it was all a fraud, a tyrant's concocted rationale for keeping and holding power, but I think he meant it. He meant it, he built it, he oversees it to this day. Most of the socialist world has given up and gone robber-baron capitalist. China has kept the official ideology and the one-party system, but invited its billion-plus citizens to make themselves fat and rich. Fidel refuses to dance that dance.

People see Cuba's material poverty and say that it would be better if Fidel would just get with the program, or if he just were a better economic manager, or if he would just remove the controls on private enterprise and stand back as the Cuban people transform the place within the course of a generation. Look what they did in Miami, people say, and imagine what they could do in Havana. But I think that when Fidel looks at the glorious shambles that is Cuba, he sees success, not failure. If Cuba were magically made rich overnight, if suddenly every Cuban had a nice house and a nice car and shopped at the Havana equivalents of Whole Foods and Nordstrom's, I think Fidel would convene crisis meetings to figure out how to put it back the way it was. He seems to believe that without hardship there can be no virtue.

A Cuban who is lucky enough to come into enough money to buy a car can't just go down to the showroom and pick out a new Peugeot. He has to apply for permission to own a car privately, and the ultimate yes or no comes from Vice President Carlos Lage, the thin, balding, brainiac former medical doctor whose cleverness is given much credit for keeping the creaking Cuban system on the road. That the third most important official in the nation decides who can buy a car and who can't is astounding, but it makes sense in the context of Fidel's Cuba. Of course permission could be given or withheld to reward the stalwart and punish the wayward, but I don't think that's the point. Being prominent and successful was usually enough; the prominent musicians I met in Cuba all had cars, including some whose lyrics often strayed from the party line. The point was simply to limit the private ownership of cars, for no good reason other than ideology. This had to be something the government really believed in, which means it had to be something Fidel Castro really believed in. Hardship was good. Public transportation was another matter; there was no excuse for cramming upwards of three hundred sweating, swearing *habaneros* onto a single bus that would take hours to crawl to their destinations. But the people standing at urban intersections and under every highway overpass, trying to hitch rides across town or to the other end of the island? That was an example of virtuous struggle, and a tool for bonding together a more communitarian society. Their fellow citizens stopped to give them rides. To each according to his needs, from each according to his abilities. Americans might need a gas-guzzling car for each licensed driver. Cubans just needed each other.

Along Cuba's streets and highways, the few drivers and the many hitchhikers alike couldn't help but notice a recent moment when the Butch-and-Sundance billboard portraits of Camilo and Che were suddenly replaced by another image, that of a young boy with an angelic face and a perfectly telegenic smile.

The Elián González era had begun. Fidel Castro was about to

show the United States and the world that he might be old, he might have his good days and his bad, but when the right opportunity came along he still had all the moves—that when Lady Luck came along he could still dance her into bed before she knew what was happening.

4. "ELIÁN, YOU ARE THE JOY OF CUBA"

At the intersection where the Prado, Havana's most formal grand boulevard, meets the broad Malecón and the sparkling sea, the shell of a derelict building marred what should have been a postcard view. Part of the structure was being dismantled at a leisurely pace, and much of the rest seemed to have just fallen down, brick by timber by tile, in a process that suggested some kind of leprosy. Rumors had it that a Chinese-Cuban joint venture planned to tear the ruin down and build a deluxe tourist hotel, one that would top the Dutch-Cuban hotel on the Parque Central, and the Spanish-Cuban hotel on the other side of Vedado, and all the other hyphenated swank lodgings that had been springing up around town. The Chinese seemed to be in no hurry, though, as much of the old hulk was still standing. One morning I saw a demolition crew at work, but they seemed to take the rest of the week off.

On one of the remaining walls, officials had hung a billboard where it was sure to be seen by each and every tourist who came to Havana, as well as all the *habaneros* who thronged the intersection day and night, waiting for Godot-like buses or trying to thumb rides with motorists heading through the harbor tunnel to the far side of Havana Bay. On the left was a portrait of a young boy—handsome, dark-haired, pensive, noble, heroic beyond his years. The rest of the billboard was taken up by three words, spelled out in giant red letters: DEVUELVAN A ELIÁN. Return Elián.

* * *

In the struggling neighborhood of Santa Amalia far from the city center, a group of friends—mostly men on the cusp of middle-age spread, including one who was once a member of the Cuban national judo team—had converted the backyard of one house into an open-air gymnasium. There are no Gold's Gyms in Cuba, and no stores where you could buy the equipment to furnish one. But in this land of chronic scarcity, about the only things in perpetual surplus are vanity, ingenuity, and time. So the men had built their own.

A 1960 Chevy Impala was parked in front of the little house, as black and shiny as the day it was made but now with an engine built in Minsk. In the front window was a sign identifying the bungalow as headquarters for the local Committee for the Defense of the Revolution, once a ubiquitous institution of state control and ritualized betrayal where neighbor nightly denounced neighbor, now pretty much a national joke. In a neighborhood like Santa Amalia, anyone who wasn't committing at least some counterrevolutionary infraction, probably involving what the government called "speculation," wasn't feeding his family. People sold food, people took in laundry, people rented their cars—people did what they had to do.

Behind the house, amid the flower beds and the chicken coops, the friends had installed a full circuit of weight machines, cleverly cobbled together from scrap steel, weathered planks, and baling wire. For weights they used massive rusty gears stamped with Cyrillic writing. Some of the improvised machines looked dangerous, like the butterfly machine that might just decapitate its user if the cable snapped, but the more immediate peril was a brisk wind that occasionally sent ripe mangoes plummeting from the leafy canopy above. There was a coconut palm in the little yard too, but all of the bulbous, potentially lethal orbs seemed firmly attached. In a corner was what looked like an old-fashioned steam cabinet, with a hole for the user's head, like the ones that the Three Stooges used to find so amusing.

This morning, two middle-aged women in warm-ups were doing lat pulldowns and squats. The owner of the house, Tamara, a tall, languid woman in a flowered dress, smoked a cigarette as she watched comings and goings from the back porch. She said that I had dropped by during one of the time slots reserved exclusively for women. Asked what had prompted this act of segregation, she shrugged. "Problems," she said. On one wall, behind the table where they kept the free weights, hung a faded, weathered poster of young Elián.

* * *

Every afternoon, around the time when people would be getting home from work, Cuban television presented a "roundtable" discussion—that's what they called it, the *"mesa redonda"*—in which a shifting cast of talking heads analyzed and reanalyzed every incremental nuance of the unfolding Elián story at numbing length. No development was too small to require extensive examination, no newly discovered fact about any of the principals in the story too minor to be placed in the context of all the other inconsequential facts that suffocated the Elián saga in a fog of trivia. Had a television station reported that one of the Miami Relatives was once suspected of drunk driving? Had Elián's family in Cuba emerged to wave briefly at the crowds? This was the place to find out. The live program—sometimes it lasted an hour and a half, sometimes two—was shot in front of a small studio audience, and sometimes Fidel Castro himself showed up and took his place on the sidelines among the patriotic citizens, raising his hand like anyone else when he wanted to make a point. He was always called on promptly. Later each evening, one channel would faithfully replay Castro's recent May Day speech before the multitudes, in which he had recounted the Elián case in excruciating detail. It was aired so often that it seemed the aim was to have everyone in the whole country learn the speech by heart.

The state newspapers *Granma* and *Juventud Rebelde* were tabloid-sized and slim to the point of anorexia because of a chronic newsprint shortage, but no issue was complete without one or two Elián stories on the front page. Cubans wore Elián T-shirts that had been handed out at the million-strong demonstrations Castro regularly called to demand the little boy's return; by now, six months into the saga, the shirts had begun to fade from repeated washings. The boy's face was like municipal wallpaper. If the Cuban government's message to its citizens in the spring of 2000 could be summed up in one word, that would be Elián.

Elián González, of course, was the six-year-old Cuban boy whose mother had taken him with her in an attempt to flee the island in a tiny, overloaded boat. Like most of the Cubans who try to escape the island by sea, they had no idea what they were doing—no experience navigating the open sea, no knowledge of the winds or currents, no sense of how seaworthy a small craft would have to be to survive the passage. Off the coast of Florida, the boat sank. The mother and the other adults perished (and were quickly forgotten, or at least ignored by the media hordes that would soon descend), but somehow Elián survived, clinging to chunks of flotsam amid an infinity of deathly blue. He was rescued miraculously by two Miami men out for a day of fishing, one of whom became known in the Book of Elián as "The Fisherman," even though there was no evidence that he had ever gone fishing before. Hagiographic legend had it that the boy, who was blessed with the face of an angel, had been kept afloat by dolphins presumably sent by the Almighty.

A better guess is that he was saved by Narcissus, the god of the media, because he was a godsend of a story. His rescuers had taken him to Miami, where every Cuban who has fled the island is automatically a hero, a freedom fighter, even a little boy who had made no conscious choice between the two warring systems—a boy whose parents were divorced, and who had been spirited away without even his father's knowledge. He was quickly given over to the custody of his relatives, loving strangers, whom the mother had been trying so desperately to reach. In Miami that seemed a natural outcome—after all, if the refugees had made it safely to shore they would have gone immediately to that little house, where Elián would have played in that same little backyard, slipping down that same little sliding board, albeit without a hundred photographers pushing and shoving to take his picture.

But the father, a loyal communist who had stayed behind in Cuba, wanted him sent home. Fidel Castro had immediately recognized the potential of the story—in another life he could have been a Hollywood producer with a shelf full of Oscars. He could see it all, screenplay, storyboard, camera angles, lighting. But first he had to be sure that everyone would play his part. As the story is told by Cubans inside and outside of the government, he arranged a meeting with the father, Juan Miguel González, to see with his own eyes whether his enthusiastic aides were reading the man right.

Juan Miguel lived in Cárdenas, a town on the north coast, and worked as a parking-lot attendant in nearby Varadero, the island's premier beach resort, where planeloads of Italians, Spaniards, and Canadians roasted themselves on miles of pristine beach and luxuriated in five-star hotels for a week at a time until they headed back to the airport and flew home, without ever setting so much as one sunburned toe in the real Cuba. As someone who every day came into contact with hundreds of tourists, Juan Miguel was de facto a member of Cuba's new privileged class, the dollar-earning class. Unlike most Cubans, he could almost see a future for himself.

The story goes that Castro sat Juan Miguel down and told him point-blank that if he wanted to emigrate to Miami to be with his son, he could leave that very day. Everyone would understand, no hard feelings, and if he wanted to return someday the door would be open. Juan Miguel told him no, he wanted to stay in Cuba. He believed in the revolution and he was rooted in his native land. He had no use for Miami. All he wanted was his son. Castro watched him, looked into his eyes, and convinced himself that this man was the genuine article.

For a believer in Marxism, which posits that the march of history is inevitable and individual actors interchangeable or irrelevant, Fidel Castro has always veered toward apostasy in his endorsement of a modified Great Man scheme of history. He has argued, though in careful Marxist terms, that while the Cuban revolution was historically inevitable, it wouldn't have actually happened unless Fidel Castro had come along, with Fidel Castro's exact profile of leadership abilities, personality traits, military acumen, and political talent. Perhaps it was by listening to the calm purpose in Juan Miguel's words, perhaps it was by looking into his eyes, but whatever the confirming evidence Castro decided that this was the right man. Here in Juan Miguel, a parking lot attendant, a *fulano de tal*, a nobody, he had the right man at the right historical moment to score a victory for Cuba as stirring as any he had won since the Triumph of the Revolution itself.

The story had vivid characters, hot-button politics, apparent miracles, and at its center a protagonist so perfect—so handsome, so symmetrical, and, not incidentally, so *white*—that he instantly became not a boy but an icon, a blank screen for the projection of faith. No one saw all this quite so clearly as Castro, who recognized the opportunity not only to shore up support for the revolution at home, but to confuse and ultimately divide his imperialist enemy.

I'm arguing for fatherhood and family, Castro effectively told the Miami Cubans and the hawks in Washington. I'm arguing to reunite a little boy with his father, his only surviving parent, so that he doesn't grow up an orphan in a foreign land. Please be so kind as to rise to the bait.

And you Cubans at home, let's not talk about the depressed economy, or more movement toward private enterprise, or loosening of restrictions on the press or the Internet. Let's talk about this beautiful boy, this stolen angel.

In Havana and across the island, Castro summoned throngs into the streets to demand Elián's return. Castro commanded, and millions of citizens mouthed the words he fed them. The images of the people's fervor over Elián were beamed throughout the world, especially to Miami and Washington, the two cities that mattered. It was grand opera on a gargantuan scale.

The thing was, though, that behind all the state-sponsored,

mandatory wailing and gnashing of teeth, Cubans really believed in the cause. This time, the Big Lie turned out to be a Big Truth.

Granted, it's hard to gauge genuine public sentiment in a place like Cuba. Only one worldview was correct—Fidel Castro's worldview—and being wrong in public about certain things was a criminal offense. There were no opinion polls, and even if there had been, nobody inside or outside of Cuba would have believed them. The news media, which might have presented a diversity of views, were among the most tightly controlled institutions in the entire society, hewing to the party line without the slightest deviation. The typical evening newscast was blanket coverage of whatever Fidel had done that day, followed by blanket coverage of whatever Fidel had said that day about Elián, followed by weather and sports. The typical *Granma* front page would feature an article about the unfairness of Elián's continued detention by the "Miami mafia"; a separate piece about the international outcry for Elián to be returned home; a brief number-filled report on the unprecedented levels of production being attained by the bauxite industry, due to the heroic efforts of the patriotic bauxite workers; and verbatim text of the opening remarks delivered at some party plenum, whatever a plenum was. Only in communist societies do they have plenums.

Even in chance encounters on the street, where Cubans seemed so irrepressible, it was difficult to know whether what you were hearing was truly uncensored. It seemed acceptable for Cubans to complain about the moribund state of housing or transportation or the overall economy, even to an American writing it all down in a notebook. But was it safe to express any sort of independent opinion on a subject as important as Elián? Nobody did to me, not even bartenders or cab drivers or other cynics about the human condition who hadn't hesitated to entertain me at length with screeds on everything that was wrong with their enchanted island. It seemed that Fidel had proved once again that he knew his constituency better than anybody did—that he might be old, but he was still Fidel.

* * *

One night far from downtown, on a dark side street in the hilltop neighborhood called Cerro, a very different music scene came alive. In the old days, wealthy *habaneros* had built weekend homes in Cerro to take advantage of the cooling breezes. Now it was one of the city's more decrepit and depressing districts. The tight rows of colonial-style houses, fronted by continuous galleries like the covered sidewalks of the Old West, were falling down from neglect, and unlike some other parts of the city Cerro had seen no restoration at all. A couple of huge, ugly apartment buildings now marred the crest of the hill, and the city's principal baseball stadium drew crowds on game nights, but otherwise Cerro had been left to slowly disintegrate.

Across from what once had been a graceful park, a small crowd stood in front of a school auditorium. Tickets were being sold at the door; admission was in pesos and amounted to four cents. Inside were a few hundred young people, almost all of them black and about half with dreadlocks, listening to an eleven-piece band onstage playing "No Woman No Cry" in honor of Bob Marley Day, the anniversary of the great man's death.

This was Havana's reggae subculture, and it looked like any other reggae subculture anywhere in the world, except that the smoke that filled the hall to the point of asphyxiation was exclusively from tobacco.

"We can't really practice the Rastafarian religion as it's meant to be," a dreadlocked music producer named Daniel Rosales told me through the din and the haze, "because they won't let you smoke marijuana in this country."

Rosales had big plans for reggae in Cuba. He had helped put together this event and managed some of the participating bands, including the one now onstage, named Reto, which means "challenge." In the streets I had occasionally noticed young black men dressed for the streets of Kingston or Mo' Bay rather than Havana, with dreads, drawstring pants, Afro-chic linen shirts or wild dashikis, and red-green-black leather caps and accessories. I'd also noticed a disproportionate number of these young men being stopped by police for document checks or other harassment. There weren't many of these Rasta-wannabes, just a few, but it was surprising to me that there were any at all. And it looked as if every single one of them had come to Cerro tonight to commemorate the death of the singing prophet.

Reto soon made way for another band, which quickly made way for another. None was exceptional in musical terms, although each was warmly received by the crowd, which sang along in phonetic English with more enthusiasm than precision. Even though Jamaica was as close to Cuba as Florida was, and even though Cuba's eastern provinces had once drawn immigrant workers from Jamaica the way California now draws them from Mexico, there wasn't much of a true reggae feel to the music I heard in Cerro that night. The bands kept making the percussion more complicated than it should have been, at times even slipping unthinkingly into the three-two *clave*, the basic Latin beat. It was interesting, but not really the way Bob Marley intended a song like "Exodus" to be performed.

More remarkable than the music, though, was the very fact of this subculture. A group of like-minded individuals had come together to celebrate a music and a culture in which they had a common interest—not even worthy of notice in most countries, but intriguing in one-party, one-worldview Cuba.

The focal point of the community was music. They gathered at one another's homes and in parks and recreation centers to listen and to play. But there were other factors that brought them together. There was reggae style—the clothes, the dreads, the attitude. There was weed—contrary to Rosales's disclaimer, and in defiance of Castro's no-strikes policy against any use of illegal drugs, Cubans had been cultivating and smoking marijuana for a century. There was art—I had first met Rosales a few days earlier in Old Havana, at an art gallery, where he had been chatting with a painter who called himself Ras Israel and whose canvases were swirling riots of Afrocentric themes.

And that was what really brought the reggae scene together: Afrocentrism. The crowd that night in Cerro was virtually all-black and had come together to celebrate a musician who had done more than any one man to disseminate and popularize the notion of the African diaspora. On one level, Bob Marley's music was about dreads and dope and the divinity of Jah and the destiny of a semi-mythical Ethiopia. On another, it was a social and political manifesto on behalf of black people everywhere, seeking justice and empowerment *as* black people.

In Cuba, where racism was supposed to have been eradicated by the revolution, this was the first time—but not the last—that I had seen and heard that orthodox view of a colorblind society openly challenged.

"They pretty much let us do our thing," Rosales said, when asked how the government regarded this little reggae nation. "We all get stopped by the police, because if you look like us, that's just the way it is. But they let us have our shows like this one. There's no support for the music, and that's a problem, but they let us do it. There's just one thing you can't do. You can't call this a movement. As long as it's just music, it's fine. But the moment you say the word *movement*, you're in trouble."

I went backstage and talked to some of the young musicians, all of whom were remarkably skilled, despite their inexperience with the specific reggae vibe. When you talked to them they were nothing at all like the genuine article you might find in Jamaica: like all Cuban teenagers I'd run into, they were well spoken, polite, respectful, even wholesome. They were also uniformly gracious and enthusiastic when I approached them—this wasn't a place they had expected to run into an American, and they were full of questions about the States.

A thin young man who played the trumpet came up nervously to say that he was particularly confused about one thing:

"Why do they keep Elián when his father is here in Cuba? I never really believed the government when they said that the United States was trying to destroy Cuba, but this I really don't understand. What is the motivation? Is it anti-Cuba, like they tell us? How can the United States do this to a little boy?"

* * *

Another day I went in search of a magazine devoted to contemporary Cuban popular music. I had heard about it, but no one seemed to have a copy. There aren't any newsstands as such in Cuba, except in the five-star hotels, where foreigners can buy week-old copies of the international editions of *Time* and *Newsweek*. I'd seen references to *Tropicana Internacional* on Web sites, but none offered any clue as to how to find it. Finally, in one of my frequent conversations with officials at the Cuban Institute of Music, a branch of the Ministry of Culture (there are officials for *everything* in Cuba) I mentioned the magazine. They didn't have a copy on hand either, but they did have a phone number. The man who answered gave me an address.

It turned out to be a house in central Havana. A middle-aged woman answered the door. Like many Cuban homes, I noticed, this one had a shrine to the Santería deity Elegguá in a corner. We strode through the living room and dining room into a small office, where a gray-haired man was waiting behind a desk. This was the headquarters of *Tropicana Internacional*, and the man, Nestor Milí, was the editor.

Milí's mission was to chronicle—and encourage—the rise of Cuban music on the world scene, following the success of Buena Vista Social Club. His instrument was something new: a private magazine whose editorial direction was charted by someone other than an agent of the Cuban state.

"We're a self-financing magazine, not a part of the government, but also not a profit-making venture," said Milí, a thin man whose movements were quick and precise, like those of a drummer. "You could say we're an NGO, a nongovernmental organization."

Perhaps because Castro remembered how important favorable media coverage had been to his revolution's victory forty years earlier, he controlled television and radio just as tightly as newspapers. The officials put in charge of every station, paper, and magazine were always people whom Fidel Castro would trust with his life.

The only newspapers that reached the streets, to be hawked by senior citizens for pennies, were published by the state or various dependencies of the Communist Party. Since the economic crisis of the early 1990s, there were hardly any magazines at all. But a very few—often more like academic journals than slick glossies—were being published by universities, think tanks, and nascent NGOs. They couldn't be called an independent press, since they didn't deal with politics at all in any critical way and had to keep within the narrow boundaries of acceptable discourse. They weren't being distributed in any effective way. But they were seedlings, and given time and nourishment they might just grow into something.

Tropicana Internacional was no threat to the government's information monopoly. Its subject matter was noncontroversial, at least on the surface, and its resources were so tenuous that it couldn't manage a regular publication schedule. An issue would come out when it came out, and the next might have to wait a few months or even a full year. *Tropicana Internacional* was founded in 1996, Milí told me; the most recent issue he handed me, dated simply "2000," was his ninth.

"I come from a musical family. My father wrote songs for Celia Cruz," Milí told me. "I spent a year in Venezuela making art—I'm an artist, really—and when I came back I saw that there was a need for publications devoted to Cuban music. Our music has always had space in the international market. But now, all of a sudden, it's much bigger."

Issue No. 9 ran to sixty-six pages and was thick with stories—with no advertising. There were features on top salsa bands, historical pieces on great Cuban musicians of the past such as Beny Moré and the pianist Bola de Nieve, tips on newcomers to watch, a top-forty list based on radio airplay, and even an editorial calling on *someone* to recognize the quality and marketability of Cuban music and make a real effort to promote it in the world marketplace. That unnamed someone being called to task would have to be the government, but of course this was not spelled out.

The lead story was about a wildly popular band called

Charanga Habanera, which at the moment was in turmoil. Led by a charismatic singer-songwriter named David Calzado, the sixteen-piece band had become a favorite of Cuba's teens and twentysomethings, with a combination of furious, danceable music and lyrics that spoke of real life, often risqué enough to provoke government disapproval. One hit song told of a woman who got so loose at a concert—a Charanga Habanera concert, of course—that she started taking off her clothes. In concert, the song had become a cue for women to do just that. Another hit admonished listeners, in frank terms, to use condoms. Sex was pretty much the band's constant theme.

They had been riding atop the Havana musical scene, but then one day Calzado suddenly fired the whole band, complaining they just weren't good enough. The angry musicians claimed it was they who had fired Calzado, in a dispute over money. While Calzado went out and put together a new Charanga Habanera with a whole new set of players and singers, the old ones stuck together and formed their own band, which they called Charanga Forever. In the article, Calzado introduced his new *orquesta* and assured readers there were no hard feelings. He'd be back soon, he promised, better than ever. The tone of the piece was somewhat skeptical. In the battle of the two Charangas, who would win?

"David Calzado's new percussionist is sixteen years old!" Milí told me. "Amazing little kid. David is smart. I think he'll be all right."

Milí was no less than an evangelist when it came to his pet subject. All of what we call "Latin" music, he said, came from one ur-source: the savory Cuban *son*, which had codified the use of the basic three-two rhythm in song form. "Others have added richness to the music, we cannot deny this. The Colombians, and the Puerto Ricans, certainly have contributed. But it all derives from the *son*."

In Milí's analysis of this musical evolution, percussion is the indicator to follow. The three-two *clave* originated in Cuba and provided the basis for *son*, which then, as any prodigy born and raised on a little island might do, went abroad: the rhythm spread throughout Latin America and into the Latin neighborhoods of U.S. cities, especially New York, where amplification and street-smart attitude turned it into the genre we know as salsa.

Salsa then filtered back into Cuba, but for many reasons—some political, involving national and communist pride, and others per- haps musical—the word *salsa* isn't used nearly as much in Havana as in, say, the Bronx. Cuban popular music has developed in at least partial isolation over the past forty years, and the result is a sound that's harder, more aggressive, more adventurous, with faster tem- pos, riskier harmonies, and undertones of the funk music of the 1970s, rather than the 1960s pop or the 1980s disco that have left their mark on salsa. In the United States, so-called traditional salsa is almost moribund, the music having been sweetened to the point of irrelevance by the application of top-forty pop conventions—and largely replaced on the Latin airwaves by more vibrant (but less interesting) rhythms like the Dominican *merengue*. In Cuba, salsa is still king, but these days it's generally called *timba*, a Cuban word for what is, once again, mainly a Cuban form of music. *Timba* is the kind of music that I had heard Bamboleo play that night at the Tropical. It's hard to describe the difference between Nuyorican salsa and Cuban *timba*, but no one who has ever heard the two could confuse them. It's a matter of stance, power, and lethal intent—the difference between a debate and a riot.

"It all begins with the percussion," Milí said. "We do it differ- ently. Our own way. It's harder. It's something we learn from the beginning. In the streets every day you see kids practicing to get the rhythms right. So the beginning is the strong, strong percussion. And then that aggression is translated to the horns."

The woman who had answered the door came in to serve cof- fee. He hardly noticed, caught up as he was in the subject that had become his passion.

"There's just something different about the Cuban music, about the *timba*," he said. "What is it? We have the best-trained musicians, that's certainly true, because of the National Arts Schools and the excellent education they give in all facets of music. But it is also true that a great number of notable musicians are without formal schooling. In all the *orquestas* you will find many of the players are trained but some are not. There's something more, something in us. Something inside of us."

Milí could be described as a Cuban nationalist, at least in his pride in his country's music and musicians, but he was no government puppet. He recognized the moment—a moment of great opportunity—and also saw that it could easily be lost.

"Look, right now there is a boom in Cuban music," he said. "Not from *timba*, not at all, but because of all the old people and the old music. You know, the Buena Vista Social Club. It's international, it's global. Look at Compay Segundo. He filled a soccer stadium in Colombia recently, and he's ninety-three years old! Cuban musicians are making more money than ever before. Cuban music is big business right now."

He described the changes that had made life better for the musicians. They technically still worked for the state, as most people in Cuba did, but they could and did sign contracts with private record companies overseas. The state music companies skimmed an agent's fee of up to 20 percent, but the rest was for the musicians to keep, after taxes. It was a more normal arrangement, one that would be more or less familiar anywhere in the world. The biggest stars lived well—although not in the style they would have enjoyed elsewhere. Milí said that Chucho Valdés, the great jazz pianist, had "a big three-story house in Miramar," one of the best-looking, best-kept parts of Havana. He reported that José Luis Cortés, the founder and leader of the group NG La Banda, "has two houses—one of them with a studio. The musicians have a high living standard and now they have great liberty to do what they want to do."

But Milí was afraid that this "very favorable moment" could slip away if the government agencies and companies that ran the music business didn't stoop to a little capitalist practice.

"We have to take advantage of the moment," he said. "The issue is not diffusion, it's promotion. Music is a product and it has to be sold. If you don't advertise it, you don't sell it. Period."

He sighed with the frustration of someone who sees an obvious fact of which others seem to be oblivious.

"People don't realize the magnitude and the quality of this product," he said. "We should be out in the world, making everyone aware that we're making some of the best music anywhere. We should help get the music into the stores in the United States and everywhere else. But as long as we do nothing to promote the music, we'll go nowhere. A few people understand this. Look at Juan de Marcos and the success he's had. Many others should be having the same kind of success as Juan de Marcos and the old people, but it isn't happening. It isn't being made to happen."

Milí gave me a couple of copies of *Tropicana Internacional* and showed me some of his artwork, which hung throughout the little house and gave it the feel of a crowded gallery. He also gave a disquisition on his shrine to Elegguá and his belief in "the Yoruba faith." Elegguá was one of the *orishas,* specifically the Lord of the Crossroads, he said. He had to be placed in a corner near the door, because it was he who opened all doors. His personal *orisha* was Changó. All this was meaningless to me, but in time I would learn how important this complex, living faith was to Cuban music in particular and indeed to the very life of the island.

Before I left, as he shook my hand, he said, "Tell me, why won't the United States let the boy Elián come home to his father? Are the Cubans in Miami really that powerful?"

* * *

I had explained to Tomás Misas, the helpful, harried international press liaison at the Institute of Music—which I'd come to think of as the Ministry of Sound—that I was primarily interested in the music of now, the music of the airwaves and the discotheques, but he kept suggesting more refined offerings. One happened to be taking place in the atrium of my hotel, so I could hardly demur. So on a Sunday afternoon I went downstairs to hear a youth string ensemble (usually an unfortunate combination of words) of which the Ministry of Sound was especially proud.

Fifteen minutes before the recital was to start, the young players were in a large meeting room on the mezzanine, being terrorized through a last-minute rehearsal by a dark-haired, cold-eyed, conceivably golden-hearted martinet named Alla Taran.

"What are you doing?" she snapped in the direction of a twelve-year-old violinist, a pudgy, brown-skinned boy who was frozen by her glare as if in the presence of Medusa. "What on earth was that? Weren't you paying attention?"

As the time approached she darted around the room, tuning instruments, adjusting ties, straightening skirts. The members of the ensemble ranged in age from eight to thirteen. As Professor Taran herded them out the door to make their entrance, she hissed, *"Silencio!"* No one even breathed.

Alla Taran was an odd name for a Cuban, and it turned out that she wasn't Cuban at all, at least not by birth. Before the whole world changed she had come to Havana as a "Soviet adviser." She was actually Armenian, and back when Armenia was a revanchist notion instead of a sovereign state, she had come to Havana along with legions of other expert Soviets to help the Cubans, brother socialists, in developing the arts and sciences. She had taken on a long-term project—development of a world-class youth orchestra—and when the Soviet Union collapsed, she decided to stay. Her work was unfinished, and the weather was a considerable improvement over what awaited her at home. Her project had been so successful that her ensemble had received lavish acclaim, appearing at music festivals around the world.

Her students, she explained, came from the National Arts Schools. Her methods were classical in every sense of the word. She brooked no nonsense. Fundamentals were everything. Practice was good; more practice was better. After practice, there would be more practice.

Her charges were a portrait of the revolution as it would most want to be portrayed. As an audience of around two hundred assembled, the young musicians arranged themselves on the hotel's grand staircase—white, black, and brown, male and female, impeccably groomed, erect of posture, poised, and confident. They looked like a propaganda poster, and in one-party Cuba, that was disturbing. It was impossible not to be impressed, but unclear whether the whole thing was worthy of unalloyed approval.

Until they began to play.

These children played so far beyond their years that it was uncanny, almost unbelievable. On their stolid but modest violins, violas, and cellos, all of which had been provided free of charge by the state, they produced not the screeching and scratching normally issued by children allowed to handle string instruments, but warm, burnished tones that had the audacity to mingle sweetly. They played Schubert's "Ave Maria," a song by the Russian composer Isaak Dunayevsky, and Saint-Saëns's "Cisne," among other pieces, followed by a crowd-pleasing finale—one of Beny Moré's more famous tunes, orchestrated for strings. In each, the technical factors such as attack, intonation, and roundness of tone were impeccable, unchallengeable. Taran had somehow instilled in these youngsters a feeling for dynamics. She had taught them a remarkably uniform vibrato. More than that, the music was actually, well, *good*. It wasn't just well played in a technical sense, it was good. It had life, spirit, emotion, the elusive feeling of dance. If you closed your eyes you were sure these were mature musicians, perhaps the string section of a regional orchestra making its move on the top rank.

The Soviet system had produced so much misery in the world, but so much beautifully played music.

Afterwards, I spoke again briefly with the *maestra*, Professor Taran, but she had little to say that her music hadn't already said. She begged off—she had to attend to the children, whom she now treated with tenderness and encouragement, and who showered her with kisses—and handed me to her Cuban assistant, Lucía Varona, a music teacher at one of the National Arts Schools.

Varona sat with me and answered my questions about the system of music education that had produced this remarkable result, and was emphatic on one point, which she wanted me to write down: "Classical music is the foundation of everything. With that background, a musician can play anything. Anything at all."

Then, as she left to respond to the *maestra*'s summons, Verona turned and asked if I would tell her one thing:

"Why are they so determined to keep Elián from his father?"

* * *

Later that afternoon, I trekked to the opposite pole of the Cuban musical universe. The journey involved a ten-minute cab ride down the Malecón, past the gorgeous Hotel Riviera—this time-warp city's most perfect museum of the 1950s, now always filled with European tour groups—and on into a far corner of Vedado, to a patio garden called El Gran Palenque. As was the case at the reggae concert, there were two admission prices, a few pennies for Cuban patrons and a couple of bucks for me.

El Gran Palenque was a venue for "traditional" music. It was a big open-air enclosure with a stage in the middle and rows of folding chairs for the audience. There were no frills in evidence, no pretensions betrayed. The floor was concrete, the walls cinderblock, the stage a bare platform filled with amplifiers and instruments. The bar offered a choice: beer or rum.

The show hadn't started, so there was time to stroll the perimeter, beer in hand, and check out the gathering crowd. There were a few tourists, but only a few. I spent a few minutes eavesdropping on a group standing to one side, two Englishwomen who had arrived with Cuban men as their escorts. The women obviously were friends—one looked to be about thirty, the other well into her forties, both trim and tanned in halter tops and shorts, both completely at ease in this exotic setting, in that way the English have of making themselves perfectly comfortable among the natives.

The Cuban guys with them were much younger, in their early twenties. The one with the older woman was tall and thin, wearing black pants, a black silk shirt, a gold chain, and a black porkpie hat; he had a pencil moustache with a gap in the middle, and carried himself as if he knew he was the coolest guy in the joint. The man attending the younger woman was shorter and clean-shaven, and he had on baggy jeans, clean white tennis shoes, and a white tank top that showed off his impressive muscles. Both were very dark skinned. Recorded music was playing over the sound system, and when a song by Bamboleo came on, the two couples began dancing. The women couldn't dance like locals, but they weren't bad at all—they had the rhythm down cold and knew enough of the steps, spinning at appropriate moments and gracefully letting the men lead. The guys slowed their moves down and kept everything simple so the women could keep up, but for foreigners they acquitted themselves quite well. This was not their first time dancing salsa, nor their first time in Cuba.

It was clear to me that these were professional relationships. The guys were *jineteros*, gigolos. The women had come to Cuba to meet tall, dark, and handsome. I'd seen lots of European men swanning around town with Cuban women draped all over them, but these were the first women I'd seen in Havana as sexual tourists. In truth, I noticed in later trips, the phenomenon isn't rare at all, but on first encounter it was jarring. These small, soft-spoken women didn't particularly look like predators, nor did these smooth, leering rakes look much like prey.

I was so momentarily unsettled that I even wondered whether I was imagining things, whether these might not simply be two sweet, lonely women who had had the good fortune to go on a sunny vacation and find true love. But any doubt was erased when the guys went off to the bar to get drinks, and a Cuban woman, evidently an acquaintance who just happened to be here, approached the Englishwomen. I wasn't close enough to hear all of what the Cuban woman said, but I understood her quite clearly when she nodded in the direction of the two guys and said, with a nudge: "*Aaaah. ¡Qué malísimas! Están con chicos frescos. ¿Les gusta bien negrito, no? ¡Que se diviertan!*"

Aaaah. You bad girls! You're with fresh guys. You like them good and black, no? Have fun! She said it with the solicitous air of a procuress.

There were young couples and groups of young people just out for an afternoon of hanging out, but there were also Cuban families, mothers and fathers with young children, and a large contingent of senior citizens that seemed to have come as a group. The seniors were wearing their Sunday best, the men in fraying suits and ties, the women in dresses and heels and even Sunday hats. It was a hot day and I was afraid they would melt in the heat, but they were much more accustomed to the climate than I was. Every once in a while I saw both men and women pull from their pockets or purses the handkerchief or bandanna that every Cuban carries, and then spend the next few minutes mopping their faces so thoroughly that not a drop of moisture remained. The procedure had to be repeated often. It reminded me of a long, hot Sunday in a Southern Baptist church.

After a long delay, having to do with some equipment problem, the show was ready to begin. An all-women *timba* group took the stage first and performed an enthusiastic set that sparked hardly any reaction from the crowd at all—this wasn't what they had come to hear. Finally the headliners appeared—a group called Canela, which means cinnamon.

Canela consisted exclusively of singers and drummers—conga and bongo players, percussionists armed with wood chocks and cowbells, *cajón* players who sat on big wooden boxes and pounded the sides—a stage full of drummers. The music they played was Afro-Cuban, and it rocked. They stripped the salsa and *timba* beats to their raw essence, powerful percussion and expressive voice, and the crowd loved it.

Everyone got up to dance but none more avidly than the senior citizens, who were clearly determined to make the most of this afternoon out, free of cares and woes, free of ration cards and dollar stores and the sad poverty that Cuba's pensioners stoically endure. Their dancing was in many ways the most wonderful I had seen. It wasn't the virtuosic spinning and twirling that I was used to seeing from the kids. It was slower and more subtle, but also somehow sexier. Big old black women moved their hips in a way that suggested the seesaw of the tides. Men held themselves in debonair poses as they led their partners, smooth and precise and irresistible like Fred Astaire. The group invited some of them onstage and they showed off their moves for the crowd. When the drummers went into a specific, complex rhythm called the *guaguancó,* a skinny old man and his fat old lady went up to demonstrate. They did a specific courtship dance, in which the woman feigns modesty while the man circles her, circles her, approaches, withdraws, bides his time, circles again, and then, when he sees the right opening, invades her space with a lewd pelvic thrust. The woman quickly turns and shies away, not me, not now, but then resumes her teasing dance, inviting him, driving him wild with passion. It was a spellbinding display.

The singers kept up a running chant, and it took me a while to realize they were improvising. I missed most of what they said—they were using slang I didn't understand—but they ended with a line that brought a huge cheer from the crowd, the biggest of the day, and told me as much about the mood of the nation as any opinion poll might have done.

"*Elián, tu eres la felicidad de Cuba,*" they chanted. "*Elián, tu eres la felicidad de Cuba.*" Over and over again, to cheers that rose into the cloudless sky: "*Elián, tu eres la felicidad de Cuba.*"

Elián, you are the joy of Cuba.

* * *

A year later, after the last notes of the opera had sounded and Elián was back home in Cárdenas, I decided to pay his family a visit, or at least try. Officials in the Foreign Ministry in Havana said that of course they had no objection to my interviewing Juan Miguel as long as he was willing to cooperate. I had friends try to reach him, but the only answer I got back was a vague "probably not." That was better than "get lost," so off I went.

Cárdenas is on the northern coast, three or four hours from Havana by rental car, depending on how many times you get lost. Fidel must have taken a page from the Spanish conquistadors, who in the early 1500s designed their most important early Cuban city, Trinidad, with odd-angled streets and an irregular grid to misdirect marauding pirates or English marines and funnel them into prepared killing grounds. Five centuries later, Cuba was a nation without highway signs. Had the invaders at the Bay of Pigs managed to break out of their doomed little beachhead, they would have wandered fruitlessly through the cane fields, asking directions from every peasant they met, until Fidel finally caught up to them. Major arterial highways go completely unheralded, unmarked, and thus often untaken. Choosing the right road is a matter of instinct and faith, neither of which is infallible. I saw a lot of the Cuban coast.

The road leads past a small oil field, whose rusting pumps worked to supply a fraction of the country's energy needs—Fidel's friend and protégé, Venezuelan president Hugo Chávez, was nice enough to supply the rest—and on through Matanzas, a port city that had been an important center of the sugarcane industry, the slave trade, and the birth of Afro-Cuban culture. Beyond Matanzas lay the anomaly called Varadero.

Varadero is a peninsula, a narrow spit of land jutting into the Atlantic that has the fortune to be lined with mile after breathtaking mile of perfect white-sand beach. The du Pont family discovered Varadero early in the century and built a grand mansion, called Xanadu, that today overlooks Cuba's only world-class golf course; Al Capone's former villa is now a restaurant. The Cuban revolution has developed Varadero into one of the Caribbean's leading resorts—but also a literal Forbidden Zone that ordinary Cubans are not even allowed to enter without a legitimate reason. If the police checkpoints don't stop them, the two-dollar toll on the road into town (the only toll road I ever saw in Cuba) surely will.

Juan Miguel González, Elián's father, worked as a parking-lot attendant in Varadero. In today's Cuba, that means with the one-dollar and one-euro tips the tourists gave him when they handed him their keys he earned more than the average Cuban pediatric neurosurgeon, aeronautical engineer, or manufacturing executive.

Varadero is like a communist Cancún, with huge modern hotels built not for beauty or elegance but to cram as many ocean-view rooms onto the property as possible. Most are joint-venture projects with foreign hotel chains. There is a lively nightlife—all the top Cuban bands play there, and foreign acts as well—and there are the usual *jineteras,* who find some way to get past the checkpoints. But overall, there is the sense of having left Cuba and entered some other country, or perhaps some other time frame—the sense of glimpsing one of Cuba's many possible futures.

Cárdenas lies a half hour farther down the main coastal highway. As Cuban provincial small towns go, it is a prosperous place, since so many of its residents work for dollars in Varadero, but the distinction is relative. Cárdenas is Cuba, not Cancún; the buildings need paint, the infrastructure is crumbling, the streets are clogged with ancient smoke-spewing buses and poke-along horse-drawn jitneys. It's a clean, sunny town, though, and the locals had a spring in their stride that you didn't often see in the hinterlands.

The one sit-down restaurant is on the ground floor of the one hotel, and both are Cuban establishments that charge in pesos. The day I stopped by, a surly waitress came over to the table—she must have worked there for years and learned her manners from *The Joe Stalin Book of Etiquette*—and announced: "Fricassee of pork, and rice." This was the entire menu, take it or leave it. The pork had perhaps one mouthful of meat amid copious fat and gristle, and there was no telling how long that rice had been sitting at room temperature back in the kitchen but the time surely was measured in days, not hours. To wash it down the waitress offered a locally bottled cola drink that tasted like medicine. The meal cost less than a dollar. Still hungry, I tried a fast-food chicken joint across the way, but alas, they were out of chicken. The man behind the counter offered directions to another fried-chicken joint a few blocks away that did, in fact, have chicken, but for some reason they served it slathered in ketchup.

I had an address for Elián's house. No one answered the door, but a passing bicyclist helpfully explained that this was the boy's grandparents' house, and that Elián, his father, and his stepmother had moved to another house about a mile away.

I expected something grander for the young icon, but Elián lived in a tiny, one-story house on the main drag, right across from a busy bus stop. The house was nice by the town's standards, immaculately kept, with a postage-stamp yard enclosed by a chain-link fence. But all the other houses on the block were equally nice. The only thing to distinguish Elián's was the uniformed policeman standing sentinel on the sidewalk in front—the policeman who came to meet me as I approached.

He was as polite as could be. I explained that I wanted to speak with Juan Miguel. He said that the family wasn't in at the moment, but he would be happy to give them the message and my business card; perhaps I could come back in a couple of hours?

With time to kill, there was nowhere to go but to the other main attraction in Cárdenas, the Museum of the Battle of Ideas.

It is better known as the Elián Museum. The government had converted one of the grandest buildings in town, a big old firehouse painted marigold yellow, into a museum dedicated to the long battle over Elián and Cuba's great victory over the exile community in Miami. Fidel himself came to Cárdenas to inaugurate the museum. "The battle of ideas cannot be lost," he said on that occasion, "nor will it be lost."

The objects on display are difficult to get your mind around, curatorially speaking. A partial list will have to suffice: the Cuban flag that flew at Elián's grandparents' house in Cárdenas. The T-shirt worn by the fisherman who pulled Elián from the sea. E-mails and letters from around the world backing Cuba's side in the dispute. Pictures of Elián at Disney World, wearing mouse ears. Photos of a multitudinous bring-him-home rally at the Plaza de la Revolución. A zootrope of a galloping horse, designed by Elián's old classmates in Cárdenas. A mockup of the Open Tribunal plaza that Fidel hurriedly built in Havana, beneath the windows of the U.S. Interests Section, so the Americans could not help but hear Cuba's demands for Elián's return. School notebooks kept by the Cuban kids who were sent to the United States to keep Elián company during the long interlude between the raid to take him away from the

Miami relatives and the conclusion of the long legal process that ended in his return. While he was waiting to go home, Elián was in the custody of the Cuban Interests Section in Washington; he and his imported classmates took the same classes they would have taken in Cuba and were taught by Cuban teachers. One of the notebooks was open to a page on which the student wrote, in careful cursive: *"Cada cubano es un soldado."* Every Cuban is a soldier.

Without a doubt, though, the museum's highlight, at least for me, was a statue titled *Dignity.* Its central figure is Elián—museum docents say it is a generic young boy, but if so it's a generic boy who looks just like Elián—sculpted in metal in a lumpy, mottled style that recalls Giacometti. He is standing erect, looking boldly into the social-realist future; he holds a Cuban flag in one hand and a toy Superman in the other. He is not standing on solid ground. At first it looks as if he's striding across waves, actually walking on water, but a closer look shows that those are hands, not waves. Elián is being supported by the many strong hands of the Cuban people.

Fidel said that when Elián came home he would be treated like a "normal" little boy. At first, he was treated more like a rock star—cheering crowds, appearances at rallies and special events. And there are not many little boys who have a museum built in their honor. Fidel so doted on Elián when the boy first returned that Cubans joked he had finally found his successor.

Whether or not the Elián case gave Fidel a protégé to groom for the next thirty or so years, it did give him the opening to score his biggest victory over Miami and Washington in years. Fidel had shown how light of foot he remained. Who else would have spotted the boy's potential so early? Who else would have discerned the primal, almost mythological power of the story? Who else would have immediately begun building the plaza next to the Interests Section, so that CNN would have dramatic pictures to show to the world: millions of Cubans, led by a vigorous Fidel Castro, united in demanding that the Americans let a lost little boy reunite with his father?

Since Elián's first few weeks of celebrity back on Cuban soil, however, Castro had been as good as his word. The appearances stopped; the reporters, both foreign and domestic, were shooed away; one by one, the billboards went back to generic slogans and pictures of the raffish young Che. Elián became a little boy again.

I went back to the house, and the policeman was joined at his post by a man in civilian clothes who turned out to be a local party official. It would be impossible to speak with Juan Miguel, the polite official said, without prior approval from Havana. I explained that Havana had told me the assent had to come from Juan Miguel himself, which meant that Havana was telling me to talk to Cárdenas and Cárdenas was telling me to talk to Havana.

"Well, there you have it," the man said. "I hope you enjoyed your day in Cárdenas. Did you see the museum?"

5. NEW BEGINNINGS

few days after that incendiary show by Bamboleo at the Tropical, Lázaro Valdés, the bandleader, was eager to talk. "Where are you staying?" he asked. "I'll come by."

It turned out to be my first close encounter with qualities I hadn't anticipated finding in Cuba—style, ambition, glamour. To paraphrase George Orwell, all Cubans are equal but some are more equal than others. The retinue that swept into the lobby of my hotel was like a flashback to Havana's glittering, decadent past. Or maybe a glimpse of the proximate future.

Valdés looked every inch the star, with his gold-colored suit, black T-shirt, thick gold chains, and sleek Italian shoes. But the commotion of jostling, rubbernecking, and finger-pointing that began outside on the sidewalk and spilled through the doors wasn't really for him. It was for his posse, which included Bamboleo's four glamorous singers: Vannia, Yordamis, Alejandro, and Jorge David. On a scorching afternoon in downtown Havana, this was a display of star power luminous enough to shame the sun.

Thousand-watt celebrity is yet another commodity in short supply in contemporary Cuba. Homegrown Cuban cinema is moribund, which means the island isn't making any new movie stars. Cuban television produces almost nothing in the way of original drama, which means no sizzle—no soap opera hunks or honeys. There are great ballet dancers, great symphony conductors, great artists and writers, but their fame is of a more refined variety. The universe that would be chronicled by Cuban *Vanity Fair,* Cuban *Entertainment Tonight,* and Cuban *Teen People,* if such bourgeois publications existed on Fidel Castro's island, is occupied almost exclusively by baseball stars and popular musicians. Pop stars are visible in Cuba—they appear on television, their songs play all day on the radio, and the nature of the business is such that they have to perform live all the time, two or three or four times a week, to make any money. By definition pop stars tend to be young and good-looking, which means glamour and sex appeal. And since popular music is the one global influence that even the most hermetically sealed society has never been able to keep out, pop stars are epidemiological vectors of foreign fashion, slang, and attitude. In Cuba they are higher beings, yet rather than dwelling on some distant Olympus they live among mortals, fully accessible, the gods-next-door. In early 2000, no pop musicians on the island seemed more nearly divine than the sex-object singers, and pimped-out *director,* of Bamboleo.

I had planned to host them in the lobby where I had chatted with Juan de Marcos, but the hotel manager dashed out when he saw them burst through the door and quickly whisked us upstairs to a quiet space on the mezzanine where we wouldn't be disturbed. I'm pretty sure he ordered security to watch the stairs.

While they were getting settled I heard the others address Valdés as "Lazarito," adding the diminutive to his name to make it "little Lázaro." At first I thought it was a reference to his height—he stood about five-eight, though he was so barrel-chested and muscular that it was hard to think of him as "little" anything; his head was shaved and he was wearing a single gold earring, and overall he looked like a successful bad-boy rapper, in some parallel universe where rappers wore suits. Later, I learned that the name wasn't a knock on his height at all. It was to distinguish him from his father, also named Lázaro, who was also a famous Cuban bandleader and musician. Big Lázaro, still active on the music scene, had been Beny Moré's last pianist. Cuban music runs in families.

Dressed in the style nightclubs call "elegant casual"—designer

jeans, tight little tops, big jewelry—the two women, Vannia and
Yordamis, looked every bit as stunning as they had the other night
in their sequined gowns. Alejandro, tall and strapping, and Jorge
David, dark and wiry, hung back a bit. Here, as onstage, their body
language acknowledged they were secondary. Bamboleo was about
the women.

"Things are going well, really well," Lazarito said. "Our latest
CD has been very well received, especially in the States. At least
that's what our record company says. Tell me, are you able to find
it in the stores?"

I told him that yes, I had bought a copy of *Ya No Hace Falta* at
Tower Records in Washington, just down the street from the World
Bank.

"Excellent," he said. "And, I mean, what's your impression? Of
the sales, I mean. Is it in other stores? Did you see our other records
too?"

I said that I had spotted a copy of an earlier Bamboleo CD in
the music section of my local Borders, but nowhere else.
Distribution seemed to be an issue, I told him, for all the Cuban
bands. There was no promotion at all, which meant that many people who would love Bamboleo's music didn't know the band existed.
Even for the few who did know, and who wanted to follow the
band's career, the music was hard to find. Lazarito nodded, shook
his head, and shrugged.

"Well, those things are hard for us to control, that's just the
way it is. Here in Havana at least, Bamboleo is going through a
great period. The public is more enthusiastic than ever. They've
accepted the changes and it seems as if our popularity has even
grown."

This was said with pride, but mostly with relief. For Bamboleo,
this was a new beginning.

The recent "changes" had been huge and potentially disastrous.
Lazarito had founded the group in 1995, building it around two
exceptional singers—Vannia and a woman named Haila Mompié.
This was novel: Cuban music had seen its share of outstanding

women singers, including the great Celia Cruz, but *timba* had been considered man's work. The music was so loud, so rough, so macho that the mere fact of attempting it with women singers was enough to attract attention. Vannia and Haila were a perfect pair. Both were tall, brown skinned, and stunningly beautiful, both displayed commanding stage presence, and both had remarkable voices. Vannia's was smooth and smoky like a saxophone, Haila's sharp and clarion-clear like a trumpet. Almost freakishly, both women had the vocal strength and stamina to sing for two or three hours straight over the banging, clattering, thumping, and bleating of a dozen musicians who prided themselves on sheer power. Vannia and Haila had given the group its musical identity, its visual signature, and ultimately its fame. But then the band's chief songwriter suddenly left to form his own *orquesta*, and he took Haila with him.

Yordamis was the substitute, and in truth she had neither Haila's voice nor her charisma. But she had done well enough, and meanwhile Lazarito had tweaked Bamboleo's sound and come up with a formula that young Cubans found irresistible. The rhythms were Afro-Cuban but the harmonies, and much of the sensibility and spirit, were Afro-American. *Timba* had been married to 1970s American funk.

"My father is a great musician, so of course he is an influence, but when I was growing up I liked to listen to American black music, like P-Funk and Earth, Wind and Fire," Lazarito said. "In Bamboleo's music the percussion is Cuban. But the harmony is American, the bass is American, and the horns have an American accent."

The group had toured the United States a couple of times, and the experience had been exhilarating but also frustrating: just as Juan de Marcos had said, people didn't dance.

"In Cuba it's very hard to win applause. When people like what you do, they get up and dance," Lazarito said. In the States, he said, applause comes easily, naturally, as a matter of course. But nobody dances. Granted, they might not have the chops to dance exactly like Cubans, but they didn't even try. They just sat and clapped, politely.

You could hear the exasperation in Lazarito's voice as he made this distinction. It wasn't just that American audiences didn't dance, it was that at some fundamental level, the whole American musical enterprise—record companies, booking agents, record stores, on down to the listeners themselves—wasn't connecting with the best of contemporary Cuban music. All the power, the speed, the funk, the *sabor* that bands like Lazarito's used to send Cuban audiences into rapture somehow wasn't doing the same to significant numbers of Americans.

Juan de Marcos's solution—reach back to the simpler, sweeter melodies and harmonies of the past, played and sung by musicians old enough to give it authenticity—had made him a millionaire. But Lazarito, like most of the other bandleaders in Cuba, had no desire to exploit the past. He wanted to push ahead, to ride this wild *timba* mixture of salsa, funk, and jazz as hard and fast as it would go. He wanted to make new music, not old.

The record companies had another solution—go with the flow. They wanted to channel this untamed Cuban sound into more familiar genres, because without a genre in today's popular music, you're nowhere. Some Cuban bands had been pushed into the Latin-pop genre, recording albums full of soft, simplistic *salsa romántica* and bombastic power ballads drowned in woefully over-done arrangements. When you listened to these records you could hear the musicians' boredom and disdain, like a concert pianist sentenced to serve his eternity in hell playing the collected works of Madonna. This Lazarito simply refused to do. If that was what Bamboleo had to put out to make it in the American market, he wasn't interested.

He wouldn't use his custom-made, turbocharged music-making machine to churn out tame, mindless pop. But he had allowed his record company—a Los Angeles–based outfit called Ahí-Namá—to experiment with another genre, dance music. Dance music at least had some *edge* to it. Ahí-Namá was about to release an album that consisted of several tracks from live *timba* performances, followed by dance-floor remixes of Bamboleo songs released on earlier albums. It was a compromise—and unfortunately it sounded like one.

Lazarito put the best face on it. "It's different," he said. "We have to try new things."

He was neither ignorant of the realities of the popular music marketplace nor implacably defiant of those commercial realities. But he knew what his band was capable of, knew the kind of magic it could make, and he wasn't ready to give that up. He was making a good living in Cuba by any standards, a terrific living by Cuban standards, and he was playing his kind of music—wild music, hot as it could be, music that made people dance all night. The band went regularly on tour to Europe and the States, and managed to find a small but devoted audience. That wasn't superstardom, by a long shot, but it would have to do until there was some way for Bamboleo to really break out of the island.

To wind things down, I asked about their personal backgrounds. The singers' act was elaborately choreographed, but none of them had ever studied dance—"It's in our feet, in our hips, in our blood," Vannia said. All had sung with other groups before Bamboleo. Jorge David said he had received his entire musical education "in the streets." The rest of the singers, and Lazarito as well, were all graduates of the National Arts Schools. Their twelve years of musical education hadn't exactly been aimed at this moment, however. Vannia's instrument in school, for example, had been oboe, not voice; singing just came naturally.

The clothes, the jewelry, the trips abroad, the adulation—these Cubans were living a life the vast majority of their countrymen could only dream of. I was curious what kind of separation this brought about. Fidel Castro had been remarkably successful in creating an egalitarian society—egalitarian in the sense that everyone was equally poor. These sleek, confident pop stars weren't poor anymore. In other countries, their lives would have changed dramatically in ways that took advantage of their good fortune. The effect would be to make them more pampered, more cosseted—to construct a bubble where life was more comfortable than on the outside. They would eat in fine restaurants. They would drive nicer cars. They would move to bigger houses, in better neighborhoods. Had this same process taken place in Cuba? Which of them, for example, had moved to new apartments or houses?

The question drew laughter, shrugs, and one attempt to explain.

"Fame doesn't change who you are," Vannia said. "That's not how it works in Cuba. If I moved to another house, another neighborhood, I'd be lost. Not to be able to go across the street to the store and see the friends I've had all my life, the people I've grown up with? How could I do that? Why would I do that?"

She laughed at the idea. "Who would I be?"

* * *

Most of the hyper-talented musicians in Cuba would have died, or killed, to have Bamboleo's problems. Artistic disagreements with one's American record label? Polite, nondancing audiences at one's European shows? The wrenching struggle to hold on to one's roots against the relentless pull of single-name celebrity? Sure, right. How about a real problem, like scraping enough money together for cab fare to get your band and all its equipment to a show? Or finding some way, some connection, some gimmick that lets you stand out from all the other hyper-talented musicians trying their best to get noticed?

The odds were impossible but the reward for success was admission to another world, a postrevolutionary world of public adoration and public income. And musicians do dream.

Later that same week, in a tiny first-floor apartment carved out of a decrepit mansion in one of the leafy neighborhoods where the sugar barons once lived, Daulema Fuentevilla reached the point of total exasperation and shot a look at her hapless bass player that made the poor woman tremble.

"It's all within the chords, we're just staying in the chords," she snapped, and then she ran her left hand up and down the keyboard through the correct bass line, the one she had been trying to teach for a good fifteen minutes. "All right, all right, let's take a break. A *short* break."

This was a beginning, and not all beginnings are easy.

I'd been asking around to find a group just starting out in the music business. On a trip out to the neighborhoods—around the corner from the backyard health club, in fact—I met a trombone player, a veteran of several prominent *orquestas,* who said his wife Moraima, a singer, was fronting a brand-new band. A couple of phone calls back and forth resulted in an invitation to a practice session.

The address was one of the baronial homes in the western neighborhoods of Havana that had been abandoned by their wealthy owners after the revolution and pressed into service by the state. Almost all had been divided and redivided into ever-smaller apartments and flats until a mansion that once had housed one family (plus servants) now was home to four, or six, or eight. To get to where Moraima's band was practicing you ignored the grand front entrance altogether and followed the sound down a narrow walkway to the left of the main house, ducking under a rusty iron bar that for me was just at eye-poking height, continuing between mottled gray stucco walls whose grimness was relieved by a red-pink spray of fragrant hibiscus, until you came to an open door and a room literally too small for the whole band to fit inside at once. Fifty years ago, this might have been where the butler lived.

A tall, mahogany-skinned woman with her hair in straw-colored braids came bounding up the walkway to meet me. "You're here!" Moraima Marín said, greeting me with a kiss on the cheek and grabbing my elbow. "Let me introduce the rest of the girls."

That was the hook, the distinction, the gimmick that was supposed to get these neophytes noticed amid Havana's overcrowded, hypercompetitive music scene: It was an all-girl *timba* band.

Together for just a few months, the group was so new that it hadn't quite settled on a name. Their first idea had been Aroma, which had a girl-group sound to it. But the players were also all black, and so they thought maybe the name should be Aroma de Ebano. The manager of some venue where they had played was pushing them to switch to simply Ebano. So the name was definitely in flux.

As was the whole enterprise: It was like a homemade airplane, slapped together in someone's garage, rattling down a bumpy runway on its maiden attempt at flight, straining for enough speed for a takeoff.

"It's impossible to get started," said the bandleader, a honey-skinned young woman named Marbis Manzaret, who played percussion. "There are eleven in the group, and most of us came from another *orquesta*. We were doing all right, but we decided we wanted to do something for ourselves, so we broke off on our own. But getting started, here in Havana, is just impossible."

The first big issue had been money. Nobody in Cuba has any. They had borrowed from friends and family. They had scraped together second- and third-hand instruments. They had dusted off an old electric piano that had been gathering dust in the drummer's house. They had sewn their own costumes. This cramped rehearsal space was the home of their manager, sound engineer, and lone roadie, a guy named Roberto, who seemed to be somebody's boyfriend. They practiced almost every day. The furniture had been cleared out of the little living room to make enough space for the players, including the keyboardist, Daulema, whose instrument was wedged in a corner beneath a picture of the Last Supper. There wasn't enough room for the singers, who had to stand outside, in the doorway. Roberto's parents were back in a bedroom, presumably with their hands over their ears, because in these cramped quarters Aroma de Ebano was loud enough to wake the dead.

Most problematic of all was finding someplace to play in public and somebody to listen. There had been a boom of all-girl groups on the Havana scene over the past year or so, and a couple had made it to the big clubs and even recorded CDs. But the novelty was wearing thin. These young women—and they were very young, all of them in their twenties, a few just barely—had to try to muscle in on the big boys, and it wasn't easy.

"First of all, the doors are closed to women in *timba*," Marbis said. "They don't take women seriously. They don't believe that women can play with the same power as the men. We want to change that. We want to show that we can be just as hard, just as fast, just as powerful."

There were amens all around.

"But the other problem is that there's no space for anyone on the Havana nightlife scene. The competition is just so tough. The same top bands—" here she was referring to the likes of Los Van Van, NG La Banda, Bamboleo, and perhaps a dozen others "—play all the time at the same places, the Casa de la Música and the Tropical and a few others. Nobody else can get in. There are bands much more established than ours that don't have work."

For the moment they considered themselves doing well just to get occasional work at tourist bars, including one semiregular gig. The work didn't come close to paying anyone a living wage, and given the overhead their net cashflow was still going the wrong way. But hadn't every successful musician started just this way?

Marbis was the bandleader in the organizational sense, but the musical director, and the real creative force, was Daulema. She had light-brown skin, curly black hair, and dark, flashing eyes. She could have decided any morning to ditch this whole music thing and become a fashion model, if Cuba had had a fashion industry. But she was also the most serious and accomplished musician of the lot, a graduate of the Instituto Superior de Arte, Cuba's national arts university. This meant she was among the best of the best of Cuba's world-class musicians, good enough to take a shot at a career as a concert pianist if she wanted. Between songs she limbered up with Bach fugues that fairly danced off her fingertips.

Most of the rest of the band members had graduated from the high-school-level National Arts Schools. This meant that every one of them could sight read Daulema's complicated charts and keep up with Marbis's furious rhythms. These women were young enough to have butterfly tattoos on their ankles and shoulders, to wear halter tops and clunky platform shoes, but they knew their way around their instruments like wizened old pros.

They ran through most of their repertoire without a hitch, but one song was giving them an inordinate amount of trouble: a new *merengue* that Daulema had written called "El Talismán." The rhythm had a devilish hitch in it, the chord changes were counter-intuitive, and the players were having trouble orienting them-selves—particularly the bass player, who seemed utterly lost. Daulema alternated between sweet patience and head-shaking frus-tration as they tried again and again to make it all the way through the piece without a breakdown. After almost a half hour on this one number, she realized that everyone had had enough. She declared victory—"That was okay, more or less"—and everyone could exhale and break for a stretch and a cigarette.

The alto sax player put down her horn, picked up a flute, and started goofing her way through *Rhapsody in Blue*. Others joined in between puffs on their smokes, until a little corner of Havana resounded to the great soar and sweep of George Gershwin.

While the youngest women played and laughed, the senior members of the group—Moraima, Daulema, Marbis, and one or two others, the women closer to thirty than twenty—each sank into her own thoughts. Already they had accomplished much. They had put together a talented group of musicians, learned an impressive body of music, designed a look, choreographed a show, and dedi-cated themselves to sticking with the enterprise as long as it took to break through. But something was missing. Despite having come so far, the road didn't look an inch shorter.

The music they made was good, at times very good. But only in brief flashes did it find a groove that was truly inspired. The bass player couldn't quite keep up, and the percussionists were sharp but light-handed, which meant that the goal of pure, macho *timba* power underlying the music was still a dream. I understood what they were up against: being good in Havana, even very good, was hardly even a beginning.

* * *

One of Fidel's creations that will survive him, if there is a God, is Cuba's peerless system of music education. The Instituto Superior de Arte is, in its Cuban way, the Juilliard of the Caribbean—except that all the instruction and all the instruments are provided to students free of charge.

One of Korda's most famous photographs is *Guerrillero Heróico*, the portrait of Ernesto "Che" Guevara with his beard and his beret, against a blank sky as background, gazing into the future with a look of strength, confidence, and inevitability. It is *the* picture of Che, the one that has graced millions of T-shirts and dorm-room walls—the one image, above all others, that took Marxism out of the library and the union hall and made it sexy, made it worthy of the bedroom. Perfect in its simplicity, the picture is actually the result of a good crop: The original, wider frame shows the profile of a second man on the left, while the fronds of a nearby palm tree encroach from the right. Korda pared them away, recognizing that in this case, less would be immeasurably more. Korda died in 2002, having made no money at all on one of the most famous photographs ever taken.

Korda, in his role as one of the semiofficial court photographers of Fidel Castro's new government in the weeks and months after the revolution, took scores of other great photographs of Fidel, Che, and their compatriots at work and play. One striking sequence was the result of an urgent summons: emissaries scoured Havana until they found Korda and told him he was to come to the Havana Country Club at once, to photograph Fidel and Che as they played a round of golf. The legend is that Fidel had seen pictures in *Life* magazine of President Dwight D. Eisenhower playing golf, and, always proud of his athletic prowess, the former schoolboy baseball star wanted to show the world that revolutionaries could play the game better than the imperialist *yanquis*. More likely, the purpose of the outing was not to play well, but simply to mock the unsympathetic Ike and all that he stood for—and also to have an afternoon of fun, away from the new pressures and responsibilities of reshaping a nation. Why else would they arrange to be photographed playing golf in military fatigues and combat boots, if not in a spirit of burlesque?

Several of the pictures show the moody Che in stitches, laughing to bust a gut. One shows Fidel finishing a swing, the club slung awkwardly over his shoulder, his whole posture not of a golfer but of a second baseman who has just slapped out a single and is about to tear off for first. It gives an idea of what Che might have been laughing at.

I went out to the Havana Country Club, and standing on the veranda of the clubhouse I could still see the outlines of the fairways where Fidel and Che had tromped and flailed and mugged for Korda's cameras. It took a golfer's (or a hacker's) eye to make out the layout of the course, since the bunkers and greens had been eliminated long ago. But you could still see the long, narrow clearings walled off from one another by stands of trees, and the way one led to another like a chain of paper clips. From the clubhouse you could see what probably had been the ninth hole, and also what probably had been the eighteenth.

But what I heard was not the low whirr of a golf cart or the metallic thwack of a titanium driver. Instead, I heard sweet, sweet music.

It was Bach, for violin and piano, and it came from a large, bright, parqueted room that once would have hosted society balls and lavish wedding receptions, but now had been transformed into a recital hall. Coming inside, I could see the outlines of what must have been the club's old swimming pool, long since filled with concrete and transformed into a space for al fresco performances. The whole place had been transformed, beginning just two years after the revolution's triumph, into the Instituto Superior de Arte. This campus stood at the apex of a system of arts education that over forty years had produced a huge surplus of musicians who could play with such assurance and technique and power that it boggled the mind.

The system produced visual artists too, and writers, and fantastic dancers. At a ballet school in Havana one afternoon, I watched as another of those Soviet-adviser émigrés put a classroom full of twelve-year-olds through their paces, smoking a cigarette and keeping time by slapping her thigh with what looked like a riding crop. The most abundant and remarkable yield, though, was of musicians. Like tobacco or sugarcane, music seemed to flourish in the Cuban climate and soil.

Alicia Perea, the director of the Cuban Institute of Music, had leaned forward across her desk a couple of days earlier and explained the system to me. She was a government bureaucrat, technically, but when she spoke of music it was with the confidence and fervor of an impresario, and that was the role her job most resembled: she was the impresario of Cuban music.

It all began with the requirement of universal school attendance, which the Cuban state took pains to enforce. In all the schools, specialist teachers came in to give each seven-year-old Cuban child a series of tests for exceptional ability in art, athletics, or music. The music test sought to discern whether the little boy or girl had a particularly fine sense of pitch, feel for rhythm, memory for melody, or suppleness of voice. Perea had spent much of her career as a music teacher. "I myself administered more than five thousand of these tests," she told me.

The talented were offered places in the elementary National Arts Schools dotted around the island, where they studied and practiced, practiced and studied, all the way through the equivalent of eighth grade. At that point they were given another test, and those who scored highest were invited to attend the secondary-level National Arts Schools. There were fewer of those, mostly in the provincial capitals. Those who graduated could take another test, if they had the stomach for it, to attend the Instituto Superior. At that point they were already fully qualified as instrumentalists, well grounded in the classics, jazz, Cuban music, and just about any other genre. To even apply to the Instituto Superior meant the intention to devote not just one's career to music, but one's whole fiber and being, one's life.

Those super-select few ended up here, amid the indelible fairways, on a campus that was like the rest of Cuba: a gorgeous wasteland of excellence and decay.

"I would *pay* to work here," said Ana María González, rector of the institute. Actually she was all but paying for the privilege already, given that her state salary wouldn't have been worth more than twenty-five dollars a month. But if you did have to pay to work someplace, the Instituto Superior looked like a good choice.

The dean of the music faculty was with her, and he elaborated the point. "Here, we are surrounded by music. We live music. If you walk around, you will hear people conversing, but in music. It's our language."

The young woman I'd heard playing the Bach partita so beautifully was a young student named Mirelys, whom the faculty deemed especially promising. She was soft spoken and seemed shy, but her playing was bold and decisive. Her accompanist, a young man named Lázaro, had done his job well, tempering his musical voice to support and complement hers; it was almost a surprise to meet him and encounter a talkative live wire who must have been one of the more popular students on campus. Their performance had been arranged as a demonstration of the musical conversation that took place on the campus night and day. In a society whose basic template had been designed in Moscow, the words "Potemkin village" had to come to mind. If that's what it was, the czar surely would have been fooled.

The music school at the Instituto Superior occupied a building near the old clubhouse that once had been an exclusive little hotel. There were fewer than five hundred full-time students. In one classroom, a young man named Melkisedek Semé—a West African, one of the thirty or so foreign students on campus—sat alone and intent before a battered snare drum, working on his technique with brushes, searching for just the right attack and pressure that would make the instrument whisper. In another room, first-year student Yordamis Oreli bit his lip as he beat out a complicated *rumba* on a much-used conga drum. There were drummers all over the place, in the classrooms and practice studios—percussion, in Cuba, is an extremely rich and rewarding field of academic study.

Down the hall, Ariane Trujillo ran through finger exercises on an old upright piano. Next door, a young woman played an air for flute under the tyranny of a big, old-fashioned metronome. One floor up, a serious young man named Aldo Salvén made his saxophone sing, cry, growl, dance, plead, and shout in a display that left me floored. He had such control of the instrument and played with such mature intelligence that I decided he must be one of the Instituto Superior's brightest stars. It turned out that he wasn't, yet—the kid was just eighteen, he said, and wouldn't even enter as a freshman until the fall. How, I wondered, could this kid get any better?

And then I wondered whether anybody would ever hear of Aldo Salvén. Would he leave Cuba in search of the wide audience he was sure to covet and sure to deserve? Or would he stay in Cuba, the equivalent of a soundproof booth, conjuring great beauty that the world would never witness? Would the music have to be its own reward?

There were four other colleges planned for the Instituto Superior in addition to Music: Plastic Arts, Dramatic Arts, Modern Dance, and Ballet. Fidel had made the development of art an urgent national priority. Before breaking ground on the Instituto in 1961, he selected Ricardo Porro, a young Cuban architect with budding fame and impeccable revolutionary credentials, to lead the design team. Porro enlisted the help of two like-minded Italians, and they designed a campus that was to be a landmark of modern architecture, a stunning achievement of the Cuban revolution. Each college was to be in a different style. Each was to be a jewel, set amid many acres of lush greenery. To walk from one to another was to be like a journey between magical kingdoms.

At least that was the idea; much of it never got built. By the mid-1960s, post–missile crisis, Soviet ideology had taken firm hold and the Porro team's sensual, tropical, essentially Latin designs looked out of place in a nation that had officially adopted Moscow's utilitarian esthetic. Besides, while Porro's political line was correct, he nonetheless was a son of the bourgeoisie—and the other main architects, the Italians, weren't even Cuban. The government stopped funding the project in 1965, and Porro, brokenhearted, left the island the following year.

Substantial portions were completed, however, including the School of Plastic Arts, which Porro himself had designed. Today it crumbles slowly, one of the most beautiful buildings I could imagine, one that—well, it sounds hokey and melodramatic, but one that haunts my dreams.

I should probably mention that when I entered college I intended to become an architect. Only gross ineptitude as an architecture student, plus a certain concern for the public safety, made me give it up for writing. An incompetently designed sentence may offend, but at least there's no danger that innocents will be crushed and buried when it fails. But I still admire, and I still dream. A beautifully designed building lifts the soul and purifies the heart. It is the closest thing to frozen music.

After touring the music school, I couldn't resist walking over to take a look at Porro's creation. It was less like a building than a village, a low-slung collection of modules like huts, connected but distinct, laid out along a wide, winding pathway. The idea had been to use native materials and respect the contours of the land, so the building was made of brick and the path meandered organically; the pieces of the building seemed to be where they had to be, rather than where someone had decided to put them. The walkway wound deeper into the school until at the center it came to an enormous *flamboyán* tree that must have been there all along, must have been a focal point of the original design. The tree was one of those ancient, gnarled specimens with branches that spread horizontally and reached impossibly wide, embracing the entire space, dominating it, filling it, completing it. The overall effect must have been dramatic when the building was new. But the building hadn't been maintained, and so now the land was reclaiming it—buckling the walkway with intrusions of root, weathering the concrete with rain and wind, slowly turning brick back into clay, seizing the walls with long, delicate tendrils of vine. The building looked as if no one had designed or built it, as if Porro hadn't existed. It looked as if it had simply grown there.

In one of the modules, I saw a couple of artists working on an abstract print. They were Cubans, which meant they were educated but poor, politically aware but unable to speak their minds, confined at gunpoint to an island that was grand and varied and lively and fascinating but, in the end, still an island. But there they were, creating art in the belly of a great work of art, and I thought, How lucky. I knew all the reasons why I should never feel envious of them, yet as was the case with the dancers at the Tropical, and with the young violinists at my hotel, envy was the precise emotion I felt.

Amid such decay, such excellence. Whatever the shape of the next revolution after Fidel's, artists of imagination and skill would surely deserve a voice, and surely find one.

* * *

Fine art can't match the power and urgency of popular art, though, and the liberating force in Cuba today is music. Cuba's music is Cuba's great freedom, its inalienable liberty, its irrevocable bill of rights. I understood this the first time—and the second time, and the fifteenth—that I set foot in the Casa de la Música, which is the Carnegie Hall of Cuban popular music, but with a dance floor.

The acoustics are contemptible. The sound system alternates between muddy and fuzzy. The layout of the room is inconvenient in every respect. The stage is almost too large, the tables too close together, the area for dancing too cramped and narrow. Waiters laden with food and drink have no easy access to any table. There doesn't seem to be a backdoor, so the musicians have to come through the rope line like everyone else, toting their instruments, and bull their way through the crowd. On a night when one of the top *orquestas* is playing, the clientele is interesting but not terribly authentic, and certainly not in the least wholesome. There are a few dozen foreign tourists, Europeans, Canadians, and Americans, mostly men. There are twice that many *jineteras*, young and not-so-young and way-too-young women in short skirts and halter tops and tight jeans and visible thongs, all sending come-hither looks across the room, advertising for business. There are VIP tables crowded with singers and bandleaders and managers from the other top *orquestas*, dropping by to check out what the competition's playing these days. What these groups of people have in common is the wherewithal to pay the cover charge, which for a top band is fifteen or twenty or even twenty-five dollars—or, in the case of the musicians, the connections to get themselves comped in. Miraculously, once the lights go down and the show begins, suddenly there materializes a sizable contingent of ordinary Cubans. Some are regulars who know the bouncers, and the rest just seem to be unusually resourceful. The shows are advertised to begin at ten thirty but the headliner generally doesn't play a note until one in the morning, which means the show is unlikely to end before three. It's too far to walk home to any hotel, and at that hour the only transportation consists of gypsy cab drivers who will charge double or triple what the fare should be.

In a word: glorious. Everything about the place is just glorious.

This hallowed shrine is in a huge old mansion in one of the best-preserved parts of Miramar, a tree-lined district in the western expanses of the city, once the exclusive preserve of the cosseted rich. Coming out from downtown has the feeling of pilgrimage, and on some nights the Casa de la Música rewards the journey with an experience that seems genuinely religious.

Charanga Habanera, the group featured in Nestor Mili's magazine—the group that had changed all its members—was giving a show, and everyone wanted to see and hear what it would be like. Haila, the singer who had left Bamboleo, was over in the corner with an entourage from her new band. Half of Bamboleo was on the other side of the room, and the two posses did not acknowledge one another. Two singers from Los Van Van sat at a table up front, and if they'd had sticks they still couldn't have beaten off the women crowding around. The Dancing Man—the guy I'd seen at the Hotel Nacional, partnering the Dancing Woman—was there too, sitting in the front, dressed in black and wearing sunglasses; he was with a woman who could dance quite well but clearly was foreign, probably English or Canadian. Every table was filled and there was still a crowd at the rope line. This concert was an event, the musical event of the month—the return of bandleader David Calzado, with a dozen unknown and untested musicians, to the toughest house in Cuba. The crowd would either embrace him or eat him alive.

The show started a little past one. The first number was high energy, as is customary. Also according to custom, no one got up to dance. It always takes a couple of songs to get a groove established. But when I looked around, I saw mostly smiles. The band was looking and sounding good.

There were four singers besides Calzado, all of them male, and their choreography was airtight—spins, leaps, shimmies, cross-steps, Cuban boogaloos, all in perfect ensemble. Their voices were a good blend, obviously chosen for pitch and timbre. Plus, they were heartthrob handsome. The horns were crisp and powerful, especially through the middle register. The new bass player seemed a definite improvement, and the old band's distinctive keyboard sound, contrapuntal and insistently propulsive, was still there. The revelation, though, was the percussion. The drumming, which Calzado had described as a weakness in the old band, was razor sharp and incredibly powerful.

At the center of the stage, wailing on his drum kit, was the sixteen-year-old drummer whom Calzado had discovered and Milí had told me about. He was about five feet two and looked to weigh a hundred pounds sopping wet; he had dreadlocks and a winning smile, and he was a monster on his instrument. Calzado is a showman; he wasted no time, bringing the kid to the front of the stage in the middle of the second tune to do a little dance. He looked like the Cuban equivalent of Lil' Bow Wow.

By the third number—a song called "Bla Bla Bla," in which a man tells his lady friend to cut out her constant harping—the room was in David Calzado's hands. The new, improved Charanga Habanera had completely won this tough audience of skeptical peers, shady ladies on the make, drunken tourists, and local party animals. The dance floor filled to capacity, and for the next two hours it just got fuller and fuller, until abandoned tables had been shoved away to make more room for dancing and the whole crowd was on its feet.

At three thirty, when the band finally finished, I was drenched with sweat from just standing at my table. As I stood outside bargaining for a cab back downtown, I saw the Dancing Man walk past. His black silk shirt and linen pants looked as if they had just been pressed, his smile was wide and bright, his manner was pure charm as he opened the door of a taxi for the blond foreign woman he was escorting.

The exciting thing, for Cuba, was that this vibrant music scene was a kind of demimonde with a collection of great artists at its center, a world that coexisted with the official, sanctioned world of Fidel's revolution but had its own mores and hierarchies, even its own economy. The *jineteras* weren't supposed to be doing what they were doing. The male hustlers like the Dancing Man were breaking the law as well, and they were doing so with flagrant insouciance. The gypsy cab drivers waiting at the door were operating outside the law, as were the snack vendors and the sellers of bootleg CDs and the touts offering cigars. The music was the draw and the inspiration, the catalyst. Because of the music, all these people were getting together in the middle of the night, making their own rules.

In Gdansk, grassroots civil society developed in the shipyards; in Prague, in the coffeehouses and drawing rooms. In Havana, I was seeing a tropical version of civil society take root in the hot, sweaty, sexy, swinging dance halls.

6. RAP AND *REVOLUCIÓN*

FUBU-clad and Nike-shod, Isaac Torres and Reynor Hernández sat at a crowded table in the inky gloom of the Cabaret Las Vegas, nervously trading sips from a bottle of rum as they waited their turn to perform. The Las Vegas opened its doors in the last days of 1953 and swung hard through the remaining years of Fulgencio Batista's reign of sin, a smoky cave where beautiful women met dangerous men and danced the night away. But forty years of revolution had their effect, and by the time I got there all that was left was the smoke. The best the Las Vegas could do was put on a low-rent floor show—competent six-piece band, three decent singers, seven chorus girls with chunky thighs and runs in their fishnet hose—for an audience of smug, rum-happy foreign men and their bored *jineteras*.

Except at the Friday matinee.

The crowd at Las Vegas this Friday was all Cuban, all black, and very young, in their twenties and teens. The men wore baggy cargo pants or droopy jeans, with NBA basketball jerseys, ribbed white tanks that showed off their muscles, polyester kung-fu shirts covered with tigers and dragons, and unblemished sneakers of a whiteness seen only on the feet of the very rich or the very poor. The women were in low-rise jeans and tight-fitting tops, with colorful head scarves, lots of bracelets and rings, and multiple ear piercings—a look that was aggressive, in-your-face. Both sexes went in for tattoos and dreadlocks, along with attitude. The exception was

Reynor's mother, a doctor who specialized in lung diseases, who sat primly in the front row and shot her son a pained look every time he took a drag on a cigarette.

Around six, the lights dimmed and the music started—not sly, syncopated Latin sounds but hard, pounding hip-hop beats—and three young black men came forward, a group called 100% Original. They had all the standard moves, the prowling, the scowling, the arm crossing, and the pushing up, and within minutes of their taking the stage the crowd was on its feet, moving to a bass line loud enough to rearrange internal organs. The rappers called out and the crowd answered back:

"Pa' mis niches!"

"PA' MIS NICHES!"

"Pa' mis negros!"

"PA' MIS NEGROS!"

For my niggaz! they were saying. For my black people!

An all-star lineup of rappers followed. Isaac and Reynor's group, Explosión Suprema, performed its brief set midway through the show, after which Reynor's mother slipped quickly out the door. The finale was a freestyling contest, won by a short, slight teenager who calls himself El Menor ("The Kid"). The sound died and the lights came up promptly at eight.

A dark-skinned young man emerged from his labors in the deejay's booth and flashed a dazzling grin—Pablo Herrera, Cuba's leading hip-hop maestro.

"Did you like the beats?" he asked, fretting that the sound levels might not have been just right.

The beats were good, I told him, and yes, the sound had been a bit unbalanced, but it had been hard to pay attention to any of that. It had been hard to hear past the *words:*

"In the eyes of the police I'm nothing but a criminal."

"Stop me on the street for no reason. Just to screw me over."

"We're fighting for equality."

"Nigga, nigga, open your eyes!'

"Fight!"

"Criticize!"

"Make a stand!"

To hear these words spoken openly in Cuba, before a fist-pumping crowd of young black people who cheered wildly in response, was surreal. Even with no direct challenge to the one-party state, no questioning of the fundamental tenets of Fidel Castro's socialism, the words that were shouted at Cabaret Las Vegas that Friday evening sounded like rap music is supposed to sound: armed and dangerous.

Amid all the energy in the club, amid the electricity, the motion, the color, and the noise, there was also the feeling that the matrix of what was possible in this country, and what wasn't, somehow was shifting.

"We like to talk about things people don't talk about," Reynor explained later. "Like how when the police see a black man on the street, and especially if he has dreadlocks or something like that, as far as they're concerned he's already a criminal. I write about my life. When I have a problem with my girlfriend, I write it. When I have a problem in the street, I write it. When I have a problem with the police, I write it."

As in this ode to the police: "Alert! Discrimination right here . . . I'm already a criminal to you, simply for being six feet tall and having dark skin . . . You stand there and follow my dark movements everywhere . . . Does the way that I dress bother you that much, ass-hole? . . . The failures of black people are due to the brutality of whites . . ."

Explosión Suprema's startling racial anger turned out to be the norm. All of Cuba's rap stars are venturing into the same Outer Limits, rampaging through areas of discourse that have been unexplored for decades: Calls for racial solidarity. Blasts against discrimination. Bitter denunciations of the arbitrary and heavy-handed police. Narrative tales of the bizarro-world travails of daily Cuban life. Cuban hip-hop sounds as if it isn't really about the music at all, but about the screwed-up present and uncertain future of the nation.

Pumped and exhausted from the show at the Las Vegas, Pablo Herrera glad-handed his way out the door and pulled up a chair at one of the club's sidewalk tables. He started to talk about his work and his vision, about the "revolution"—his word, not mine—that Cuban hip-hop was creating. But every few seconds he had to interrupt his flow and bump fists with well-wishing fans. They were filing out and heading en masse to another spot, a mile or so up the street, where the second hip-hop show of the night was about to start.

"You know, most people have in their head an idea of what Cuba should sound like," Herrera said between show-the-love hugs, flashing the million-dollar grin once more. "And Cuba right now is *none* of that."

* * *

To get to Pablo Herrera's "right now" requires a little background, starting with the fact that Fidel Castro's invasion and conquest of Cuba began in an utter and complete fiasco.

In December 1956, his revolutionary army set out from Mexico in the legendary "yacht" *Granma*—really a weekend skipper's cabin cruiser that had no business venturing onto the open sea. The little craft was absurdly overburdened with men and material, straining and wallowing even as it left port. Miraculously it survived the crossing, but the future liberators of Cuba miscalculated and landed at the wrong place at the wrong time. Actually, it was the worst possible place at the worst possible time. The *Granma* foundered on hidden shoals and promptly sank, taking most of Castro's weaponry and supplies with it. Castro and his fourscore *guerrilleros*, most of them still seasick and dehydrated, were left to slog and slash their way through dense mangrove thickets until, utterly exhausted, they finally staggered onto the mainland. Whereupon they immediately came under attack.

Castro escaped, of course—he always managed to escape, somehow. He made it to a meager little thatched house, typical of Cuba's desperate rural poverty, startling the woman who lived there.

Instead of sounding the alarm and turning him over to the soldiers who were combing the area, she offered him food and shelter.

Her name was Leocadia "Chicha" Garzón, and she was a black woman, the descendant of slaves.

That was the beginning of Fidel Castro's revolutionary engagement with black Cuba. His mother, nominally white, was said to have had at least a bit of African blood in her. It's hard to discern any blackness in Castro himself, and in any event he has much less claim to mulatto status than the man he deposed, Batista, whose brown skin and broad nose famously disqualified him for membership in the sanctums of the white elite, such as the Havana Yacht Club. In his youth Castro was something of an outsider in the big city because he was a country boy, a hick from the folkloric east, but he had the cachet that money always conveys and nobody ever doubted he was white. He never doubted it either: his unsympathetic biographers never fail to cite an alleged early boast that someday he would kick "that nigger" Batista out of power.

Actions do speak louder than words, though, and Castro not only denounced Cuban racism immediately upon taking office, but did something about it. Arguably this was a matter of collateral benefit; Castro's efforts to alleviate the worst, most grinding effects of poverty and ignorance on the island were inevitably bound to have a major impact on black people, since most of them were among the poorest of the poor. Still, whatever the degree of intent, for black Cubans he changed the world. He gave them access to education. He gave them access to jobs. He gave them access to health care. And he began a Long March to replace the fetid shantytowns, like the one his savior Chicha Garzón lived in, with sturdy, safe, clean modern housing.

The apotheosis of this effort, for better or worse, was the creation of a place called Alamar.

A half dozen miles east of Havana, right on the coast, is the fishing village of Cojímar, where Ernest Hemingway kept his boat, the *Pilar*. From this little harbor he embarked on his excursions for marlin—and, during World War II, a comical patriotic foray in search of German submarines, which he failed to find. Now, more than half a century later, busloads of tourists still flock to Cojímar to eat seafood and drink daiquiris at the dark little waterside restaurant where Hemingway ate and drank; to occupy his seat at the bar and soak up the great writer's inspiration; to pose for pictures with the ancient man who claimed to be the inspiration for Santiago in *The Old Man and the Sea*. Now, as then, Cojímar is reasonably picturesque.

Alamar isn't. Just past Cojímar on an expanse of desolate dunes, Fidel Castro decided to build a new city, one worthy of the new Socialist Man his revolution was creating. He intended Alamar to be a lasting monument, one of the greatest public and social works of the Cuban revolution, a shining example to the world. He ended up building the South Bronx, minus the guns.

The labor was provided by volunteer construction brigades from across the island, aided by solidarity brigades from overseas, idealistic young leftists from Munich or Muskegon who desperately wanted to help the Cuban revolution but found pouring concrete more amenable than cutting sugarcane. Throughout the 1970s they worked, directed by Soviet advisers, whose first order of business had been to build a row of comfortable houses for themselves. Thus settled, they began on the apartment buildings for the Cubans.

Soviet Premier Aleksey Kosygin visited the Alamar construction site in 1971. According to the Soviet news service TASS, the unfinished buildings were festooned with banners that said: Welcome to Cuba, envoys of the fraternal Soviet people. Workers shouted "Long live communism!" and "Long live Soviet-Cuban friendship!" At least that's what the TASS reporter said they shouted. Kosygin uttered the normal bromides about the eternal bonds between these two great, peace-loving, communist peoples, and then retired to the comfort of his air-conditioned car.

Alamar grew to become the biggest housing project in Cuba and one of the biggest in the world, a vast reservation of squat Soviet-style apartment blocs. By the time I saw it, Alamar was unbelievably grand in scale, and in all other aspects unbelievably sad.

It was hard to tell just how many people lived there—at least a hundred thousand, maybe twice that many, maybe more—but it was clear, even by Castro's own admission, that very few lived in Alamar by choice. There were huge tracts where five-story and six-story concrete apartment buildings had been plunked down apparently at random, some in thick clumps, others in isolation, separated by weed-choked empty lots. In other parts of Alamar, identical buildings were arranged in a tight grid, making a search for a specific address like a trip through a maze. Most of the construction was shoddy; the volunteers and amateurs who built the place may have had their hearts in their work, but they apparently didn't know much about modern building techniques. Perhaps they did the best they could with the materials they were given. In any event, almost immediately the place began to fall apart. Roofs leaked. Electricity flickered. Water pressure failed.

The apartments were small, but because housing remained in such short supply across the island they were chronically over-crowded. Every view in every direction from every window was bleak, and the faded beauty of Havana was a long, uncomfortable bus ride away. There was basic shelter and basic hygiene for all, so in this sense Alamar was a vast improvement over the little slum it had replaced. But it was ugly and depressing, and the eruptions of the human spirit evident there—kids playing baseball on a scruffy field, old men enjoying a game of dominos, young lovers strolling hand in hand, soldiers on home leave whistling at the pretty girls—were in spite of the place, like grass pushing through broken concrete.

Alamar was different from most other Cuban communities in many ways, but two of those distinctions were particularly relevant in the birth of Cuban hip-hop. First, since the need for decent housing had been particularly acute among blacks before the revolution, and since this disparity had proved tough to eradicate, it ended up that a high percentage of the families who moved into Alamar's just-completed apartment blocs were black. Second, the beachside location away from Havana's congestion and clutter meant that residents often were able to get decent radio and television reception from Florida. Those factors explain why, in the early 1990s, Alamar's teenagers came to be seduced by messages from the imperialist enemy to the north.

They tuned to Miami radio, and through the static they heard music that took them to a different world—hip-hop music by N.W.A, Public Enemy, L.L. Cool J, Eric B. and Rakim. The kids memorized the lyrics, at first with only a vague understanding what they meant. They discovered *Soul Train* on a Miami television station and began to mimic the rappers' ghetto-fabulous wardrobe. They made cassette tapes of the music they liked and shared them with friends, who shared them with other friends, and soon the tapes spread across Havana and the rest of the country, like the way Russian *samizdat* used to circulate under Kosygin's red nose.

Alamar is where I first met Isaac Torres and Reynor Hernández. I'd gone out there because I'd been told that Alamar was where Cuban hip-hop had been born and where many of the rappers lived. People I asked on the streets kept pointing me toward a sector called Micro X (the "X" meaning *"diez"* or "ten"), which proved to be a dense and baffling labyrinth of cookie-cutter buildings. A guy buying fried chicken at a fast-food stand sent me to a specific courtyard, and a kid in that courtyard led me to a tall, skinny, dark-skinned guy with his hair in braids. He was Isaac, and when I told him what I wanted he led me over, under, around, and through a half dozen of the innumerable Micro X buildings until we got to Reynor's and climbed the stairs to his apartment.

It was a tight squeeze. The door opened on one small room, bisected by a big armoire into an entrance area and sleeping area. Beyond was a narrow hallway that led to the kitchen, and presumably on to other rooms. The sleeping area was mostly filled with a double bed, on which Reynor had been napping in drawstring pants and a ribbed wife-beater undershirt. He immediately apologized for the apartment, which he said was in chaos. His mother had decided to do some remodeling, he said, so that he would have a bit of the privacy that a man of twenty-two needed. This area looked as if it once might have been a living room.

Reynor was tall and dark skinned like his lifelong friend Isaac, but he was slightly more muscular and much more expressive. He was the wordsmith, the one who wrote the songs that Explosión Suprema performed—he showed me a drawer crammed full of sheets of paper filled with lyrics, written out in handwriting so small and neat that it would have been an anachronism in any country where average people owned computers to do their neat writing for them.

"Right here in Alamar is the center of rap in Cuba," he said proudly. "Here is where it was born. Rap is different. Most Cuban music talks about women, how beautiful they are, how *fine* they are, but that's something you see every day. We talk about things you might not see, or you might not hear about. Like discrimination."

Reynor and Isaac saw themselves as among the prime targets of this discrimination. They fit a certain profile: young, black, tall, dark skinned, and perhaps a little arrogant. This combination of characteristics, to a Cuban policeman, was like a red flag. In the United States, commentators have written volumes about the risks inherent in the simple act of Driving While Black. In Cuba, where hardly anyone owns a car, rappers like Reynor and Isaac were exploring a parallel phenomenon, the danger of Walking While Black.

"The police have their job to do, but when they see somebody who looks like me, they assume I must be guilty of something," Reynor said. "They stop you for nothing. It's not fair."

The very first Cuban rappers mostly imitated what they heard on the radio from the States, rapping about bitches, ho's, guns, luxury cars, jewelry, and gettin' paid. Then, in the early 1990s, a few of the crazy rappers of Alamar—there was actually a group by that name, Crazy Rappers of Alamar—did something unprecedented, something liberating: They rapped about discrimination. They slammed the police and called for justice. They talked about their frustrations as young black Cubans. They identified themselves that way, as *black* Cubans, in a society where race wasn't supposed to matter. They stomped and they cussed and they glowered. And in song after song, they slammed the police.

The police were not amused. More than once they waded into concerts at Alamar's central amphitheater and shut them down, sometimes hauling the performers away. But the authorities didn't seem to quite know what to do about the whole annoying little phenomenon. Sometimes they ignored it, other times they tried to wipe it out, but they never treated the rappers the way they would treat, say, someone who tried to found a new political party based on a platform of ending racial discrimination and reining in the police—which is to say, they never just tossed them in jail and put an end to the whole thing. The rappers, for their part, kept pushing the envelope. It was a constant, low-level struggle that went on throughout most of the 1990s.

Then one day the rappers looked up, and they'd won.

Suddenly the harassment stopped. Suddenly there were new venues for performances—not many, and only during a few time slots, but there were places to perform. Suddenly the government was offering the use of professional sound equipment. Suddenly the government had put Alamar's annual grassroots rap festival on the official cultural calendar. I didn't quite understand this sudden détente, but by the time I got to Alamar it had been in place for three or four years. Rappers like Isaac and Reynor were able to look ahead to a new phase of artistic development—and commercial development as well. Cuban rap was out in the open, people were starting to notice, and the artists were entertaining new ambitions.

"We've been in *Vibe* magazine!" Reynor told me, and he dashed over to the armoire—the dash was all of two feet—to pull some clippings out of a drawer. The hip-hop bible had done a recent piece on Cuban rap, and Explosión Suprema had been one of the featured groups, complete with photographs of Reynor, Isaac, and friends looking ghetto tough. He showed me clips from a few other publications in the States as well, and on the basis of this evidence he could dream of a day when Cuban hip-hop would be more than a man-bites-dog novelty.

His mother came home from work, apologized again for the state of the apartment, told me how genuinely proud she was of her son, and went back into the kitchen to make coffee. When she came back out to serve it, she sat with us and listened as Reynor talked about the future he imagined. He was studying computers and studying English, he said, but he was convinced that his future was in music. Cuban rap was good and getting better. With a little promotion, with a little exposure, Cuban rappers could penetrate the international market. They had to improve, though, he knew that. They weren't quite ready.

"What we want to do with Explosión Suprema is something new, and we know that's not easy," he said. "We want to change the cadence, the flow, make it better, make it ours. Our style, not anybody else's. And always we want to continue to teach with the music. We want to teach the little that we know."

He was speaking these words in a tiny apartment in an anonymous building in the bleakest, most sterile housing project in Cuba, and it sounded like a new beginning. This was not yet, and may never prove to be, the actual seedling of a new Cuban revolution. But would anyone who stumbled across the kids listening to folk music in Greenwich Village in, say, 1962 have had any idea where *that* was heading? These young Cubans had something to say and had found the voice to say it. They shared a feeling of alienation and a sense that the society in which they lived offered them no good options. They felt their elders weren't hearing them when they spoke, so they raised their voices.

"For me, the future is unknown. I hope the future has something good for me. I'm working to become a great artist. I want to realize all my dreams, both artistic and otherwise. Someday I'd like to touch snow. Someday I'd like to sing on a stage as big as Michael Jackson. I don't know if I'll make it there, but that's where I want to go. I just have to try. Life is like a puzzle, a labyrinth, in which you don't know how you'll make your way through."

* * *

Given the Cuban government's complete lack of humor when it comes to anything that remotely sounds like dissent, it made sense that the likely reaction would be to squash the hip-hop movement like a bug. But that's not what was happening at all.

The star attraction of the Museo de la Revolución in downtown Havana is an exact replica of the sainted *Granma*. The historic craft is shockingly small and thoroughly unimpressive, almost unimaginable as the ship that launched a revolution. Most visitors don't even bother to go inside the museum because you can see the *Granma* from the street—the front of the building is walled with glass. Walking past is like seeing Lenin's corpse in Moscow or Mao's in Beijing, or for that matter seeing any venerated saint's forelock or shinbone in any of the great churches of Europe. You almost want to genuflect as you pass by.

Down the street, toward the Malecón, stands a building that houses part of the bureaucracy of the UJC, the youth wing of the Cuban Communist Party. On one of the upper floors is an office suite belonging to the cultural arm of the UJC, a subunit called the Asociación Hermanos Saiz. In one of these offices, with a commanding view of Havana Harbor and the Florida Strait, I met the Cuban state's official Minister of Hip-Hop, Ariel Fernández.

That wasn't his actual title, but "Official Promoter of Hip-Hop for the Asociación Hermanos Saiz" hardly rolls off the tongue and in fact is less descriptive of what he did. Ariel Fernández was the Cuban official in charge of hip-hop.

He didn't look like the official in charge of anything. He was twenty-five but looked younger, a thin, light-skinned, baby-faced Afro-Cuban who looked, well, fresh outta Compton—jeans, baggy shirt, clean sneakers, studied air of hip-hop cool. To manage the hip-hop beast the Cuban state had chosen someone who fit the demographic. And someone with credibility on the street: Ariel had been one of hip-hop's Cuban pioneers.

"I always liked American music, because I could hear and feel the African roots, just like in Cuban music," he said. "I was seventeen or eighteen years old, in high school, when I met some friends who liked hip-hop. We listened to the music in our homes. We started going to performances."

This was back when the rappers began slamming the police and complaining about the shortages, hardships, and indignities of daily life in Cuba—and the Cuban authorities struck back.

"You have to remember that rap came along at the same time as the Special Period," Ariel told me. "It was a very difficult time for the Cuban revolution. The rappers were expressing their support, but they also had to be critical of what was going on."

"The Special Period in a Time of Peace" is Fidel Castro's euphemism for the years of woe that have followed the collapse of the Soviet Union and the Eastern bloc. Moscow had given Cuba a hefty annual subsidy until Mikhail Gorbachev cut it off. At least he had the decency to give his comrade Fidel the bad news face-to-face; photographs taken immediately after the encounter show Castro barely able to suppress his anger. Eastern Europe had joined its Soviet patron in providing markets for Cuban goods and a flow of tourists. Suddenly Cuba's sugar daddies disappeared. The U.S. trade embargo, previously a major nuisance, became more like a noose. There were sudden and desperate shortages of everything—food, fuel, electricity, soap, money.

Fidel weathered the crisis by doing things no one thought he'd ever do—things that *he* never thought he'd do. He made it legal for Cubans to hold and spend U.S. dollars, in effect welcoming a monetary invasion by the hated *yanquis*. This made it possible for some Cubans to get by on money sent by relatives in the States. Fidel also sanctioned much more private enterprise than ever before, giving farmers the right to sell some of their produce at new nonstate markets and issuing licenses for small private restaurants, *paladares*, in some Cubans' homes. He built tourism into the island's biggest earner of hard currency, forming the joint ventures with European firms that had produced all the new five-star hotels. Gradually things got better, although when I landed, the crisis still hadn't ended. Many people said their lives, in material terms, were still much poorer than in the 1980s.

Fidel's survival strategies had turned the society upside down. The most honored and accomplished pillars of society—surgeons, engineers, scholars—found themselves struggling to make ends meet on their state salaries of twenty dollars a month. For young people assessing their career options, street hustling and prostitution began to look like viable choices. And the new elite were the musicians and artists whose work could find markets overseas where people had disposable income, an economic variable that in Cuba had been zeroed out. But there were only a few of these super-elite stars. The lumpen elite was made up of the maids, waitresses, doormen, and parking lot attendants at the new luxury hotels, because the hotels were reserved for foreigners only and foreigners tipped in precious dollars. Many black Cubans came to feel they were being overlooked for these jobs in favor of whites. They began to say so out loud.

So it turned out that the young rappers in Alamar and across the island had a lot to talk about.

Ariel had this take on it: "As Fidel tells us, culture is the soul of the people. This is a cultural movement that focuses its message on improving the nation's social health. The rappers are not trying to escape from society's problems, they're trying to solve them. Being revolutionary is to recognize things as they are and not be afraid to say it." And as he framed the whole thing in impeccable official rhetoric, at times quoting Fidel himself, I began to understand why he had been chosen for this job. As a diplomat, he had mad skillz and righteous flow.

No one had been more surprised than he at his appointment. In 1998 he had been working at a Havana radio station, trying—unsuc-cessfully—to persuade the managers to give him a little airtime for a hip-hop show. "The management said it was just black music," he re-called with a smile, "and not popular with the listeners."

Frustrated, Ariel wrote a manifesto setting out his view that hip-hop was an important cultural phenomenon and that the Cuban state should pay attention. He started showing his essay around, figuring it would just be ignored, but an official of Asociación Hermanos Saiz for some reason offered to publish the piece in a prestigious state-run journal, *El Caimán Barbudo*—"The

Bearded Alligator." That article led to other writing opportunities, more chances to preach the hip-hop gospel, and soon another radio station asked him to start a program called *The Rap Corner.* He did the show for three years, at the same time organizing and deejaying live rap shows, and in December 2000 he was offered his job with Hermanos Saiz in charge of hip-hop.

He had been talented and ambitious, but also lucky enough to benefit from an abrupt change in the government's attitude toward this loud, insulting, unruly phenomenon.

The key moment came in the spring of 1999, and like many key moments in Fidel Castro's Cuba it involved a speech: Minister of Culture Abel Prieto declared that hip-hop would receive state support as "an authentic expression of Cuban culture." That changed everything. It meant that rather than try to shut hip-hop down, the Cuban state had an obligation to give it money and other resources, as it did with other officially "authentic" art forms.

It looked like the classic calculation that Lyndon B. Johnson once made about J. Edgar Hoover: better inside the tent pissing out than outside pissing in.

Why the change? There are reasonable theories. Abel Prieto is seen as one of the smartest and most progressive members of the Politburo (yes, they still have one in Cuba). But the consensus of government officials with whom I've talked is that no reversal of this magnitude could ever happen without Fidel's personal approval. There must have been a meeting at which he said, "Hip-hop? Yes, all right, go with it."

However he got it, Ariel had a mandate and was using it. He was responsible for the weekly hip-hop show at the Las Vegas, another weekly show at a recreation center near the University of Havana, the yearly festival in Alamar, and other events both in Havana and around the island. Part of his job, though he didn't put it quite this way, was to make sure that the rappers didn't cross any uncrossable lines that would put them in direct opposition to the state, because that would end the era of good feeling. Contextual criticism could not turn into dissent.

Ariel preferred to phrase it in terms of keeping "negative influences" out of the music and promoting "positive messages." Among his tasks was to find ways to coax the more strident rappers back onto the reservation. These kids had never known any other system than Fidel's, and if you'd asked them whether they were socialists, they probably would have answered honestly that they were. But they were also Cubans, and they felt that all Cubans should have the right to criticize the things that were wrong in their society. There was a fine line between slamming the police who acted on behalf of the state and slamming the state itself. But it was there, and to the mature and observant, like Ariel, it was perceptible. The trick seemed to be to move the line itself.

And that was what the rappers had done. They had found a way to get together several times a week to speak out about the bad things in their society—by implication, the wrong turns the revolution had taken—without being shut down. They were doing something nobody else in Cuba could do, something nobody else in Cuba could even imagine.

I asked Ariel whether hip-hop culture was effectively standing in opposition to the government, and he replied that of course it wasn't. They only wanted to make things better, but always—and he emphasized *always*—within the context of the revolution. Then he sat back and smiled.

"Hip-hop is a completely revolutionary culture," he said, "in the broadest possible meaning of the word."

* * *

Santos Suárez is an average neighborhood south of the city center that happens to be where the great singer Celia Cruz grew up. It is also where Pablo Herrera lives, and where one afternoon he was putting 100% Original, one of his stable of hip-hop groups, through some grueling paces.

One of the songs they were practicing was a gritty narrative of life on the margins in the big, bad city of Havana. They talked about a couple deeply in love, "like Romeo and Juliet," only Juliet went out at night to prostitute herself with foreigners and Romeo was acting as her pimp. They talked about a pickpocket who got caught, was sent to a notorious local prison, and found himself doing a hard fifteen years. They talked about a self-proclaimed gangster who went around acting all big and bad, figuring all the angles, when what he couldn't see was that he had no future. They talked about Cubans lining up to participate in a lottery for the sought-after papers that would let them emigrate legally to the United States. All this over a respectable hip-hop beat that Pablo had produced on his mixing board and was playing over big, window-rattling speakers—not on the level of the best cutting-edge hip-hop producers in the States, but better than average by any standards.

"Now is the moment when Cuba can afford to have that kind of self-criticism," Pablo said in a quiet interlude. "With the crisis in the socialist bloc, the Special Period and all that, there was a real turmoil. With the situation now more stable, it's brought back the need to talk about things that weren't talked about before, things like racism, sexism, homophobia. Cuban hip-hop speaks to the need to talk about issues that haven't been dealt with, in a process that's healthy for the revolution. There are two discourses about these issues, and they're not antagonistic, man. One comes from the top down. The other comes from the bottom up, and that's hip-hop."

He said this in perfect, unaccented, American-style English—not good but perfect, the English of someone who had spent at least part of his youth in the States. But Pablo hadn't. He was an amazing linguist, both by natural ability and by training: he'd studied languages and linguistics at the University of Havana, becoming fluent in Russian and English before deciding to become the Cuban Dr. Dre.

His house stands on a corner. To gain entry you stood on the sidewalk and yelled "Hey, Pablo!" until he came down from the second floor by way of an exterior staircase and led you up to his studio, a big room with a couple of couches, a couple of chairs, lots of full ashtrays, an Akai drum machine, a Roland multitrack recorder, a Behringer mixing board and turntable, and speakers big enough and loud enough to rock the whole neighborhood.

If Ariel was Mr. Inside, in the Cuban hip-hop universe, then Pablo was Mr. Outside. He held no position with the state, but he had an almost monopolistic dominance of the Havana scene. He managed four or five of the most popular groups and deejayed a lot of the regular shows: his booth, his rappers, his party. He knew everyone, and everyone knew him. At any show, there were always two knots of ambitious people trying to get into the scene, or trying to get ahead in it, or just trying to log some face time. One was around Ariel, the other around Pablo.

Pablo said he was a socialist, by upbringing and philosophy, and didn't have the "mind-set" for capitalism. He did have big plans, though. He had an overseas record contract; the company had paid for the equipment in his studio. He had an agent who lived in L.A., a smart and stylish Eurobabe named Grixuelle. He and Ariel had teamed up to produce a sampler CD of Cuban rap called *Cuban Hip-Hop All Stars Vol. 1,* which remained the only homegrown album that the Havana scene had produced to date. He was working on *Vol. 2,* which he promised would be much better. He wanted to break away from imitation of American hip-hop and synthesize a uniquely Cuban version of the music. For the "samples"—bits of appropriated recorded music—in his own compositions he had already stopped using American music and instead turned to the Cuban greats, Beny Moré and the rest, in hopes of adding a new depth and authenticity. He was thirty-four years old, and he was sure he was going to take the world by storm.

The afternoon I dropped by, he was coaching the three members of 100% Original. One of them, Edrey Riveri, was his godson; the other two, Ulises Quiñones and Rafael Reyes, were friends from the 'hood. The Romeo-and-Juliet piece they were practicing was a new work, and they didn't have it just right. Pablo would crank up the music and they would run through a phrase, and he would rap along and show them where the emphasis should be, how the flow should go. Some of the lyrics were impossible for a non-Cuban to follow without translation, because they dealt with experiences no outsider could relate to, using slang no one else would understand—trivia from the Soviet era, for example, when Havana had been full of Russians.

To me, that sounded like a problem. Cuban rap, thus far, had achieved no penetration of the world market at all. The only success story was a group called Orishas, and they had had to move to Paris to get their CD professionally recorded and adequately distributed. I wondered if part of the problem wasn't the fact that Cuba just wasn't like anyplace else. The extreme specificity of the Cuban rappers' lyrics seemed to me likely to exclude, rather than invite.

But to Pablo, it just sounded real.

"I always tell my rappers to talk about reality, their reality," he said. "They come in trying to sound like American rappers, all the gangsta shit, and I tell them it sounds wrong. It's a bunch of negative stuff, and it's not authentic. I tell them, look, you don't live in the Bronx, you live in Havana. You don't *have* a car. You don't *have* a gun."

* * *

They didn't have cars or guns, but the Cuban rappers and their fans had something more powerful: a sense of identity.

A few days later at the Las Vegas, everybody waited while Ariel and Pablo stood outside and finished a private conversation. Pablo's group 100% Original performed, but only two of the three rappers could make the show, so they were only 66.6% that day. Explosión Suprema, the duo I had met in Alamar, was there, and a new group called Familia Cubana. There were also assorted rappers who worked alone, including an incendiary little guy who called himself Papá Humbertico. He was witheringly sharp in denouncing the police, maybe dangerously so. He got the crowd going with a message that seemed almost political, that strayed dangerously close to the bright white line labeled "dissent."

The biggest response, though, was when 100% swung into a number whose refrain, in English, was "Black people!" The rappers would call out a line and then the whole room would respond, "Black people! Black people!" The hip-hop movement in Cuba was certainly not able, and maybe not willing, to delve too far into politics. But it had gone deep into culture—specifically, into questions of race and racism. They were claiming space for themselves in the society as black Cubans—as part of the African diaspora connected to other black people around the world, victims of racism, constituents of a group to which not all Cubans belonged, inheritors of a unique culture, possessors of their own special blackness. This was a powerful display of culture.

As Fidel was always reminding his citizens, in Cuba culture is political too. And this particular bit of culture seemed thrillingly out of control. The hip-hop scene was growing every day, and I was seeing just its most public manifestations. All around Cuba, in apartments and on street corners, young people were trading cassettes and practicing their rapping skills; all around Cuba, kids were wearing baggy jeans and oversize shirts and growing their hair so they could braid it into cornrows.

This was something new for Fidel Castro's revolution. Never before had a generation of young people developed a culture of its own that established such distance from the dominant culture, and never before had young people been so openly critical of the stewardship being exercised by their elders. Maybe this wasn't the beginning of a new revolution, maybe it wasn't the start of a cultural upheaval like the one America saw in the 1960s. But Fidel is a student of history. He had to realize that maybe it was.

7. MUSIC OF THE SAINTS

The proto-dissent of the rappers and their fans was growing but still corralled within a young, black subculture. Another set of ideas fundamentally antagonistic to Cuban communism, however, was spread throughout the whole of Cuban music—and the rest of the society as well—like a stubborn infection. Communist Cuba was riddled with religious faith. And since faith feeds on hard times and desperation, it was growing stronger every day. I saw its power one night at the Casa de la Música.

José Luis Cortés pimp-walked on to the stage with the swagger of a man doing something illegal and getting away with it. He looked like an extra in an old blaxploitation flick—tomato-red zoot suit, matching fedora, high-heeled Italian boots with pointed toes. Beneath this Cotton-Comes-to-Havana outfit he was short and stocky and baby faced, with caramel-colored skin and the cocky posture of the street tough who knows he can beat up all the other street toughs on the block. His nickname was "el Tosco," or "the Roughneck," and for two decades the group he led, NG La Banda, had been the tightest, the most streetwise—in a term befitting his wardrobe, the *baddest*—in all of Cuba. The fact that Tosco held under his arm a flute, never considered a particularly threatening instrument, somehow only heightened the effect. It said: Yes, I play this dainty, chirpy, tweety little thing, and I'm *still* Mack Daddy.

After some introductory banter he raised the flute and gave a nod, and his sixteen-piece band swung into a devilishly intricate jazz-fusion number, Chick Corea's "Spain," followed by an amazing two hours of funkified salsa, with interludes of salsified funk. By this point, I was accustomed to shows that ended at three thirty in the morning with the whole audience on its feet, dancing as if to hold back the dawn. But when NG finally finished, precisely at four ten, at least half the audience was *up on the stage*, such a crowd that you could no longer see the band, dancing and singing with such complete abandon that it seemed a miracle no one fell off.

The really strange thing was that the number that brought the Casa de la Música to this apotheosis was not so much a song as a chant:

> *Despójate,*
> *Quítate lo malo.*
> *Échalo pa'trás,*
> *Límpiate, mi hermano.*

Over and over again they said those words, over a buttery bass line and a pounding beat, not the type of chant that brings peace but the kind that incites frenzy. *Strip yourself. Remove the evil. Throw it behind you. Cleanse yourself, my brother.* Each line was accompanied by a specific movement. You rubbed your arms to scour off the evil. You tossed it over your shoulders, leaving it behind, moving forward toward something new, something pure.

The song was called "Santa Palabra," which means "Sacred Word," and it only stretches the point a bit to call it the rough equivalent of a gospel song. In this most secular of settings, with its hoochie mamas and sugar daddies, its hustlers and ho's, its pungent atmosphere of booze-fueled licentiousness and general lowdown raunch, I was glimpsing something unexpected.

It was worship. It was the tip of the iceberg of faith.

* * *

You didn't hear people speak of anything called Santería in Cuba much at all, but the phenomenon itself—the faith—was more pervasive than you ever could have imagined. The word *Santería* had taken on more than a whiff of the pejorative, and in any event was seen as more of an American term; people on the island spoke instead of "Regla de Ocha" or "Regla Lucumí" or "the Yoruba religion" or "Ifá" or just "the saints." Sometimes they didn't call it anything at all, just went about the business of observing as many of its rites, instructions, and proscriptions as they chose to observe. But even if it often went unnamed, it was everywhere. The Afro-Cuban faith was like a parallel system of belief, organization, and authority on Fidel Castro's island. And now, with the economy in ruins and the people desperate and without rational hope, this church without walls was gaining new members every day.

The faith had always been somewhat problematic for Castro and his revolution. It's true that there were long-standing reports, fairly credible, that Castro himself was at least a casual believer, but publicly he seldom acknowledged the faith at all and when he did never showed more than a distant, purely academic interest. For good reason: as a matter of definition (as well as red-scare slogan), communism is godless. Cuban communism could not be an exception, and so for years the revolutionary government frowned on the *santeros* and their unenlightened superstitions. For the first decade or more following the triumph of the revolution, the faithful felt actively hounded. But that aggressive position by the new government, always untenable, eventually came to be *seen* by everyone in Cuba as untenable, and thus it had to be abandoned. In 1992, finally, Cuba abandoned atheism as its official ideology and Cubans were free to practice their beliefs, primarily Roman Catholicism and the Afro-Cuban faith. Trying to discourage religion had been like pressuring people not to eat or breathe—nothing but a guarantee of dangerously widespread disobedience.

By now, Cubans who once might have gone through the motions of some of the Afro-Cuban faith's traditions or given lip service to some of its beliefs—*"por las dudas,"* they said, meaning "just in case" this exotic family of African deities turned out to be the real deal—were throwing themselves completely into ritual and ceremony with heart and soul. Everywhere you looked, if you knew what to look for, you saw the faith in action.

In the lobby of the Ministry of Culture, you were greeted by a receptionist dressed head-to-toe in white; this attire signified that she was undergoing an important yearlong purification ritual in which she would take one of the Yoruba deities as her personal protector. In the home of a bandleader you took note of a china cabinet containing an unusual collection of decorative objects; on closer inspection this display revealed itself as a *canastillero*, a shrine assembled of various idols and fetishes representing the deities, carefully placed in relation to one another and to the configuration of the room in a kind of Afro-Cuban *feng shui*. In a dance hall you saw a rum-swilling party animal romancing every woman within romancing range, and you noticed he was wearing a yellow-and-green-beaded bracelet; this proved that he had gone through an advanced and demanding rite involving the complex art of divination. On a busy sidewalk you saw a man—it was always a man—wearing a much bulkier bracelet, made of a dozen or more yellow-and-green-beaded strands, that marked him as a *babalawo*, or priest. You noticed the deference others paid him, the instant respect. You overheard their whispered requests to the *babalawo* for prayers or advice, which followed the greeting they offered him in an archaic version of a language that no one outside an oil-rich corner of distant Nigeria really spoke anymore, liturgical words that had survived the crossing of an ocean, two hundred years of slavery, another hundred years of racism, a dictatorship, a revolution, three decades of obeisance or at least lip service to communist ideology, and a final decade huddled around the corpse of communist ideology, waiting for the miracle of Lazarus or the coming of another revolution. Three ancient words of greeting: *iboru, iboya, ibocheche*.

The faith was especially evident in Cuban music. Celia Cruz had recorded albums of sacred music. Los Van Van's songs were riddled with references to the saints; one of their most-loved pieces, "Soy Todo"—"I Am All"—was nothing but an explicit prayer which in concert the band stretched to ten minutes, fifteen minutes, twenty minutes of hypnotic chant, circular and cosmic, until at the climax the lead singer dropped to his knees and demanded that the audience do the same. The story was much the same with all the other groups, or at least all the ones I knew about. I went systematically through my growing collection of Cuban music and played a little game, trying to find a CD that didn't have a single reference to the Afro-Cuban faith. I'm still looking.

As it happened, it was a vision—an apparition, but one of the flesh—that really opened my eyes to this spiritual world.

It was on my second trip to Cuba. As I had promised a host of musicians, I brought down copies of the newspaper articles I'd written about them after my first trip. I started calling the people whose words or pictures I'd featured, and for my convenience they all volunteered to come by my hotel and pick up the clippings at the front desk—all except one. Vannia Borges, the singer for Bamboleo, had been the central figure in a big photograph covering the entire top half of the front page of the *Washington Post*'s Sunday Arts section—the most important publicity boost she and the group had ever gotten. But when I phoned her and suggested she might come pick it up at her convenience, she said she couldn't.

"I'm sorry, but I have to stay in," she said. "Is there any way you could bring it by?"

The address was just off a busy thoroughfare called Infanta. My first thought was that it was odd for such a star to live in such gritty-looking surroundings, as opposed to the leafy, suburban-style neighborhoods out around the Casa de la Música, where I knew a number of other prominent musicians lived. But I remembered her telling me how unthinkable it would be for her to ever leave her old neighborhood and her lifelong friends. The two-story house was stately and narrow, and like every other house in sight—with its flaking plaster, chipped tiles, broken concrete, shutters that sagged away from the tall windows as if stricken by a great sadness—it had seen better days. Upstairs there was a large balcony, across which laundry had been hung to dry.

There were two doors. I rang the bell on the right, as instructed, and a young man answered, Vannia's brother. He took me up a narrow stairway to the family's flat. By Cuban standards it was impressive. The ceilings were high, the rooms light and airy, the furnishings solid and comfortable. There was a stereo in the corner and attractive pictures on the walls. The best thing about the place was that unlike so many other vintage flats in over-crowded Havana, it hadn't been divided and subdivided into a warren of smaller apartments, with tiny rooms overhung by home-made sleeping lofts. Vannia's family home was spacious and pleas-ant. But still, I couldn't help noticing that the living room gave on to the balcony where the laundry was drying, and that beyond the clothesline was a view not of the sea or even the skyline, but of a five-way intersection crisscrossed by several of the city's busiest bus routes. I also couldn't help noticing that the cooling breeze carried more than a hint of diesel exhaust.

Vannia's mother arrived from somewhere back in the house to greet me. She was a striking woman, tall and dark, with the regal bearing of the impossibly idealized Noble Queen in some overearnest Afrocentric painting. She wore her hair in an Afro, and she had high cheekbones and flashing dark eyes; I could only imag-ine what she must have looked like in her day. Right behind her came a younger woman, who was so occupied in bouncing a baby that she could hardly find a hand to shake mine—Vannia's sister, maker of the family's first grandchild. She said hello and then quickly retired to make the obligatory coffee. It was another few minutes before Vannia came in, and I had to work hard not to do a double take.

She was dressed head-to-toe in white—a long, lacy white dress over white tights; white sandals; and a white scarf covering her hair. She wore no makeup, nail polish, or jewelry. It took me a moment to realize what her appearance meant: she was in the process of tak-ing her saint.

I presented the newspaper clippings, and then sat back for a moment to enjoy the charming scene. Her mother sat in the room's biggest chair—her throne, I gathered—beaming with pride; the brother puffed out his chest, then came over to shake my hand a second time; they called for her sister, who came back, without the baby, and clapped her hands with delight. Then, for a moment, they talked among themselves as if I weren't there. I heard Vannia tell the others she couldn't wait to show her boyfriend.

"I'm sorry I couldn't pick this up from your hotel, and you had to come all the way over here," Vannia said to me when the spell had broken. "It's that I'm not supposed to go out at midday. During these months of initiation, you are not supposed to let the sun shine on you at noon. You're not supposed to go out at night, either, after six o'clock."

I asked how the band was, how her career was going. She was full of excitement about the recent Bamboleo album, the collection of live performances and remixes that Lazarito Valdés had told me about (and that I had found wanting). There was talk of a new U.S. tour; it would be the band's fourth, but this time they had hopes of playing bigger halls. Lazarito would have all the details, she said. After some small talk over sweet coffee, which the sister had served, I asked how she managed to keep up her demanding schedule with Bamboleo given the strictures imposed by the rite she was undergoing.

"Oh no, it's not a problem," she said. "You're allowed to go out at night if you have to work. But only to work. You have to go and do your job, and then you go right home. It's understood that one *has* to work. I don't know, maybe at some time in the past the *babalawos* were more strict. But with the situation in Cuba now, it's necessary for everyone to work if they can. The intention is still there, the sincerity is there for the *orishas*, and that's the important thing."

"Which saint?" I asked.

She smiled. "Yemanyá."

Her *babalawo*, through the practice of *ifá*—a complex system of divination—had determined that the powerful *orisha* named

Yemanyá would forever be Vannia's personal guardian. Yemanyá is our common mother, the goddess with dominion over the sea. She is strong, nurturing, and wise, although like all the *orishas* she has human qualities as well as divine qualities, and sometimes she displays a fierce temper. She has to be respected, but if accorded the proper respect, she gives of herself completely.

I offered Vannia my congratulations. But I was still curious about her decision. She was the star attraction of the fastest-rising band in Cuba. Her career was taking off, her options had suddenly multiplied beyond imagination, her potential seemed almost limitless. Yet here she was, taking this demanding and inconvenient spiritual detour. Even though allowances were made for her unorthodox work schedule, it had to cramp her style. Why was she doing it? What was the power of this calling?

"I don't know, it just gives me peace," she said. "There is just so much going on in my life right now, so much going on in Havana, in Cuba. Things are so difficult for so many people. Look at the way things are right now. Things are so confused. And the music business is so rough, so complicated, even so dangerous. This choice gives me a sense of balance. It gives me something to hold on to in my life."

"Can you feel a difference?"

"I do. I know it's not something I can explain, but I feel better. Now, with the way things are in this country right now, it is just something I have to do."

The sultriest singer in Cuba smiled as beatifically as a cloistered nun, her brown skin swathed in purest white, looking not of flesh but of spirit, like an angel. That was my apparition.

* * *

All of this struck me as more familiar than exotic. Years earlier, while researching a book on Brazil, I had gone to an Afro-Brazilian priestess and had my future told.

In Brazil, as in Cuba and the other Caribbean islands, the slaves imported from West Africa had managed to hold on to more of their

African heritage than their brothers and sisters in the British colonies that eventually became the United States. We African Americans ended up with none of our ancestral languages or beliefs; some customs survived, but even these were westernized and modified. African Americans have no Yoruba words of greeting, no pantheon of exotic saints.

Adherents of the cultural-determinism school of development would chalk it up to religion. The British were parsimonious Protestants who knew the value of a pound sterling, or a slave, and took pains to keep their unpaid workforce alive long enough to produce offspring, which would grow up to provide more no-cost labor; this meant acculturating them by forbidding any expression of their native religions and forcing them to believe in Christ if they believed in anything. The laissez-faire Catholics who ran Latin America and the Caribbean, this theory would argue, saw slaves as disposable and simply worked them until they died, at which point they were buried—God rest their heathen souls—and simply replaced. A disposable slave does not need to have his culture taken away. It doesn't matter so much what God he prays to, as long as he works himself to death.

Some scholars point to another factor. In North America slaves were individual pieces of chattel and family units were broken up, often intentionally; with no warning, a slave's son or mother or husband could be sold away to another plantation many miles away. This had to contribute to the eradication of traditions, beliefs, and patterns of group identification. Slave owners in the rest of the hemisphere were not nearly so assiduous in destroying the black family.

As a result, African religions had survived in these other parts of the New World. Along with the faiths had survived elaborate ceremonies and rituals, almost all of them accompanied by music—African music, based on intricate, virtuosic drumming. It's not much of a leap to posit that this might be the reason why black music in Brazil, Cuba, and the rest of the hemisphere is more overtly based on African drumming, including the use of hand drums such as congas and bongos, than black music in the United States. Faith kept the rhythms alive.

In Brazil, *candomblé* and *macumba* are versions of the same faith I saw in Cuba. Some of the practices were different—in Brazil, for example, women tended to be the priests, whereas in Cuba only men could become *babalawos*—but the deities and the faith were essentially the same.

In an almost all-black Brazilian town named Cachoeira, tucked away in one of the black-loam valleys of Bahia that look and feel so much like the Mississippi Delta, a portly priestess named Mae Dionisia had tossed her cowrie shells and promised I would have a long, happy life. But then she had frowned. "Your wife is very sick," she said. This got my attention, because I had met this priestess for the first time ten minutes earlier and neither she, nor for that matter anyone in all of Brazil, could have known that my wife, indeed, was being treated for a life-threatening illness. I was not much of a believer in any form of spiritualism or divination, but I confess that I shuddered. Dionisia threw the cowries again. "But she'll be all right," she said. She told me to make an offering to the *orixa* named Iemanjá—the Brazilian incarnation of the sea-mother-goddess Yemanyá—and so, feeling a bit ridiculous, I bought some mangoes on the way back to my hotel and that night I tossed one of them as far as I could into the ocean. As it turned out, thanks to the wonders of modern medicine, my wife was cured.

I have never read any measure of literal cause and effect into this sequence of events. I'm too much of an empiricist for that, too much a product of my Western education and belief system. But neither have I ever again been tempted to denigrate any of the Yoruba-inspired New World faiths as bizarre superstitions—which is a long, roundabout way of explaining why, when Tosco led that chant at the Casa de la Música and all those people were scrubbing the evil from their bodies and tossing it over their shoulders, I was scrubbing and tossing too. *Por las dudas.*

* * *

The anthropologist who had agreed to spend a few hours with me explaining the Afro-Cuban faith said he would meet me in the hotel lobby. We had only talked by phone, though, so we'd have to pick each other out.

"I'm mulatto," he said. "Tall, thin, and I'll be wearing a blue shirt."

"I'm black," I told him, "and I'm also tall, and I'll have on a white shirt and navy blue pants."

But we passed each other in the lobby a couple of times before making the connection. In describing ourselves I had been using the American color scale and he the Cuban, and so when we finally resorted to clothing, height, and the process of elimination to make a positive identification, the black man was a good deal lighter skinned than the mulatto.

Rafael Robaina was a scholar at the Center of Anthropology, a state-run institute, and he specialized in the Afro-Cuban faith. I had called him after running across a couple of his papers on the Internet. From his writings, I knew he would be full of facts, figures, history, and context, and also that he would have the ability— rare in academics—to assemble his knowledge into a coherent, flowing narrative that a novice could understand. What I hadn't anticipated was that he would be a believer: on his wrist he wore the beaded bracelet that marked him as having undergone *mano de Orula*, the divination rite.

He was young, in his thirties, and thin as a whippet. Even in a country where decades of socialism had grievously wounded the fashion instinct—even very high ranking government officials seemed to have a strange affinity for brown polyester—you could still tell immediately that Rafael Robaina was an academic, a man who lived the life of the mind and considered clothing mere covering for nether parts and limbs. His blue polo shirt was worn, faded, and much too small; his jeans weren't remotely the right size; and his angular, probably handsome face was obscured by an anachronistically large pair of aviator glasses with gold frames, listing slightly to port.

He began by apologizing for being a half hour late. He had gotten a late start, and since he didn't have a phone at home he couldn't call to let me know. Then he had had to wait for the bus, and it had taken an hour to arrive, which was a bit longer than he had allowed for. And then the bus, which in any event would have taken a while to come all the way across town from his neighborhood, called Víbora, had proceeded even more slowly than he had expected. Thus did one of Cuba's leading young scholars travel to his appointments.

Then he saved me the trouble of posing an opening question. "Are there more believers in this period of crisis?" he asked. "Yes. I think obviously yes. It isn't really anything particular about the faith, so much as human nature. When a man sees his life come to such a point, and has no way to affect the situation on his own, he looks for superhuman intervention. So yes, we don't have absolutely current research, but a lot more people are turning to the faith."

He walked me smoothly through the basics. The Afro-Cuban faith derives from the faith practiced by the Yoruba people of what is now Nigeria, as passed down by generations of slaves and melded with Roman Catholicism so that the slaves could worship without appearing to commit blasphemy. The faith is actually monotheistic, in that there is but one creator, whose name is Olodumare. With him in the spirit world are a number of semi-deities called *orishas*, a few dozen overall—the exact number is a matter of some debate but only around fifteen of them are in any real sense present in the daily life of the faith, and only seven are routinely taken by worshipers as their personal guardians.

Each of the *orishas* has his backstory—Changó, for example, is the great warrior who sends the lightning; Ogún, the forger of steel; Obatalá, the serene fountain of knowledge. Each has his own personality. Each has his own sphere of authority over human affairs, such as lovely, sensual, riverine Oshún's dominion in matters of the heart. Each has his favorite color—white for Obatalá, blue for Yemanyá, and of course red for Changó. If the Afro-Cuban *orishas* ever found themselves as contestants on the *Saturday Night Live* spoof quiz show *Quién Es Mas Macho?*, Changó would win every time. He was the favorite *orisha* of Cuban men, by far.

And each was associated with a specific Roman Catholic saint—Saint Barbara for Changó, the Virgin of Charity for Oshún. These correlations allowed the slaves to pray to the *orishas* in a way that their Spanish overlords not only had to tolerate, but encourage. They probably knew, but were not forced to acknowledge, that the slaves who came to the churches to pray so fervently before the statues of the Virgin Mary were in fact praying to a sultry black demigoddess who would help them find their way in affairs of love.

The *orishas* were in a sense the principal actors in the faith, but there was much more: a duty to practice a form of ancestor worship, a fully elaborated system of divination that took years of study to master, a reverence for nature as a storehouse of spiritual treasure. There were ceremonies in which worshipers were possessed by the *orishas*, channeling their succor or vexation. There was the business of animal sacrifice, which turned out to involve mainly chickens and other fowl, but which, yes, meant the untimely, bloody extinction of the occasional goat. The squawks and bleats at the coup de grâce were ghastly. Most of the animals were eaten afterwards, though—no one was going to waste that much protein in Cuba—and somehow this seemed to ameliorate the violence and injustice of the knife. In the final analysis, it was just getting in touch with one's lunch.

And there was music: the faith did not exist without its chants, accompanied by complex and specific rhythms played on sacred *batá* drums that had to be made in a certain way, by specially trained craftsmen using the proper materials, and then elaborately consecrated before use. Each *orisha* had his own rhythms, used to summon or to flatter these vain beings. Each had his own melodies, and some of these praise songs were as familiar to the Cuban ear as "Twinkle, Twinkle, Little Star" was to ours. Charanga Habanera ended one of its blazing hits with an abrupt switch into a lilt used to herald Elegguá, the lord of the crossroads, the *orisha* who was always summoned at the outset of a ceremony because only he could open the pathways to the spirit world and allow mere mortals to converse with the pantheon.

Still, Rafael said, the true heart of the faith lay closer to home.

"It is an anthropocentric religion," he said. "Man is at the center of the universe. Man lives and dies, and everything occurs within that space. Not before and not after. This faith is really about each person living according to his individual way of life.

"In this religion," he concluded, "the real god is man."

Rafael said there weren't any good figures on the number of new adherents since the Special Period began, but he was confident there were a lot of them. He wasn't one of them, though; his own faith had been with him since childhood.

"I was very ill when I was young," he said. "The faith brought me through. And since I have been studying it from the academic perspective, my own faith is stronger than ever. This isn't a faith in which we proselytize. No one tries to convince anyone else. It's something that a person has to come to on his own. It's your individual decision. But if that's the decision you make, you find great peace."

* * *

There are Cubans of all colors who practice the religion but it is fundamentally an Afro-Cuban faith, a *black* faith. In a sense it is becoming blacker all the time, as religious leaders in Cuba seek a stronger and more organic connection with the roots of the faith. The best place to see this movement in action is the Yoruba Cultural Association, located in a beautifully restored building near the old Capitol. The association is many things: an administrative headquarters, a performance space, a temple. But first and foremost, it is a hall of truly bizarre statuary.

The entire second floor is devoted to a museum of the *orishas*. Olodumare, the supreme being, is represented by a spill of glittering white fabric. The rest of the *orishas* are represented by life-size statues arrayed in dioramas that illustrate each distinctive story and mission. Here stands warrior Changó, fierce and menacing; there stands all-embracing Yemanyá, serene as the seven seas. The demigods are portrayed in their heavenly raiment, each in his preferred colors, and the statues are painted to give them lifelike human form—African human form, with brown skin and kinky hair. For a couple of dollars, a guide will walk you through the exhibit and tell you about each *orisha* in turn. The effect is of walking through a Cuban version of Madame Tussaud's.

"This is a defense of negritude," Antonio Castañeda, president of the Yoruba Cultural Association, told me. "The *orishas* are not just gods, they are black gods. We feel that nobody who truly is ready to accept black gods can be racist."

The museum, which was brand new when I visited, represents Fidel Castro's final surrender to the overwhelming power of the saints.

For decades, he refused to allow any official state support or acknowledgment of the faith, even after the liberalization of 1992. But a few years ago, the Yoruba Cultural Association—mindful of the growth of the faith, and sensing that the political wind was due to shift—had the temerity to ask Fidel not just for permission to establish the museum, but also for money to acquire and renovate a grand building in the heart of Havana, a building that would make an unmistakable statement about the centrality of the Afro-Cuban faith to life on the island.

Fidel declined to give direct support in the form of a government appropriation. But he told Castañeda that the state-run banks might be willing to help with some financing. The banks, it turned out, fell over themselves to offer the necessary funds. As of my visit the state-run media still hadn't announced the museum's existence, but the faithful knew. Everyone knew.

"I thought we would never get to this point," Castañeda said. Once the faith was strongest among the working class, but now "you find believers who are doctors, lawyers, professionals." The faith that he called "one of the oldest religions in the world" had a new lease on life, and a new lease on a dandy piece of real estate.

* * *

Seek stability in all things.
Take special care with documents.
Be obedient.
Be careful with your stomach; really know what you are eating.
Pray often to Changó for all your needs.

These are among a set of personalized instructions from Orula, the divine oracle, and I was cautioned to ignore them at my own grave peril.

When I pulled up at the little blue house in Guanabacoa, a gritty suburb on the other side of Havana Bay, I was lucky enough to find that the *babalawo* was in.

Seventy-five years old, but with a teenager's bright and darting eyes, José Lino had been a priest of the Afro-Cuban faith for three decades. He certainly looked the part, as he sat there in his easy chair, carefully sizing me up. He was shirtless and barefoot, his skin a walnut brown, his hair nearly white, his face deeply lined. You'd expect a prophet who wandered in the desert for forty years to come out looking exactly like José Lino. Except for those lively eyes: this was not a prophet who condemned the world, but one who celebrated it.

Across the tiny living room was a framed picture of a Caucasian, airbrushed Jesus with flowing hair and a copiously bleeding heart. In the middle of the floor, like an altar, sat a round table with a child's black baby doll positioned in the center.

This room was just for sitting and talking, for greeting the many supplicants who dropped by. When it is time for the actual reading—the session during which he tells you who you are and what will be—José Lino takes you into a back room that seems more workshop than sanctuary, unadorned and filled with so much random clutter that you hardly notice the modest shrine in one corner that looks at first like a junk pile.

He is efficient and practical at his work. One of his sons acts as an assistant, taking notes in a neat hand.

Avoid war.
You may not betray anyone.
At your place of work, not everyone is trustworthy.
Bathe yourself with the herb paraíso *and ordinary unscented*
soap.
Be especially careful on staircases.
Sweep flower petals through your house from back to front and
out the door on two successive days.
Beware of envy.

The Brazilian priestess I consulted had relied on atmospherics to create a sense of mystery in the room where she tossed her cowrie shells—beaded curtains, religious posters and paintings, incense and candles and carefully timed gasps and sighs. The *babalawo*, by contrast, made the experience about as occult as a trip to the corner store. First we chatted for a while—when I asked how he managed to look so youthful, he lowered his voice so his wife in the other room wouldn't hear and said the credit was due to his new girlfriend, who had just turned twenty. He also thought that smoking the occasional joint might help, and at that he laughed out loud, revealing a paucity of teeth.

When he sat down to do the actual reading, he was all business. He used a chain on which there were eight lozenges of coconut shell, each with a dark side and a white side. He would ask the oracle a question and then drop the chain, and his son would note which pieces of shell had landed dark side up and which white side up. Then the son would consult a thick reference book: each conceivable pattern—dark-dark-dark-white-dark-white-dark-dark, for example, or white-dark-dark-white-dark-dark-dark-dark, all the many possible arrangements—was a specific sign with a set of possible interpretations, depending on the context. José Lino knew most of them by heart, recognizing the sign before his son could look it up. The system was not just scientific but binary, with each piece of shell the equivalent of a byte of information in a computer. The notation the reference book used, in fact, looked just like computer language, a matrix of ones and zeroes. This either hinted at some deep, universal truth about linguistics and the nature of information, or it suggested that the inventors of modern computer science could have saved themselves a lot of work by consulting an anthropologist versed in the religious practices of West Africa.

> *Throw cold water and hot water into the street.*
> *Be a good son.*
> *Be aware of where you eat and drink.*
> *Be aware of whom you have dealings with.*

* * *

In the end, the *babalawo* gave me this list of instructions, along with the general assessment that as far as he could tell, things were going pretty well for me. Then, toward the end, he frowned; he saw something inauspicious. In truth, I had half-expected something like this. In Brazil, the priestess had claimed to see a similar potential problem but assured me it could be completely eliminated with a ceremony that would cost a mere thousand dollars. I gathered that every rich tourist would be found to have such a shadow looming over his life, and that a few would even shell out the dough to have it removed. I wasn't one of the few; at those prices my interest in the whole thing was purely journalistic, and I was willing to take my chances. I had liked José Lino an awful lot, though, and was a bit disappointed that he seemed to be running the same scam.

But I was wrong. "This isn't any big thing, but it really should be taken care of," he said. "All we need is a few pieces of fruit. I don't have any here, though. We need to go find some."

So we got into my rental car and drove the length and breadth of Guanabacoa in search of fruit. It was Sunday, which meant nothing was open. Finally, in the next town over, we found a farmers' market and I spent all of two dollars and fifty cents on an assortment of fruit. When we got back to the house he placed it around me, then had me hold it, then said a few words and announced that the problem, whatever it was, had been eliminated. Before I left, he spent a few words talking to me the way a concerned Methodist pastor might have done, explaining that I really might want to think about investing more of myself in the faith and taking the first official steps toward becoming an active practitioner. He understood that this was difficult, since I lived in the States, but there was no real hurry. Whenever I was ready, he and the faith would be there. The faith would wait for me.

* * *

At the beginning of each year, the leading *babalawos* in Cuba issue a pastoral letter predicting what the next twelve months will be like, based on their consultations with Orula. The letter speaks of spiritual matters, prayers that should be said and ceremonies that should be conducted, but it also talks about general conditions. Will there be more hardship, or less? Will things get better, or worse?

The Cuban government exerts tight control over anything that could loosely be called "information technology," so that the state has an effective monopoly on media of mass communication. This includes obvious info-revolution items such as computers and satellite dishes, but also prosaic devices such as photocopy machines. If someone wanted to distribute an antigovernment broadside, he'd have a hell of a time finding a copier to use as an instrument of counterrevolution.

Yet the *babalawos'* letter manages to circulate. During the early months of the year the religious often carry a copy at all times, so they can show it to others they encounter as they go about their daily business. In Cárdenas, for example, while I was waiting to be definitively turned away from Elián's house, I saw a group of a dozen men at a little corner bar, crowded around a guy who was holding a sheaf of well-thumbed papers. He turned out to be a *babalawo,* and he was sharing his copy of the letter. His audience was rapt, hanging on every word. Occasionally an animated discussion would break out over the interpretation of a difficult passage. Every phrase, every word, mattered intensely.

I never saw anybody reading the official newspaper *Granma* that way.

The Afro-Cuban faith is not a hierarchy, but it is organized. It is not an alternative to the state, but it exists as a parallel construct. It does not compel allegiance, but it inspires belief and participation. It was important to Cuba long before Fidel's revolution and will be important to Cuba long after he is gone. The more difficult life on Fidel's island becomes, the stronger the faith continues to grow. Whenever the next Cuban revolution comes, the faith will be a factor—a source of comfort, a path to enlightenment, or maybe something more.

I've been back to see José Lino, and I've met other *babalawos* as well. I've come to admire the faith more and more—the intricacy of its theology, the beauty of its parables, the comprehensiveness of its engagement with daily life. I haven't taken any steps to be initiated, but I did buy a little statue of Elegguá, *por las dudas.*

And I still have the list that Lino gave me.

Beware of enemies.
Beware of hemorrhoids.
At all times, in all things, beware of arrogance.

8. "LOOK, THERE'S ONLY ONE LEADER"

antiago de Cuba is the anti-Havana—tight instead of sprawling, cramped instead of wide, hilly instead of flat, Caribbean in flavor rather than Hispanic. The population is overwhelmingly black and a surprising number of people have surnames like Malveaux or Johnson or Robinson, descendants of immigrants from nearby Haiti and Jamaica who came generations ago to prosperous Cuba to work in the cane fields and sugar mills. Historically Cuba's second city is prone to upheaval and revolution, which is one reason Fidel Castro chose to launch his epic campaign right here; his raid on the impregnable Moncada Barracks ended in abject and almost comic failure, but it made Castro a star and sent him on his way. In Santiago's central square, Céspedes Park, you can sit on the terrace of the city's best hotel and look out over Cuba's entire bloody history. Across the park is the oldest house on the island, a gloomy sixteenth-century pile where the conquistador Diego Velásquez once lived. Looming to your left and lording over the graceful square is the massive cathedral, built to be one of the grandest in all of New Spain. To your right is the flag-draped building where Castro announced his victory, hours after the dictator Batista had fled, coming out onto the balcony to give his first speech as Cuba's Maximum Leader.

The music in Santiago is anti-Havana too. It's like Delta blues as opposed to Chicago blues—less amplified, more acoustic, in some ways more authentic, anchored by deep roots, evocative of long days in endless fields under the scorching sun. Around the corner from Céspedes Park is the Casa de la Trova. It's a performance space and cultural center, established by Castro's revolutionary government and dedicated to the preservation and celebration of traditional Cuban music. There is a Casa de la Trova in every provincial capital, but the one in Santiago is the most famous because Santiago is the source of most of the island's musical heritage. Every afternoon, musicians come to the Casa de la Trova to jam—grizzled old guitarists, slick young trumpeters and drummers, bassists with thick layers of hornlike callus on their fingers. Locals drop by to listen and, of course, to dance. Someone always produces a bottle of rum. It's a pleasant way to pass the afternoon before night falls and the real party begins.

Céspedes Park is headquarters for Santiago's hustlers, and a couple of them latched on to me and offered to show me the city. I was in town to do a story on race and racism, and these two young men were black, so I let them walk me around for a while through the city's compact downtown. Their names were Ariel and Osmel. Both looked about twenty, both were high-school graduates, neither had a job or was bothering to look for one. They spoke passionately about the discrimination they felt as Afro-Cubans, and even more passionately about the despair they felt when they tried to imagine what kind of future they might have.

"What about the black leadership?" I asked. "What are black leaders saying and doing about the problems you face?"

Instead of answering, they looked at each other and laughed.

"Amigo," one of them finally said, in the tone one uses with a slow child. "Look, in Cuba there's only one leader."

* * *

This had been true of all communist countries, but Fidel was different. He actually *downplayed* the cult of personality. In the cities and across the countryside there were thousands of posters and billboards of Che Guevara, Camilo Cienfuegos, and the other revolutionary heroes, but not of Fidel. Occasionally you would drive past

Havana's famed seawall, the Malecón, is a dramatic backdrop for the city's changing moods. Storms send waves crashing across the four-lane boulevard, but when the skies are clear the Malecón becomes a place where lovers stroll, children play, and dreamers dream.

Old Havana is the colonial heart of the city. Away from the tourist zones, the neighborhood moves to local rhythms.

Cubans dance the way others breathe, but Fidel Castro may be the nimblest dancer of all. He still wears his trademark green fatigues at times, but more often than not these days he conducts his public life in a well-cut suit. His private life remains strictly private.

(Opposite, bottom) *Singer Vannia Borges struts across the stage as the band Bamboleo plays a sold-out show at one of Havana's legendary dance halls, the Tropical. Within a year she had become an initiate in the Afro-Cuban faith; a year after that, she left the band to launch a solo career.*

Juan de Marcos is one of Cuba's most farsighted, enterprising musicians—
and one of its sharpest minds.

La Charanga Habanera, one of the most popular salsa bands in Cuba, raises the temperature at Havana's Casa de la Música.

Moraima Marín (left) and Daily Suárez of the all-girl group Ebano share a laugh during a rehearsal. The fledgling band could only find a tiny apartment to use as a practice space—so tiny that the singers, including Marín and Suárez, had to stand outside.

Santería, more commonly known in Cuba as Regla de Ocha or simply the Yoruba faith, is an important facet of Cuban life—even more important, say scholars, as people seek solace amid a long-running economic crisis that shows no signs of ending.

A woman whirls in a trance at a religious ceremony after being possessed by one of the Yoruba gods.

Huge crowds gathered in Havana and other cities for the visit of Pope John Paul II in 1998. It was a hopeful moment, but predictions that the visit would lead to greater openness and prosperity have not come true.

Charlie Hill relaxes in a private moment with a girlfriend. A fugitive from American justice who arrived in Cuba in 1971, he lives in a three-room house in one of Havana's less desirable neighborhoods and spends much of his free time studying the Yoruba faith, in which he is a babalawo, *or priest.*

A typical street in Alamar, the neighborhood where Cuban hip-hop was born. Alamar, built on Havana's eastern fringe as a model of socialist development, is the biggest housing project in Cuba, and by most measures the bleakest.

Pablo Herrera, Cuba's leading hip-hop impresario. Herrera was a linguist at the prestigious University of Havana before finding his musical and entrepreneurial muse. He speaks English as if he'd grown up in the South Bronx, but he comes from Santos Suárez, the same Havana neighborhood where the late, great salsa singer Celia Cruz grew up. Pablo Herrera rehearses and sometimes records his rap groups at his home. Here, he works on a new song with the trio 100% Original.

The collapse of the economy has eliminated so many options for classical musicians that many have turned to popular music to subsist. Though the government still supports education in classical music, the foreign tourists who prop up the economy will pay for salsa, but not for sonatas.

the home of a loyal patriot who had taken it upon himself to display the leader's likeness, but that was about it. There was no industry cranking out images of Fidel; street vendors in Old Havana would sell you as many T-shirts and hats with as many different images of Che as you wanted, but not a single one depicting the man who had been Batman to Che's Robin, the man who had made Che the second most powerful man on the island and allowed his revolutionary style and fervor to define the world's image of revolutionary Cuba and then later sent him to his death in the jungles of Bolivia. Spend all day looking for a Fidel T-shirt; you won't find one.

This was either an extraordinary act of self-effacement or an extraordinary act of arrogance. His portrait didn't even hang in the offices of the government officials I visited, unlike the photograph of George W. Bush that looms over the bureaucrats and soldiers of the United States. His picture wasn't on all the money, unlike the regal profile of Queen Elizabeth II that gladdens the pockets and purses of her subjects. But even though he had banished the trappings, Fidel had hardly prohibited the cult of personality itself. Another way of looking at it was that his position was so preeminent and so secure that he didn't *need* to plaster the landscape with his famous bearded face. He had no rivals, no visible opponents, no one to share any real power with except his septuagenarian brother Raúl, who long ago had accepted the fact that his entire life would be spent in Fidel's shadow. People didn't need to see Fidel's face all the time to know who was in charge.

Whatever the reason, the effect was almost mystical. Fidel was nowhere and everywhere, felt more than seen. He was a presence in every Cuban life, an intimate presence, and whatever people thought of him, they had to acknowledge he was there.

"I hate him," a gay Cuban man told me. "I mean that with all my heart. I *hate* him. Look at us. All of us, we are nothing but prisoners on this godforsaken island."

"He's a good man, and I genuinely feel that he's done a lot for the people," said a Cuban celebrity who has known Castro personally for thirty years. But then the celebrity became concerned that I had arrived at his house unannounced. "They know about this interview, right?" he said. "I don't want to get them mad at me."

"He has defended our nation for forty years," a cab driver said. "Yes, we have problems, but remember that we're basically at war with your government. Anywhere in the world, a blockade like the one the Americans impose on our small island is an act of war. Fidel has done the best he could do under the circumstances. I'm with him to the end."

"He has ruined this beautiful country," another cab driver complained. "Look around you. Really look. It's fine for tourists, but it's intolerable for those of us who live here, and Fidel is the one to blame. I'd leave tomorrow if I could. Take me with you!"

"I hate that man," an unemployed engineer said. "And I sincerely hope he lives forever. That's how afraid I am of what will happen after he dies. Things are bad now, but I fear they will get much worse without Fidel. Much worse."

Actually, I found that a surprising number of Fidel's bitterest critics on the island felt the same. They were petrified of what might come after he was gone. His designated successor was his brother Raúl, age seventy-two. Raúl kept mostly to the background, having quietly run the Cuban military for decades, apparently with an iron fist and a good deal of skill. His reputation, dating back to the time of the revolution, was as much more doctrinaire and Stalinist in his approach to the whole communist enterprise than his mercurial older brother. In the mountains, he had been the one pushing to execute suspected traitors at the slightest hint of betrayal; after the triumph, he and Che had lobbied hardest and most remorselessly for the firing squads that eliminated many of Batista's thugs and henchmen—the ones who had been too stupid to hop a plane for Miami or Tampa—and probably quite a few innocent people as well. Raúl had negative charisma. He absorbed the limelight like black velvet, giving back no reflection at all. He wasn't tall and handsome like his brother (there had long been rumors that in fact he had a different father), and without any evidence people had always made disparaging remarks about his sexual preference, a public relations catastrophe in *machismo*-drenched Cuba. Those whispered slurs, plus his oddly almond-shaped eyes, had led people to call him *"la china"* behind his back—"the Chinese lady." The consensus was that the nation would never, ever follow him the way it followed Fidel. The nation might obey, to a point and for a time, but it would never follow him. And if it wouldn't follow Raúl, where would it go? Would neighbor turn against neighbor? Would there be riots in the streets? Would the army remain loyal? Would Cubans fire on other Cubans? And when the Miami Cubans tried to come back to reclaim what they felt was rightfully theirs, as everybody knew they would someday, would they be met with open arms or barricades?

Even this worrisome succession plan depended on Raúl's outliving Fidel, and with both men in their seventies, that seemed no better than an even-money bet. If he didn't, the future of Cuba after Fidel was completely opaque. For forty years, Fidel had assiduously avoided naming a next-generation heir. Pretenders came along every few years, the incumbent being Felipe Pérez Roque, the eager-beaver foreign minister. Fidel always tolerated them for a few months or a few years, then mercilessly cut them off at the knees. Pérez Roque was universally seen as living on borrowed time. Everyone seemed to know that but him, *pobrecito*.

There were bright and capable people in the government, though, even in the high-and-mighty Politburo. People like Pedro Saez.

I first met Saez at a party in the grand old Washington, D.C., mansion that houses the Cuban Interests Section, the quasi embassy that handles Cuba's diplomatic, cultural, and commercial affairs with the imperialist hegemonic power to the north. The Cubans in Washington, like the *yanquis* in Havana, are not allowed to have a proper embassy, since the nations do not share diplomatic relations; but the two Interests Sections are really embassies in all but name. The Cuban mission is on Sixteenth Street, the monumental boulevard that defines a straight line from the portico of the White House to the city's northern tip. The mansions around the

Interests Section, with their gorgeous hilltop views, were once the favored precincts of the aristocracy—*Washington Post* publisher Katharine Graham grew up in one of them—but after the 1968 riots most of the rich people and most of the other embassies abandoned the zone. Recently it has been gentrified, or regentrified, and young hipsters and gay couples now share nearby Meridian Hill Park with blacks and Latinos whose landlords are just itching to install Sub-Zeros and Vikings and quintuple the rent.

The party was in honor of the first legislative delegation from Cuba ever to come to Washington on an official visit, courtesy of an invitation from the Congressional Black Caucus. I hadn't bothered to ask the press officer from the Interests Section just what it was that legislators in Cuba did. The ranking official, I was told, was the Communist Party chief for Havana Province, who also served as a legislator. When I arrived at the mansion the press officer took me to meet this important figure, Pedro Saez. I was charmed.

He was about my age, in his late forties; he was smooth and confident, carrying himself like a man in charge; he was engaging in a way that projected sincerity; and, perhaps most interesting, he was black. Unlike most Cuban officials—and this is no slur on my friends in the government, just reported fact—he was wearing a suit that fit properly and a shirt and tie that didn't clash. There were hundreds of people at the party and we didn't have much time to chat, but he made me promise that the next time I came to Havana I would look him up.

So that's what I did. I called his provincial office, I called his downtown office, I got to know his chief of staff and several of his secretaries on a first-name basis, and I heard a succession of promises that the very busy Mr. Saez was *extremely* busy at the moment but wanted to see me and firmly intended to do so. In truth, he *was* busy—another of the frequent hurricanes that assaulted the island had just come through, providentially missing the big cities but devastating parts of the agricultural countryside, including Havana province. Saez had been busy coordinating relief efforts; one evening I saw him on the news, standing at Fidel's side as the

commander-in-chief inspected the damage and praised the remarkable evacuation effort that had resulted in zero fatalities—a true
accomplishment, the kind of thing that Cuba does better than any
poor country I've ever seen. Clearly, Saez had more on his mind
than a vague commitment to see an American reporter, so I decided
that I'd probably try him again next trip.

But a day before I was scheduled to fly home, he called.

"I couldn't let you leave without honoring my word," he said.
"I'll be there this evening at seven. We can have a drink and maybe
something to eat. Done?"

Done. I told him that there was a quiet corner in my hotel lobby
where we might talk.

"No, there's a hospitality suite on the top floor," he said. "We'll
talk there."

I decided to go down and meet him in the lobby anyway, and at
a quarter after seven the waters parted. A big black car pulled up; a
plainclothes security man jumped out to hold the door, which the
doorman already had but immediately surrendered; the hotel manager practically hurdled the front desk and sprinted over to greet
Saez with his most unctuous smile. All this happened before I could
move a muscle. Saez accepted the manager's greeting and then
came straight over to me, the manager trailing behind as if on a
string, all the while continuing his effusive welcome. In the elevator
Saez clapped me on the back as if I were an old friend.

The hospitality room on the executive floor was luxuriously
stocked with food and drink. The manager led us to a cozy inner
sanctum, took our drink order personally and then asked with ceremony to be able to take his leave so that we could talk privately. He
all but backed and kowtowed out of the room.

None of this was excessive for one of the two dozen most powerful men in Cuba.

Like a pro, Saez began by establishing the ground rules. This
wasn't an interview for the *Washington Post*, he said, but neither
was it off the record. It was more of a friendly chat between brothers. In other words, no notebook or tape recorder. I ended up hav-

ing to commit as many quotes as I could to memory, and then reconstruct the conversation as best I could as soon as I got back to my room.

He started by giving an unintentional insight into the way Cuba works at the top.

"You know, I really wanted to see you because I thought we had a lot to share, you and I, but I wasn't sure. This American reporter for a big newspaper, at a moment when relations between the two countries are problematic. I didn't know, so I asked Fidel. I told him there's this reporter, he seems like a good guy, I think it would be fine. And he said sure, go talk to him. No problem."

I told him he must be exhausted, and he said he was. There was the hurricane relief effort, which was sending him all over the province. There was much work to plan a special upcoming "open tribunal" that Fidel was scheduled to hold soon in a provincial town. And last night, he told me, Issac Delgado had dropped by.

Issac Delgado was one of Cuba's biggest stars, the handsome singer whose immaculate phrasing and silken baritone I'd heard on "La Vida Es un Carnaval." He was a good friend, Saez said, and so Issac had dropped over and they had got to talking, and maybe they had had a bit of rum, and it had gotten late. "Issac finally fell asleep on my couch," he said. "That's where he stayed the whole night."

I asked about his background. Pedro Saez was born in 1954, which made us the same age. He grew up in a little town in the interior, a black boy with no prospects except a life in the fields. But then came the revolution, which gave him the opportunity to go to school. He excelled in both academics and politics, becoming the head of the communist youth organization in his province. A talent spotter from Havana noticed him, and he was brought to the capital for more grooming as a young man on the rise.

His military service included a stint in Angola, site of one of the Cold War's bloodiest skirmishes, when thousands of Cuban soldiers were sent to stand alongside Angola's Marxist government against rebels supported and armed by South Africa's apartheid regime. It was one of the more obscure, but also one of the bloodiest, of the proxy wars that the United States and the USSR fought over the long years of the Cold War. I eventually came to think of Cuba's experience in Angola as roughly equivalent to the American experience in Vietnam. A generation of Cuban men went to an alien and distant land to fight and die in the name of ideology. They saw horrors they could never have imagined. Their bodies were punished, their minds were stretched, and when they came home to their little island they were utterly changed. Saez didn't talk much about Angola, but he got that distant look you see in the eyes of men as they read the names on the wall of the Vietnam Veterans Memorial in Washington on the Mall.

I asked about trends in Cuban society—the dollarization of the economy, the rise of tourism, the emergence of a tourist-sector elite. What effect would this have on the revolution?

His answer was thoughtful. He said that tourism had brought prostitution and even drug abuse to Cuba, and these were obviously problems. But he said he thought this would change when the U.S. travel ban was finally lifted and "ordinary people" could come down on vacation, middle-class families with wholesome values. And anyway, he said, not all of the liaisons that came from *jineterismo* could be labeled prostitution. "If a man comes down here and happens to fall in love with a Cuban woman, really in love with her, then what's wrong with that? What could be more natural? I can imagine that a lot of American women, if they came to Cuba, might fall in love with Cuban men as well. That's just the way things work between a man and a woman."

After his military service, Saez began climbing the party ladder as a municipal official. Then his fast-track career was suddenly boosted into overdrive. In short order he became the top party official in Sancti Spiritus, a small central province, and then was given his current post in Havana province and his seat on the Politburo.

The event that gave Saez such a boost to the very top of the Cuban power establishment was a riot, perhaps the most serious challenge Fidel Castro has faced in his many years of rule.

It happened in August 1994. By then, the Cuban economy had

bottomed out from the vertical dive it had taken during the Special Period. Macroeconomic numbers had even started to get a bit better. But for the Cuban people, life was nothing short of desperate. The whole country, used to middle-class living standards, suddenly had had to endure an awful poverty. There was no gasoline to fuel the trucks that brought food from the countryside to the cities, so people were hungry for the first time since the revolution. There was no fuel for the generators, so officials had to ration electricity and people suffered blackouts almost daily. The infrastructure began to decay—roads, bridges, water mains, sewers. There was no toilet paper, no underwear, no meat, no milk, no hope.

A Cuban friend of mine tells a story from those awful days. His neighborhood hadn't seen food for so long that a community decision was taken to break the law. My friend and another man were chosen to go out into the countryside, buy a fat pig, and bring it home for slaughter. Such private commerce was illegal, but there was no choice. These men were city kids—their idea of the country was an afternoon in Lenin Park on the outskirts of Havana—but off they went. They hitched a ride and wandered through rural Cuba until they found a farmer who indeed had a fat pig he was willing to sell. They bought it, then faced the question of how to get the animal home. After standing beside the road for quite a while, they were finally picked up by a trucker who let them and the pig ride in the back, along with a host of other hitchhikers who were using the only available transport to go from town to town.

They were home free until the overloaded truck went into a curve too fast and skidded off the road. In the bed there was a bedlam of shifting passengers and cargo, and my friend and the pig both fell out.

"Don't worry, I'm okay," my friend yelled up from the bushes where he'd landed.

"I don't give a shit about you, just save the fucking pig!" his buddy yelled back. Somehow the rope by which they were restraining the pig had wrapped itself around the pig's neck, and the animal was strangling itself. They rushed to cut the rope, but by that time the pig was in such distress that it defecated all over the two city boys trying so desperately to save its life. When they finally got the animal untangled it did the only sensible thing, which was to light out as fast as it could down the hillside. The two men had to spend an hour scrambling to find, secure, and retrieve the pig. They emerged looking as if they'd been through a war, covered with mud and scratches, but they nabbed the porcine fugitive. And eventually they had their revenge, in the form of *puerco asado* with black beans and rice.

Cubans can laugh at stories like that now, but in 1994 nothing was funny. One solution that occurred to many Cubans was simple but impossible: leave the island. Go someplace where there was food, where there was light, where there was a future.

A group of would-be escapees hijacked one of the ferryboats that crisscross Havana Bay and ordered the captain to sail to Florida. It was not a seagoing vessel, and Cuban military ships overtook it before it had gotten far into the Florida Strait. What happened next is the subject of dispute. The Cuban government says that the boat was mishandled by the hijackers, foundered, and sank. Others say the pursuing Cubans sank it. In any event, more than thirty people died.

When news of the sinking reached the city, in Centro Habana, a dense and overwhelmingly black neighborhood in the middle of town, people did an unprecedented thing: they poured into the streets. They refused to disperse when police ordered them to. Their grievances were mostly economic, but there was a racial element as well. Fidel Castro's regime was confronted with something that looked very much like a race riot. There was a melee, the dimensions of which are still not well known; two policemen were killed, and there might have been civilian casualties as well. The legend is that Fidel himself went down to the scene of the violence to quell the disturbance, but an official once told me that in fact he directed the police operation from his office.

Afterwards, Fidel did three things. He allowed an exodus of boat people, a kind of mini-Mariel that brought thousands of refugees to Florida's shores. He grudgingly gave more ground on economic reform, sanctioning more limited private enterprise, like small family-owned restaurants, and ordering officials to turn a blind eye to unlicensed entrepreneurial ventures. And he rapidly began to promote black officials into what previously had been an overwhelmingly white leadership group—people like Esteban Lazo, the party chief in Havana city, and Juan Carlos Robinson, party chief in Santiago. And Pedro Saez.

Saez and I talked a bit about the racial issue in Cuba. I told him about a woman I'd interviewed, a scholar at the Cuban Institute of the Book named María del Carmen Caño. She was a black woman who studied race, and she'd told me that her husband, also an Afro-Cuban and very dark-skinned, was a colonel in the Cuban army and had never taken her work seriously. He believed Cuba was a color-blind society—until one day, dressed in shorts and a T-shirt, he had been walking down the street and a policeman had picked him out of the crowd and ordered him to produce his documents. He was carrying a package, and the policeman wanted to know what he had stolen. The cop backed off when he saw the identity documents and realized who he was dealing with, but the colonel understood for the first time that without his rank he would be just another black man, a suspect even before any crime has been committed.

Saez thought for a while. He said that I had to understand how pervasive Cuban racism had been before the revolution. He said that speaking just as a black man, not as an official, he genuinely believed the revolution had made giant strides toward ending discrimination. His own life, he said, was an example—never could he have achieved so much under the old regime. Had every trace of racism been eliminated? Sadly, no. Things were so much better, but no, they were not perfect. Fidel himself was very aware of the race issue, he told me. The commander in chief was aware, for example, that some neighborhoods were more heavily populated by blacks than others, and that some of these areas were lacking in basic services. Fidel was personally involved in trying to redress these inequalities. And yes, as tourism grew as an industry the government had to assure that blacks shared in the wealth. "But I tell you honestly, my brother, Fidel is no racist and this government is not racist. You have spent time in Cuba. What have you heard from black Cubans?"

I told him I had heard exactly what he said—that black Cubans now had opportunities that were unthinkable before the revolution. But I told him I had also heard from many black Cubans that both racism and inequality seemed to be getting worse. The two main supports of the economy were tourism and remittances from over-seas relatives. Since most of the Cubans in Miami and elsewhere in the States were white, most of the remittances were going to whites. And if black Cubans were justified in their complaint that they were being shut out of the lucrative jobs in tourism, as many had told me and my observations confirmed, the racial situation was indeed get-ting worse.

It was his turn to direct our conversation. He wanted to talk about his recent trip to Washington, which had been his first trip to America. He said that one of his first impressions was an odd one—that black Americans were taller and of bigger frame than black Cubans. "Do you know why?" he asked. When I said no, he gave his explanation, which he said was confirmed by scholarship. When slave ships made the Atlantic crossing, they stopped first in the Caribbean. Those who had died in the stinking, sardine-packed holds during the passage were offloaded and buried. Then the weakest and smallest of those who had survived were taken off and sold, leaving the biggest and strongest aboard since they were the most likely to survive the subsequent leg of the journey, to Charleston or Savannah or New Orleans. It was thus a matter of genetics. I nodded, but told him I thought it might also have some-thing to do with nutrition. Big Macs make you big.

He said that riding around Washington he was struck by another thing, and he wanted me to help him understand it: What was the nature of the reverence that Americans obviously had for the American flag?

"Go to the memorial to the patriot José Martí here in Havana and you'll see one flag. At the Washington Monument there must have been a hundred flags. There were flags everywhere, it seemed, on every building in the city. And not just one flag. Why is that?"

I tried to explain the American flag as a symbol, an almost sacred icon that helps hold a huge and diverse and fractious nation together. He listened with genuine anthropological curiosity, as one might listen to a lecture on the mating habits of Amazon Indians— as if he were hearing about a practice so foreign and exotic that it beggared belief.

I'm not quite sure what I expected a member of the Cuban Politburo to be like, but I know I didn't expect relative youth or intellectual curiosity—or dark skin, for that matter. There are those who suggest that there are younger officials in Cuba who advocate taking the Chinese path of development, meaning continued one-party rule coupled with free-market liberalization. Saez gave absolutely no hint of such deviationist thought. He struck me as a true believer.

Still, I'd met lower-ranking officials who, when they expressed the required optimism about Cuba's future, spoke in terms of what an outsider would have called economic reform—more space for private enterprise, the right to buy and sell property. I'd heard these officials confidently predict that next month or next year some big change was coming, only to be proved wrong. What struck me about those conversations, and about my encounter with Pedro Saez, was how thoroughly Fidel controlled his government and how tightly he played his cards to the vest. Saez consulted him about trivial matters, like whether or not to talk to me; the loyal public servants who were charged with carrying out his policies had no idea where those policies were heading. The vacuum he someday leaves behind will be total.

* * *

On the theory that biography at least hints at destiny, and in the hope that there might be some undiscovered aspect of a man about whom millions of words have been written over the years, I jumped at the chance to meet a man who knew Fidel when the legend was being written.

Félix Martínez hasn't been anywhere near Fidel's inner councils for many years, but there was a time when Fidel's life and the survival of the revolution itself were in his hands. He was El Guía, the guide.

He knew the peaks and folds of the Sierra Maestra as well as any man alive, and could find his way from farm to farm and town to town in the pitch black of night as surely as if the route were lit by neon arrows. In the early days, when Fidel had just a handful of guerrillas bivouacked in craggy mountains surrounded by thousands of Batista's soldiers, the entire army was just one wrong turn away from annihilation. El Guía's knowledge kept the revolution alive.

Félix Martínez is an old man now, of course, and the years have been ungenerous. He lives on the outskirts of Havana in an unimportant neighborhood with streets so rutted a taxi practically has to drive on the sidewalk. The first time I tried to visit him, a middle-aged man stuck his head out of the empty window frame and said that Félix wasn't in. The second time, I called first and the old *guerrillero* was expecting me. It turned out that he had been there the first time I came, too, but he had been napping and his son—the man in the window—had decided for whatever reason to send me away. Guía didn't seem to much like the son, who fortunately wasn't at home when we finally met.

His two-bedroom apartment, in pitifully bad repair, spanned the ages. There was a portrait of a much younger Félix Martínez on the wall, wearing the full beard and green fatigues of Fidel's revolutionary army. The few pieces of furniture were from the 1950s, with spare lines. A crystal chandelier, missing most of its bulbs, was reflected in an ornate gilt mirror. The apartment was small enough that you could look into the bedrooms and see that the plaster had fallen from the ceiling, exposing bare joists. A lot of plaster was missing from the bedroom walls as well. The kitchen was in a corner of the main room; Guía kept his food from spoiling in a

Kelvinator refrigerator that he remembered acquiring in, let's see, it must have been 1959. In the middle of the room, with pride of place, sat a new Chinese-made television, Panda brand. In honor of some recent commemoration, identical televisions had been presented to all the surviving *combatientes* who had shared those halcyon days with Fidel up in the Sierra Maestra. The remote control was enclosed in a clear plastic sheath, presumably to protect it and possibly extend its life. The whole place was spare, spartan, spotless—an old soldier's home.

But not an old soldier's last home, if he could help it. At seventy-two, Guía had plans to move back home to the foothills of the mountains, where his girlfriend was waiting for him. The first of his treasures that he showed me was a picture of the girlfriend, who looked to be in her late thirties. The first of his precious stories that he shared was of a little-known mountain herb that "works better than Viagra."

Guía has treasures and stories of a less racy nature. Chief among them are yellowing pieces of paper, signed and stamped, in which various revolutionary commanders attest that Guía was an authentic *combatiente,* which was the term for those who fought in the Sierra; and a gold medal awarded to each *combatiente* years ago at one of the many revolutionary observances.

And of course he has his memories.

"Let's talk first of Fidel the soldier," he began. "He is the sort of commander that when he gives an order, it must be obeyed. It cannot be changed. Even Che could not change it. He gives an order, and you must follow. If anyone was going to make a mistake, it was going to be Fidel. He had a way of turning defeats into victories. And when he did make a mistake, he admitted it. He'd say, 'I screwed up,' and when he admitted it like that, everyone would applaud and smile."

He gave an illustration of Fidel's military thinking. "We could come across a thousand Batista soldiers. The rest of us would be afraid, but for Fidel each one of them was just a frightened, illiterate young man with a rifle. We might have only a hundred armed fighters, but Fidel would inspire us. He would say that we were going to be better than those thousand soldiers, because we were going to split ourselves into ten troops of ten men each. We were going to surround them and shoot from all angles, and they would be confused and frightened, and they would disperse, and we would win. *And we did."*

Fidel "hated to lose"—he seemed to love winning for winning's sake—and inevitably, sometimes the enemy would get the best of an engagement. "When we lost, that put Fidel in a bad mood," Guía said, shaking his head. "No, he didn't like that at all."

The young Fidel that Guía described was a man so sure of himself, and so able to transmit that certainty to others, that he inspired men and women to put themselves at mortal risk with no rational expectation of victory or even survival, and to feel *good* about the whole endeavor. "He has a virtue that nature gave him, *una simpatía,*" was the way Guía put it. "Even his enemies, they may hate him and have good reason to, but deep inside they admire him too."

Che didn't have that special quality, but Guía admired him as well for being "a true revolutionary, and never an egotist." But he was a serious man to the point of being dour, Guía reported. "I think the whole time I saw him smile once. Laugh, no, but I did see one smile."

Guía was one of the many, many *campesinos* who were fed up to the point of insurrection with the brutality and corruption of the Batista regime, ripe fruit for this magnetic rebel who could make people believe in the unbelievable, and in themselves. He joined the rebel force when it numbered just a few score men and a couple of women. He wasn't much of a fighter—he was a skinny little guy who had trouble carrying the antiquated blunderbusses the rebels had to haul around, to say nothing of firing them—but Fidel didn't need him for his strength or his marksmanship. Guía's job was to be a living map of the unmapped mountain range, to shuttle platoons or messages or even Fidel himself from redoubt to redoubt past legions of enemy soldiers. Had he decided to betray Fidel, the revolution and its commander surely would have been extinguished and Guía would have been so richly rewarded by Batista that he'd probably be spending his last years counting the money from a string of hotel-casinos. But he had no betrayal in him then, and none in him now.

Guía made clear that he didn't think he had been taken care of as well as some of the other *combatientes*. He didn't resent the largesse shown to others. He spoke, for example, of one guerrilla who had done something to get on the good side of Celia Sánchez, Fidel's aide-de-camp who most biographers believe was his most important adviser during and after the revolution, as well as the one great love of his life (notwithstanding his other lovers and wives, before Celia and after). After the triumph, Celia gave this man a signed chit to receive one of the farms that were being expropriated from bourgeois landowners. The *combatiente* went back to his hometown for thirty-five years, then one day showed up in Havana and began to go from office to office to see about claiming his house. In the interim, Celia Sánchez had died. But when he finally reached the proper housing bureaucracy, the official in charge took one look at the chit and a week later had the man escorted out to his new farm.

Still, he had no disparaging words to speak of Fidel or the revolution. Some other *combatientes* had joined the Miami-bound exodus in the early '60s, but Guía had decided to stay and now said he had no regrets. He wished he were living in a decent apartment, he wished there were some food in the empty refrigerator, he wished he had a car, he wished he were thirty again or even sixty again—he wished a lot of things. But he didn't regret.

He hadn't really talked to Fidel for years. Every once in a while, at a parade or a rally, Fidel would see him in the crowd and say, "Guía, how are you, how's the family?" But then he would move on, and that was that until the next chance encounter.

Even in his dotage, Guía had a near-photographic pictorial memory. He could recall every detail of the main rebel camp at La Plata—how it was tucked into a steep little valley, where the hospital was, where the mess hall was, where the troops slept, how the headquarters building where Fidel worked had been wedged into the bed of a dry arroyo and then covered with branches and loose foliage to hide it from Batista's spotter planes.

His gift for navigating the unnavigable Sierra Maestra was legendary. He was particularly adept at ferrying messages between the various rebel camps. Others weren't willing to take on the task, which inevitably involved crisscrossing enemy lines, but Guía always raised his hand.

"I wasn't brave, I was hungry," he said. "We were always cold and we were always hungry. There was never enough food. I figured that wherever they wanted to send me, along the way there would be some food. So I was glad to go."

Despite his talents Guía never sought promotion, nor was it offered. He was always just a rebel grunt, subject to the moods and whims of the officers. Twice, he was sentenced to be executed by firing squad—once for going AWOL from camp to drink rum and chase women in a nearby town, the other time for lighting a cigar while malingering in a dark little shack that he didn't realize was the rebels' main ammunition depot. Both times, Fidel arrived just in time to rescind the sentence. The kangaroo courts-martial might have been staged just to teach him a lesson, given Fidel's suspiciously timely last-minute reprieves, but then again maybe not—Guía did see comrades-in-arms led to a post and shot, sometimes for lesser offenses than his.

Guía's life as an old man was hard. The revolution had promised him the world and delivered almost nothing except a Chinese television set, some old medals and papers, and, once every few years at official ceremonies, exalted status as a *combatiente*. He hadn't bolted to Miami, like some of the rebel soldiers in the years after the triumph. He hadn't pestered the bureaucracy to give him his due, the way some had managed to cadge new houses or cars. He was living in threadbare poverty, amid falling plaster, straining to raise his voice over the loud, grinding hum of a refrigerator older than the Cuban revolution itself. He could hardly see, more of his teeth were AWOL than accounted for, and his talk of moving back home to luxuriate in the arms of his young girlfriend sounded like nothing more than an old man's dream.

Yet still he believed. After all that, he believed in Fidel.

Maybe it was the hammock.

One night, after a long and exhausting day's march, the main rebel column finally stopped for the night and pitched camp. Guía had just settled into his hammock when the brass arrived—Fidel and one of his top commanders, Juan Almeida. This night, for some reason, no one had brought a hammock for Almeida to sleep in. Guía's immediate superior officer looked around and yelled, "Guía, get up and give your hammock to Almeida!"

"I said *coño*, buddy," Guía recalled, using the indispensable Cuban curse word, an obscene reference to female genitalia. "I said, 'Jesus, we've been walking all day without food or rest, and you want me to give up my hammock?' And my commander cursed me out. He said to me, 'Guía, you will never amount to anything.' Then he turned to all the others and said, 'Look at Guía, the illiterate, the idiot. No one will ever give him anything.' By this time, everybody was listening, including Fidel. I stood my ground. I said nobody had to give me anything. I said that I came here of my own will, that it was my decision and I would take the consequences."

Fidel walked over.

"That's a good answer," he said. "Almeida can sleep on the ground. Guía doesn't have to give the hammock to anybody."

And Guía slept.

* * *

Which goes to show that Fidel really may be the best dancer on the island.

Whenever I went to hear music in Cuba, I tried to pay close attention to the dancers in the vain hope that someday I might be able to pull off at least a few of their moves. The best dancers come in different sizes and shapes, and they all have different styles and tendencies; some like to spin left and some right, some hold their partners close and others at arm's length, some respond precisely to shifts in the music and others let their dancing flow according to its own logic.

The thing they all have in common, though, is the ability to surprise at just the right moment. You think you have them figured out, you think you know where they're going, and suddenly they head off in another direction, somehow managing to engineer the move so that inevitably their partners, who haven't seen it coming either, still end up just where they're supposed to be. Some people have the gift of heightened spatial awareness, I suppose. I certainly don't.

Fidel has that gift. Think of all the U.S. presidents, secretaries of state, national security advisers, and directors of central intelligence he has sent to bed cursing and muttering over the decades with his sudden reversals. Think of the ambitious young-buck Cuban apparatchiks who've thought they could surely outmaneuver and outlast the old man, only to find themselves cross-legged and off-balance and finally sprawled on the floor. Think of the Cuban people, always waiting for an unannounced shift of direction. They have to follow his lead but provisionally, tentatively, in a state of dependence, because they know that soon they'll be dancing to a new tune.

Fidel's brilliance is that, like those good dancers whose level I'll never reach, he leads and seduces not just with skill but with emotion as well. This is perhaps his most remarkable talent: that he can make a gesture that seems so admirable, so tender, that he disarms a lot of the anger and resentment that otherwise might build against him. The gesture can be grand, like the way he sensed and represented the true feelings of his nation during the Elián affair. It can be as small as a warm smile aimed at a young comrade at a rally, or as tangible as a new house for a great Olympic champion. But it always comes just at the right moment for maximum, sustained effect. The right gesture at the right time can buy loyalty, or forbearance, or at least respect for a lifetime.

He knew when to lift up a young black boy from the hinterlands and bring him to the top echelons of power, just as he had known years earlier when to let a bone-tired warrior sleep in his own damn hammock. Always, even now in his last years, he would be planning his next move.

9. THE BUSINESS

The music business in Cuba is so intertwined with religion, culture, and politics that it's hard to look at any of those elements in complete isolation. But there's another factor that does stand apart, and for the musicians trumps everything else in terms of urgency. Unlike medicine or law or plumbing or almost any other career in Cuba, music is indeed a business. Put in terms any musician around the world would understand, at some level it has to be all about getting paid.

That's tough anywhere—just ask the parking lot attendants of Los Angeles, the waiters of Nashville, or the buskers strumming their guitars down in the Paris Métro—but uniquely so in Cuba. Musicians function largely in a sector of the economy that barely exists, the private sector, and as on any frontier rules are improvised and recourse for the aggrieved is minimal. The supply-demand equation is brutal, with thousands of skilled musicians chasing just a few well-paying jobs. For the most talented and successful, the major markets are overseas; the biggest and potentially most lucrative of all is in the United States, a nation that officially refuses to do business with Cuba. The trade embargo can be skirted, but this necessarily makes business dealings across the Florida Strait opaque, which means it's hard to know how many records you're really selling, how much money you're really making, where you really stand.

And even for those who are talented, clever, and lucky enough to surmount all these obstacles, politics can come into play at any moment and put you back at square one.

It's enough to make you pray for divine guidance.

* * *

"I thought you knew," Lazarito Valdés told me, "I'm a *babalawo*."

"I am too," his father, Lázaro Valdés, said proudly. "Both of us are *babalawos*."

I was *en famille* with the Valdés clan, sitting around a long table at a *paladar* not far from the Hotel Nacional, where Meyer Lansky once presided over his casino. A casual question about religion and music had brought out the surprise that father and son were both Afro-Cuban priests in good standing. But at the moment, all that spiritual power wasn't providing enough of a boost to propel the son's band, Bamboleo, to the next level of stardom. Two years after I'd first met Lazarito, he and the group were stalled. Worse than that, they were losing altitude.

The place he'd picked for lunch was popular, and our group of six (there was also a manager, a friend, and a significant other) had to wait for a table. *Paladares*, licensed private restaurants run out of Cuban homes, were supposed to limit themselves to seating for no more than twelve diners at a time, but the rule was routinely stretched. The little dining rooms were always crowded, since no Cuban with even a couple of dollars in his pocket would ever eat at one of the official, state-owned restaurants, the ones that charged in Cuban pesos, unless he had a powerful urge for grease, gristle, and bone. The food at most of the *paladares* was nothing special, just wholesome Cuban fare—chicken, pork, and maybe fish, served with black beans and rice, sometimes enough fresh vegetables for a salad, and always the irresistible fried plantain rounds called *tostones*, which I gobbled by the plateful. That's what this *paladar* was serving, but the quality of the food was better than most. The meat came from animals only recently deceased.

I was meeting Lázaro, the father, for the first time. I hadn't realized what a famous musician he'd been in his heyday. He was

Beny Moré's last pianist, before the genius drank himself to death, and later a noted bandleader in his own right. Even now he still performed the Cuban classics with a small combo. He was hale and dark, with a round face and a thickening belly, and despite his own renown he seemed more than content to be eclipsed by his son.

Lazarito was in his usual chipper mood, but he was still trying to rebound from a heavy blow: Vannia, the shining star whom I'd last seen dressed in white to honor her *orisha* Yemanyá, had left the group.

In the beginning the whole thing that made Bamboleo special, that made Lazarito's group stand out from all the rest in the crowded and competitive Havana music scene, was the starring role of the two lead singers Haila and Vannia. Haila had already left to go out on her own, first to front another group and then to work as a solo artist. She was being marketed as "the next Celia Cruz," and it was working; her penetrating voice and her indomitable sauciness did call to mind the young Celia. She had even put out a well-received album full of covers of Celia's old songs. In Cuba, at least, she had attained one-name celebrity: if you said "Haila," everybody knew who you meant. She hadn't conquered the American market, but that's what she had her eye on. And she had demonstrated with her marketing strategy that she would do what it took to get there.

Now Vannia, the other dominating presence, had gone solo as well. She hadn't recorded anything yet and didn't seem to be performing anywhere around town at the moment, but that would come. She, too, was setting out for the Grail.

Which meant that Bamboleo was suddenly bereft.

In response, Lazarito had made what amounted to a radical set of changes. Yordamis, Haila's first substitute, was gone too, as was Jorge David, one of the original male singers. Bamboleo was now fronted by three men, two of them brand new to the group, and one woman—an accomplished singer named Yurianna, whom Lazarito hired away from another band.

I had seen the band perform the night before at the Casa de la Música, and at first it had been a little weird. Yurianna had been groomed into the classic Bamboleo siren, her hair cut super-short. She had learned her predecessors' moves and added some of her own; she had presence and polish, vim and verve, sassiness and a winning smile. From the VIP table where Lazarito's people had installed me, she could have been any one of her female predecessors in the group; she definitely had the Bamboleo look. She had a strong voice, too, one that could slice through the roar and rumble of the band's powerful rhythm section. The new male singers seemed fine in their second-banana role, and Alejandro, the only singer left from the original lineup, had been elevated to costar with the ingenue Yurianna. He held up his end quite well, although he had put on a few pounds that conspired against the sex-machine image he intended to project. Some of the musicians had been replaced too, but the band was as hot as ever, and judging from the whirling, twirling multitude on the dance floor, everyone at the concert was having a great time. It was a great scene, but there wasn't quite the same magic as before. This was a new band, and it would have to discover its own magic.

I asked Lazarito about the changes, and he brushed them off with a confident wave.

"In Cuba, the musicians are so good that you don't change because you want someone better. It's just that musicians here are somewhat," and he sought the right word, "somewhat, let's say, undisciplined. You have conflict over how much to practice, how often to play. A band is like a family, and you have disagreements."

There hadn't been any conflict over Vannia's departure, he insisted, just an amicable parting of the ways. Life, and the band, would go on.

He agreed, however, that something had been temporarily lost—"that empathy, that instantaneous communication when you look each other in the eye and everyone knows what everyone else is about to do"—but only temporarily, he was sure. That was the magic that I had missed, he said, and they'd get it back. There had been changes before, and each time the band had emerged stronger, not weaker.

I wasn't sure about that. Haila's special voice and presence had never been replaced. And wasn't this a much more radical change? Wasn't this abandoning the identity that made Bamboleo famous, the dominance of a matched pair of women singers? Wasn't it like serving coffee with no sugar?

Lazarito gave another shrug.

"That was important until the public got used to the sound of our music. The singers are the visual element, but you really have to get people accustomed to your particular sound. The force of the group is in the music, not the singers."

He was sincere. If he was whistling past the graveyard, he didn't know it.

There had been one other thing about the previous night's concert: only two of the songs were new. All the rest was familiar. It had been nearly four years since Bamboleo released a full album of new material. About this, Lazarito admitted his frustration.

"If I do what the record company wants me to do," he said with some passion, "I lose my identity. That I won't do."

Bamboleo's U.S. record company wanted something more commercial. In the American market, the "traditional" and "tropical" genres—music-speak for salsa—were growing weaker every year. The airwaves and record stores were dominated by Latin-flavored pop, and that's what the music executives wanted Bamboleo to play—undemanding *"salsa romántica,"* maybe, or better yet something along the lines of what Carlos Santana was putting out, something that might cross over into the larger marketplace and blow up. Lazarito had shaped and reshaped Bamboleo to be a turbocharged *timba* machine, based on speed, power, and precision. He had no intention of using this honed instrument to stir a vat of syrup.

"That's not Bamboleo," he said. "We're at a standstill over a new record. That's just the way it is right now."

At a standstill, Bamboleo was doing surpassingly well by Cuban standards—and just fairly well by world standards. Lazarito had a car and could afford to put gas in the tank. He bought rounds of overpriced drinks at the Casa de la Música and insisted on paying for the lunch we all shared at the *paladar*. But he still couldn't afford to buy a professional sound system for Bamboleo; the one they used for their concerts was rented. In Cuba he and his group were rock-star famous, but only in Cuba, and that meant there definitely wasn't rock-star money attached to the fame.

When they played at the state-owned Casa de la Música, Lazarito told me, 20 percent of the gate went immediately to the house and nearly 50 percent to the Ministry of Culture. That left just over 30 percent for the band. So if Bamboleo drew, say, three hundred people, paying a sky-high twenty dollars each, that would mean the group would take home less than two grand for the night. Any way you split that up among fifteen or sixteen musicians— more for Lazarito and the star singers, less for the relatively anony- mous percussionists—no one could walk away more than a few hundred dollars richer. If Bamboleo played as often as three or even four times a week, Lazarito would be ultrarich in Cuba. But in absolute terms, it would be hard for him to make more in a year than an electrician in Chicago or a fairly successful insurance sales- man in a suburban Jacksonville office park.

There were of course other sources of income. Money from overseas concert tours didn't have to be tithed so heavily to the rev- olution, and there was more of it to start with. Bamboleo had toured the United States four times, with another tour coming soon. The band was hardly a big concert draw in the States, though, and since its music was so specifically wrought to make people dance, booking agents for sit-down concert halls were often luke- warm; the band drew more consistent interest from big warehouse dance clubs, which paid less. To reach the next level of popularity and success, Bamboleo had to sell records.

You couldn't sell records in Cuba because nobody could afford them, and in truth not many people wanted them. The market for compact discs in Cuba, at sixteen dollars apiece—a month's salary in pesos—was limited to foreign tourists and successful Cuban musicians for whom buying music was a necessity rather than an unthinkable luxury. All the top-rank Cuban musicians I'd met had reasonable stereo systems in their homes, and the most successful, like Lazarito, even had CD players in their cars. Ordinary folks, if they had music systems at all, had cassette tape players, hissy old relics that elsewhere in the world had gone the way of the electric typewriter and the mechanical adding machine. Cassette tapes were not only cheap but recordable, which allowed the flourishing of a huge black market in bootleg tapes. That was how the music of the great Cuban bands circulated throughout the island. Tapes of albums, live performances, even television appearances and radio shows were sold or shared, then copied and recopied and passed along again, moving from hand to hand, tape deck to tape deck, until the umpteenth-generation copies were more white noise than music. It was file sharing without the Internet, a giant, low-tech Napster. Like the high-tech version, it didn't make any musicians any money.

The musicians didn't really mind. They wanted their music to be heard, they realized it wouldn't be heard at all if it had to be bought and sold, and like most Cubans they had genuine affection for the egalitarian, nonmaterialistic qualities of their society. In short, most of them didn't have heads for business. A few did—Juan de Marcos, arguably Chucho Valdés—but most just wanted to play and make people dance, and to the extent they wanted fortune to go along with their fame, they had no stomach for squeezing it out of fellow Cubans who had so little to give.

Music lovers overseas, by comparison wealthy as Croesus, were another story. That was the place to sell records. But all the Cubans could do was sign a contract, make a record, and then hope. They couldn't be sure whether the record companies told them the truth about sales, and they were convinced their records weren't getting proper distribution or promotion. Musicians all over the world are eternally suspicious that glad-handing, Gucci-wearing music company executives lived only to cheat them out of their due. But because of Cuba's relative isolation, and because the U.S. trade embargo provided both good reasons and convenient excuses to eschew full transparency in business dealings, it was more likely to be true in this case. The Cuban musicians trying to sell into the American market were completely in the dark.

For ten minutes, Lazarito grilled me: Where had I bought their latest album? How big was the store? How many copies were in the bin? Was Bamboleo in all the stores, or just some? What about in other cities?

I told him that in Washington, New York, and Miami, I'd had to look hard for Bamboleo records and found them only in the biggest, best-stocked stores; smaller outlets, like the chain stores in shopping malls, never had them. I told him that on a business trip to Houston, I'd been unable to find any of the band's records at all. Never had I seen more than one or two or three Bamboleo records in any big-city store in the States. There were a couple of Web sites that sold Cuban music and were always well stocked, but those were for fanatics like me. So yes, distribution was problematic. But at least there *was* distribution; promotion, on the other hand, was simply nonexistent.

He listened intently, shaking his head. "That's what I thought. That's what I thought."

The whole business was so opaque. "You listen to what the record company tells you, and what can you say? They tell you, 'We're sending eight hundred records to Japan,' and then later they tell you they sold them but that's all they sold. And then we go there and we do a concert, and people come up for autographs and everybody has all four of our records. All four of them, every person who comes up."

I sensed that as well as things were going for Lazarito, the dream was at a crossroads. Bamboleo was drawing its usual huge crowds at the Casa de la Música and the other venues around town. But the group had lost its two most brilliant stars, and while the local public seemed to accept the changes, they didn't seem wild about them. At the show I saw, I heard mild but ominous grumbling. The dream had been to make great music and by the way become rich and famous throughout the world, but Lazarito's record company was telling him that the rich-and-famous part couldn't come unless he changed the music. In a business where presence in the marketplace is a prerequisite, Bamboleo hadn't made an original record in four years. Everything was locked in a standstill.

Lazarito had to make a move. Something had to give.

But not today.

He peeled three twenties off his modest roll, refusing to let me pay a penny, and we left the *paladar*. He had gotten home at five that morning, slept for a few hours, run some errands, and come to this lunch. "We've got a practice now," he said by way of apology.

Bamboleo usually practiced for five hours at a time. And of course, that night the band would be playing a show.

* * *

Juan de Marcos was busy, as usual. He had said he would meet me for lunch one day, then he canceled and said dinner, then lunch the next day, and finally lunch the day after that. When Hurricane Juan blew into the restaurant, a vortex of energy and cheer, he explained that he had been in his home studio for he-didn't-know-how-many-days solid, remixing an album.

"It's a bunch of classical musicians who decided they want to play dance music, and they're awful," he said. "They're great musicians, but they have no idea what they're doing. The rhythm is all wrong, they keep missing the beat, there's no bottom, it just doesn't swing. I had to strip out all the percussion and all the bottom and rerecord it, trying to make it into something. Shit, after a week of trying I'm still not sure we have anything, but they're friends and I told them I'd try, so what can I do?"

Juan lived in the unlikeliest place for a Cuban millionaire to live, the wasteland of Alamar. But not in one of those Gulag-style apartments, like the rapper Reynor Hernández: he lived in one of the nice houses the Soviet advisers had built for themselves, and he had a home studio to work in.

He arrived with a middle-aged woman who sat quietly while we talked. She was a Cuban who now lived in England, home for a quick visit. Even if she'd wanted to say something she couldn't have gotten a word in, because Juan was on a roll. It had been a while and we had a lot of catching up to do.

The last time I'd seen him had been almost a year earlier, at the legendary EGREM recording studio in Centro Habana. If you've seen Wim Wenders's *Buena Vista Social Club* film, you've seen the studio. It was where Juan and Ry Cooder had recorded the album, and in the movie it was where Ibrahim Ferrer and Omara Portuondo sang that lovely duet that made you want to cry. Wenders kept cutting from the studio to fifty-year-old cars rolling down the narrow streets to shots of big waves crashing onto the nearby Malecón. In reality the seawall is blocks away, and newer cars probably outnumber the old. But the studio itself is even more atmospheric and magical than he made it out to be.

Juan had been at EGREM recording an Afro-Cuban All Stars album. When I arrived it was crowded and smoky, the way you'd imagine a jazz session in the '50s to look and smell. The studio was a museum piece, small and snug and sweet, lined with wood and acoustic tiles. There must have been two dozen people crammed inside, musicians and hangers-on like me, all wedged around a grand piano. The Buena Vista old-timers were absent; these were younger musicians, a couple barely out of their teens, playing the music of their grandfathers. Inside that venerable wooden box the sound they made had a roundness, a softness, a yearning quality. All you had to do was close your eyes and you were transported. The equipment at EGREM was primitive—the mixing board in the booth was a hand-me-down from Billy Joel, who had come to Cuba to play sometime in the '80s, gotten a tour of the studio, seen the Marconi-era piece of junk they were then using, and decided to leave behind the portable board he brought down for his concert. By now there were other studios in Havana, much more modern and better equipped, but none of them had the right sound for Juan. "I like wooden studios," he told me. "It's got to be wood."

During a break, Juan's wife had arrived with lunch for all the musicians and engineers. That time, Juan had only a few minutes to talk—he had to finish the recording session, and then in a couple of days he and the band were off on a tour. He was particularly excited about one thing: Pedro Calvo, the longtime lead singer of Los Van Van, had left the group to go solo and was joining the All Stars for this tour. Pedrito was a good singer, not a great one, but he made up for a lack of range with a surplus of charisma and stage presence. He was one of the few singers around these days who could reliably sing the classic Cuban love songs, front such a large band, and hold an audience rapt. Juan had taste.

Since that time, he'd had a couple of setbacks.

"I got fucked," he told me. "The shit with the visas. I got fucked two years in a row." It was a measure of his resilience, and his ample bank accounts, that he was able to laugh his way through the story.

"Last year, not that long after I saw you, I was all set to go on my U.S. tour with the All-Stars, right? The whole band, twenty people, whatever, I don't even know how many. Everything was all set up to go. We had the U.S. visas and everything. All set to go. But the year before, we had played a concert in Tel Aviv, and some people didn't like that."

He wasn't any more specific, but he meant that some people in the government didn't like it. Cuba's relations with Israel were problematic, because of a long-standing policy of solidarity with the Palestinians as well as force of habit from the Cold War era. There was no official censure or anything like that, but for some reason the Ministry of Culture was less effective than usual in expediting the All-Stars' exit visas, without which they wouldn't be able to travel (not to be confused with the U.S. visas, which would allow them to enter the United States *after* leaving Cuba). The musicians would show up every day and be told to come back tomorrow, but in the end tomorrow never came. "We never got the visas, man, can you imagine that? Never came. Tour canceled."

By the time the next tour rolled around, all had apparently been forgiven. The exit visas sailed through, and all the musicians had them in hand with time to spare.

"But then there was September eleventh, man. Now there was a problem with the Americans. I knew this would be a hassle so we applied early, plenty early. Waaaay early. But the Americans stalled and stalled, and the visas never came. Can you imagine that, man? We never got them. Tour canceled, two years in a row."

The ostensible reason for the delay was Cuba's inclusion on the U.S. "terror list" of so-called rogue nations. "It's a political game," he said. "They know that Cuba is not a dangerous country to the United States. It's all a game."

But that wasn't the end of the game. "The thing was, we always play the States and Canada on the same trip. We had the visas for Canada, and these are places where I play every year and I have relationships with people and I just didn't want to cancel. So I had to take the whole band all the way to Canada, man, and then play two dates, and then bring everybody back home. All the way to fucking Canada for two dates. Can you imagine what that cost me? I lost so much money on that trip, I don't even want to count it."

But as he rued his losses, he was still laughing. "Shit, I guess that's the cost of doing business."

Next time, he was sure, things would work out, and anyway the truth was that he could afford it. The band was doing well, as were his other bands—the various groupings of Buena Vista musicians whom he kept on the road, in constant crisscrossing motion, like the old Red and Blue units of the Ringling Bros. Circus. Like a good CEO, though, Juan was already looking over the horizon to try to discern what was coming next.

He was branching out into video; his next release, a live album recorded in Japan, would be marketed together with a DVD of the concerts. "I think that's the way to go. You know as well as I do what's happening to the music business all around the world, because of the whole piracy thing. I'm sure that CDs are going to be nothing but shareware in the future. Whatever you do, the hackers can break the code. You can rip a DVD too, but not with any kind of quality. I think that's what we have to do, at least for now. In any event, the business is never going to be the same, never going to be the way it was."

Unlike Lazarito, Juan had the luxury of simply not dealing with the financial headaches of the music business in Cuba: the taxes, assessments, and confiscations that left the musicians with much less at the end of a night's music than they should have had. "I just don't play here in Cuba, at least not for money. When I play in Cuba, I play for free. I pay the musicians out of my own pocket. That's the only way I can do it and keep my sanity. Believe me, this is the most surrealistic country you've ever been in your life."

Buena Vista and its offshoot records had sold nearly ten million records around the world, making Juan rich—and a host of Cuban senior citizens into megastars throughout the world. But now, he said with cold-eyed certainty, it was over.

"The Buena Vista thing is dead," he announced. "We still get good crowds, we still sell records, but the wave has passed. I'm trying to figure out what's next for Cuban music, and I think it might be the hip-hop thing. I think there's a real chance for Cubans to do something original there. I don't know what, and maybe I'm wrong, but I'm getting interested in it. I like what they have to say. They have a kind of street poetry that I like."

I had a hard time imagining that—Juan de Marcos, despite his untamed hair and disheveled clothes, was one of the most disciplined people I'd ever met, while hip-hop is all about indiscipline. I wondered if he could bridge to the younger generation as he had to the older one, and if he could meld his ultraprofessional style with the erratic habits of a bunch of kids. I wondered if he could really capture the hard edges of hip-hop, when so much of his heart was in the butter and silk of old songs played in a wooden studio.

"I've got nephews who are doing hip-hop," he said. "I listen to what they're doing. I think Cuban hip-hop will sell."

He had to run. His errand for the afternoon was to buy some Internet cards. Laws and regulations made it almost impossible for individual Cubans to have personal Internet access. At workplaces, for example in government offices, computers were few and e-mail accounts were shared with colleagues; a note to a friend in, say, the Foreign Ministry would be read first by a secretary, and then probably by a couple of other people before the recipient ever laid eyes on it. Some young hackers had managed to set themselves up in their homes, but they were violating the law and risked arrest. There were a handful of Internet cafes (without the coffee), offices where there were three or four computers with Internet access, but those were restricted to foreigners—you had to show a foreign passport—and going online cost a prohibitive six dollars an hour, which eliminated almost everyone.

There were also Internet cards with a dial-up access number and password that you could access from home or anywhere, but these were also just for foreigners. They cost fifteen dollars apiece but gave you five hours online, a bargain given the absurd cost of any form of electronic communication in Cuba. But you had to show a foreign passport to buy them. I realized that this was why the woman from England was along to run this errand with Juan—she could use her British passport to buy Internet cards, which he could then use to go online with his computer at home in Alamar.

The strange thing was that while the spirit of the law was that only foreigners could use these cards, it was perfectly acceptable to satisfy only the letter of the law. Thus Juan and his friend could walk up to the counter, he could ask for the cards and put them in his pocket and even talk about how he was going to read e-mails from all his friends around the imperialist world that night, and as long as his friend produced a valid British passport, the whole transaction was just fine. The clerk selling the cards would know exactly what was happening, and it would still be just fine.

It was as if there were a giant, pervasive conspiracy to obey the law in contexts where it had to be obeyed, but only in the narrowest, most technical sense.

I saw this conspiracy all the time, once most poignantly. I came down with a bad cold and had already given away to friends all the patent medicines I brought down with me, so I had to set out on that unlikeliest of quests, the search for some Coricidin and some Advil in Havana. The Cuban pharmacies never had such things, so I didn't even try them. I knew of a couple of so-called international pharmacies, reserved for foreigners and usually well stocked, but for some reason none of them had cold medicine that week either. Finally I ended up at an international hospital, not far from the Casa de la Música, where my cab driver said the dispensary surely would have something to make me feel better.

I found what I was looking for and was about to leave when a Cuban man came in, haggard and distraught. He began arguing with the dispensary clerk, who kept shaking her head with the grimness of a Stalinist prison warden. No, no, no, she kept saying, as the man grew exasperated and left. He was waiting for me in the hall, and he was desperate. "I've been trying to buy medicine for my six-year-old daughter all day," he said. "I've been all over the city, and I finally found it here, but they won't sell it to me because this pharmacy is reserved for foreigners. I have the money, too. Look!" He held a worn five-dollar bill. "I hate to ask you this, but could you buy the medicine for me?" We went back inside, he asked again for the medicine, I said I would buy it, and the clerk produced it without another word. I think she almost smiled as we left. The man seemed ready to cry.

It was the same with the Internet cards, but to buy them you had to know where to look. I told Juan that I happened to know that the telecom office he planned to go to was out of Internet cards, and that the clerk there was maintaining the line that they had been discontinued. *"No hay,"* she had told me a couple of days earlier. "There aren't any." But I had happened to ask at another telecom office down near the port, and there they had plenty of cards. *Stacks* of them.

In another country it would have been appropriate to ask why at one office Internet cards no longer existed and at an identical office across town there were multitudes, but that wasn't the kind of question worth pondering in Cuba. Juan just set off to get what he wanted. Don't ask why, because nobody's going to tell you.

* * *

The female *timba* group Ebano would have loved to have Juan de Marcos's problems. The months since I'd met them had not been kind.

Just a couple of blocks from the EGREM studio and shrine, I stood on the designated street corner at the appointed hour, looked around, and wondered what to do next. "We'll be right there" had been the promise, but they weren't. In dense Centro Habana, where each building is a warren of little apartments, just knocking on doors didn't seem promising. But then I heard someone calling and I looked up, and there, on a third-floor terrace, was Moraima Marín, yoohooing at the top of her lungs. A woman I'd never met before let me in and led me upstairs, and then again up another stairway so narrow I thought I might fall off, and finally into a small living room where Moraima and what was left of the band awaited my visit.

What had started as an all-female group of eleven members was down to six women, joined now by four men. Daulema Fuentevilla, the bandleader and pianist who had dreamed of proving that women could play *timba* with just as much speed and power as men, had thrown in the towel. Now, sitting on a couch next to Moraima and smoking cigarette after cigarette, she sounded like a musical Phyllis Schlafly.

"We added the guys out of necessity," she said. "We had to keep going, but the timbal player left and we needed somebody, and then the *tumbadora* went, and then the bass player, and there were men who could come in. For me, if I'm honest, the benefit is that men are much faster, especially in the rhythm section. I guess tradition imposes itself. Also, the truth is that men have fewer problems, fewer personal problems that affect the band." She gave a Bette Davis, film noir laugh, kind of a rueful snort. "Women *look* for problems. And if they don't find any, they *invent* them."

Truth was, the all-girl gimmick had never done a thing for Ebano. They were still banging on the door where the Havana music establishment was having its party, and nobody was letting them in.

They hadn't found a regular gig. They hadn't been able to crack the big music halls. No established group had taken them under its wing and asked them to open a show. They hadn't managed to get themselves on radio or television. They hadn't recorded anything except one homemade CD—one actual disc, a single copy—that Moraima thought she had somewhere around her house but hadn't been able to find for me. Most frustrating of all, they had no idea how to accomplish any of these things. They didn't even know anybody who knew how.

"We need someone to represent us, a good manager," Moraima said.

Daulema gave her Bette Davis laugh again. "We've had more representatives and managers than members of the group. Only none of them knew a thing."

Moraima had streaked her hair a different shade of blond and done it in cornrows and braids. Daulema looked the same as she had looked that afternoon when I had watched her march the band through its rehearsal in that spooky Vedado mansion—raven haired, dark eyed. But all the optimism and cheer were gone, all the excitement of the new. The woman who had answered the door, and who now sat listening to our conversation, was a relatively new member of the group, a singer named Raquel Ayala. Next to her sat a slight young man, one of the new drummers, whom nobody bothered to introduce and who said nothing the whole time.

"There's always some reason why we can't move forward, why we can't finally arrive," Moraima said.

"Why do I go on?" Daulema said. "I ask myself that question every day."

The change in mood reflected an actual worsening in Ebano's prospects of ever hitting the Cuban big time. In the beginning, there had been more places to break in. But now, some clubs that used to take an occasional flyer on untested talent—the Café Cantante in the basement of the National Theatre, or the hallowed Tropical— seemed so intent on drawing tourists and their dollars that they only wanted the big-name groups to play. The economic situation was such that those big-name groups wanted to play all the time, leaving no empty time slots to be filled. Some other venues, such as the Hotel Lincoln, had stopped having live music altogether. It seemed that clubs were shutting down all over town. With no places to even play before audiences, no places to become known and to hone their act and polish their skills, how could they ever take the next step?

"If we had a place where we played regularly, on a schedule, it would be worth it to spend some money on publicity to let people know when they could see us," Moraima said. "Without that, what's the point?"

What was the point? And by the way, where was the money? Ebano was at the bottom of the musical pecking order in Havana. In a socialist state where exploitation was by law a thing of the past, their lot was something much like peonage.

When they actually got a gig, it paid next to nothing—like a recent sixteen-day engagement at a club called the Oasis, for example, which paid the band a grand total of $150, which then had to be split ten ways. Fifteen bucks apiece for sixteen nights of work, and that was a relatively good deal compared with others they had taken. Some clubs had contracted to pay a certain amount in pesos, but then offered them a choice: accept a kind of scrip that could only be used in ill-stocked stores to buy things they didn't need, or take less money in dollars. Other clubs paid so little that after transportation to and from the gig—bus fare for most, cab fare for bringing the larger instruments—they actually lost money by working.

"It attacks your spirit," Daulema said, as if this fact weren't apparent. She was a graduate of the Instituto Superior de Arte, Cuba's elite arts university; she was one of the best of the best, with talent and learning that must have put her in the top 1 or 2 percent of musicians in the world. Here she sat smoking her cigarettes, snorting her Bette Davis laugh, trying to keep her eyes forward but seeing nothing there.

"I loved classical music," she said. "If you get to the ISA, you already have the technique. What you want to learn is how to open your mind. I never wanted to be a soloist. Chamber music was what I loved. I always dreamed of playing with a chamber group."

She laughed. "But then came the Special Period. And then came everything else."

* * *

A few nights later, Ebano was to play at a club called Amanecer, just down the hill from the Hotel Nacional. It was a small room, only half-full that evening, and the crowd was younger than I would have expected and more heavily Cuban, especially in light of the hefty ten-dollar cover charge. It was also predominantly white. When I arrived, the kids were dancing to recorded American hip-hop; I got the sense that this was an elite scene, that some of these kids were probably sons and daughters of the Cuban nomenklatura. Goofing and preening and showing off, they acted like spoiled, privileged kids the world over.

When Ebano took the stage, I counted only nine in the group; someone hadn't shown up. When they played their first tune, I could hear the influence of the new members in the rhythm section. There was a new sense of urgency, a new drive, a new churn down at the bottom. The acoustics in the little club were atrocious, though, and there seemed to be something wrong with the mix. Daulema kept gesturing—more bass, less brass, where were the vocals?—but to no apparent effect. Moraima and Raquel seemed distracted as they sang, as if confused.

The kids in the audience weren't feeling it. Cuban audiences always take a few minutes to warm up and begin dancing, but Ebano was midway through its second number before anyone started to dance. The point where the music should have taken off and found a steady groove came and went, and still nothing sounded right.

After the second tune the musicians put down their instruments and went around the stage unplugging cables and plugging them back in again. After five minutes most of them went to a table and sat down while Daulema and a couple of the men in the group continued to work on the equipment. After another ten minutes, the house lights came on.

With no explanation, and apparently no available fix for whatever was broken, Ebano packed up and left.

10. EXILES ON MAIN STREET, HAVANA

They moved the hip-hop scene and didn't tell anybody, or at least didn't tell me.

About a year had passed since I'd been introduced to Havana's smart young rappers and the provocative, high-wire act they put on with their sharp words and their bad attitudes. I'd heard the scene was growing faster than ever, but when I went to the Cabaret Las Vegas on a Friday afternoon to catch the regular show, the place was closed. According to the signboard, the entertainment that evening, and apparently all other evenings, would be a "gala" floor show performed by happy people wearing feathers and frills. One of the regular bouncers, a taciturn block of a man whom I had never seen crack a smile, was nursing a beer at one of the sidewalk tables. He recognized me and offered a handshake, but when I asked about the hip-hop show he put on his game face, the one he showed to rowdy drunks and wannabe toughs, an impassive but focused stare warning that a line was in danger of being crossed and that the crossing held consequences. He said Cabaret Las Vegas was out of the hip-hop business. No, he didn't remember when this change had taken place. No, he didn't know if it was permanent. No, he didn't know where the weekly event had relocated, or even if it was still being staged at all. No, he didn't know anything else about anything.

But he did wish me a nice day.

A few phone calls from my hotel room sketched the changed

landscape. The hip-hop scene was getting bigger all the time, thriving in the organic sense, but recently had been under pressure. There were more fans and more rappers but fewer venues for performances, and there was less accommodation of ad hoc shows; the authorities were trying even harder to confine all the inchoate energy of hip-hop into official channels. The Las Vegas show had been moved and the day had been changed. Nobody knew why. It seemed like just an arbitrary move to keep everyone unsettled, to let everyone know who was still boss.

Two days later I pulled up at Café Cantante, one of the last places on earth I thought I'd ever find myself at four o'clock on a Saturday afternoon. Café Cantante was one of the elite clubs that Moraima and Daulema had been trying so desperately to crack, and it stood out in my mind as the most night-owlish roost on the Havana scene. Once, in search of a minor *timba* band that I thought might be going places, I had arrived at twenty before midnight and been disappointed to see only stragglers at the entrance. The show must be over, I reasoned, only to learn that the place hadn't yet even opened its doors. I'd have bet that most of the people who worked there would just be struggling out of bed at four in the afternoon.

On top of that, Café Cantante was in the oddest of locations, the basement of the National Theatre of Cuba. You might imagine Cuba's temple to the thespian arts as a lavish old hunk of wedding cake, crumbling nobly to dust, but actually the National Theatre is a modern, '60s-style building on the grand ellipse of boulevards surrounding the Plaza de la Revolución. In the center of the vast plaza stands an enormous beige tower, kind of a cross between an obelisk and a ziggurat, that rules the Havana skyline in honor of the independence hero José Martí. The whole complex was built by Batista, just before he got chased off the island, but since the revolution it has been Fidel's greatest stage. The plaza is where Fidel summons the people in their millions to honor Cuba's socialist miracle. His office is in a building on the plaza, as are a host of other government departments, including the Interior Ministry building faced with a huge neon sketch of Che Guevara in his trademark beret, inspired by the Korda photograph. The whole thing is impressive but spooky, one of those too-grand public spaces built on the monumental scale rather than the human, a tropical Tiananmen where the individual is but a tiny flyspeck on the vast, featureless plain of the Big Idea.

Fifty or so kids were milling around the parking lot of the National Theatre. The entrance to Café Cantante was around the side, and there I found more loitering kids. I figured that the show was late getting started. I'd been told to arrive at three, which I took to mean that four would be plenty early. I asked one of the hangers-around, a lanky guy wearing cornrows and baggy jeans and a Michael Jordan jersey, when he thought the music would get under way.

"It's already started," he said with a shrug. "We can't get in. The club is full."

I walked over to the stairway that led down to the basement club, and there, filling the steps all the way down the well, were another few dozen kids pleading to be let in. Their way was blocked at the foot of the stairs by two fed-up security guards who kept repeating one word, like a mantra: *"Capacidad, capacidad, capacidad."*

"Capacity," they were saying, meaning the club was full and no one else was getting in. They were not smiling; their patience with pushy young hip-hop fans had long since worn thin.

Generally, the way to handle a situation like this in Cuba is simply to stay put and wait. Eventually the guards would get tired of saying no, or the naysayers in management would relent, or the interpretation of whatever rule was being applied would suddenly change, or most of the other people waiting with you would drift away, leaving a handful whose admittance wouldn't even be noticed. If you were patient and refused to go away, you'd get in. Only today, that wasn't working. Nobody was relenting, nobody was leaving, nobody was getting anywhere.

After about ten minutes Reynor Hernández, the poetic young rapper from the group Explosión Suprema I'd met in Alamar a year earlier, arrived. He started trying to bull his way down the stairs, his former shyness replaced by a little rock-star arrogance—rappers qualified as stars now, and were moving beyond the anti-police lyrics to cultivate an image of young rebellion and danger. "I'm performing, you idiot," he shouted at the guards. "I'm supposed to be onstage. This is the stupidest thing I've ever seen. You go in there and get the management because I'm supposed to be inside. Now!" This just pissed the guards off, naturally, and they shoved him back. He finally gave up and went to try the stage entrance, somewhere on the other side of the building.

The only option I could see was to politely pull rank. I pulled out my U.S. passport, my Cuban press card, and my *Washington Post* business card, and made polite but deep-voiced excuses as I threaded my way through the crowd and down the steps. I asked the head guard in a respectful but insistent tone to take my card inside to Ariel Fernández, the Minister of Hip-Hop, who was expecting me. That wasn't exactly true—Ariel didn't even know I was in Havana—but I figured he had to be there, would have invited me if he'd had the chance, and enjoyed more than enough pull to get me past these officious guards. The guard took the card, looked at it for a moment, shrugged, and went inside to look for this Ariel, who was sought by this American.

Just then, a woman's voice rang out from behind me on the steps.

"Gene Robinson!" the voice called, and it wasn't a Cuban voice. "If *you* get inside using that *Washington Post* press card shit, and *I'm* left sitting out here on these steps, then *I'm* going to be *pissed!*"

I turned but already knew who it was: Nehanda.

Nehanda Abiodun, *née* Cheri Dalton, was an intellectual, a compulsive former of human networks, a talented student of political organization, a chestnut-skinned black woman, a fan of old-school rhythm and blues, a twelve-year resident of Havana, an earth mother to the Cuban hip-hop movement, and—almost incidentally in this context, sitting on the steps of the Café Cantante—a fugitive from American justice whom the FBI considered armed and extremely dangerous.

Nehanda was an honored figure in hip-hop circles, so this was an extremely bad sign. If she couldn't get in, I probably couldn't either. Sure enough, the guard came back and told me that Ariel or no Ariel, I wasn't going to see that afternoon's show. I ended up going back to the hotel.

Nehanda gave up too and went home, back to her bittersweet life of exile.

* * *

The Thomas Wolfe line about not being able to go home again was never more literally true than for the American fugitives who had fled to exile in Cuba. For all of them, more than seventy at last count, going home to America would mean years in prison. For some, it would probably mean death by lethal injection. There were notorious figures like Robert Vesco, the crooked financier whose millions won him a cosseted tropical holiday in the Havana suburbs, beyond the grasp of his pursuers, until he managed to get on the wrong side of Fidel Castro; he was last seen somewhere in Cuban custody. At the other end of the scale there were anonymous criminals on the lam, people no one ever heard of and nobody really missed. And then there were the political exiles, the black Americans, like Nehanda.

Once they had considered themselves soldiers in the black revolutionary underground; some still did, but not all. The Cuban government considered them political refugees and guests of the state, though it declined to give them full rights of citizenship. The U.S. government considered them hijackers and armed robbers and murderers, and the shelter they received in Cuba was a constant irritant in relations between the two countries, a point of tension even in those rare moments of partial, halfhearted, we-don't-really-mean-it rapprochement. The FBI kept them on its wanted lists; U.S. diplomats issued regular demands for their return; senators and congressmen took the time to read extensive accounts of their alleged or proven crimes into the *Congressional Record*. Most of the country had long since forgotten them.

The most notorious, or least forgotten, was a woman named

Assata Shakur, formerly known as Joanne Chesimard. A member of the Black Liberation Army, she was tried and convicted for the 1973 killing of a New Jersey state trooper and sentenced to life in prison. Six years later, comrades disguised as visitors pulled out weapons, took hostages, and busted her out of prison—an unforgivably audacious act, the kind that lawmen take as a personal insult—and she made her way to Cuba. In interviews she has claimed that she didn't kill the state trooper in the first place, leaving the implication that it was a fellow Black Liberation Army soldier who pulled the trigger. Partly because of this claim of innocence, and partly because she was a woman with considerable skill at public relations, her case became a minor cause célèbre for the contemporary African-American radical left, a female Mumia Abu-Jamal who was already free. By virtue of this attention she vaulted past other exiles in Cuba, guilty of equal or greater crimes, to become the fugitive whose return the United States demanded most frequently and most angrily. Her profile finally got so high that she became concerned about Fidel's reaction, worried that he might disapprove, and so she shut up and went to ground. Once listed in the Havana phone book, visited regularly by fight-the-power pilgrims from Brooklyn and Stockholm and Caracas, suddenly she was nowhere to be found. Fidel's disapproval was one of two things the exiles desperately feared, with good reason, because only he could send them home.

The other thing the exiles feared, with even better reason, was Fidel's death. When that happens, *anyone* could send them home.

Nehanda had been my first point of contact with the important figures in Cuban hip-hop—Ariel, Pablo Herrera, a dozen of the more established rappers. They trusted her because she had been one of the few adults to embrace their cause and help them fight for it. "These are my children," she told me once, and that's the way they treated her, like an unnaturally hip parent—a fifty-ish mom who wore dreadlocks, helped them pick out new African names to replace the slave ones, listened to their problems with genuine interest, and liked to dance all night. Oh yes, and was on the lam.

She used her credibility as a dedicated revolutionary to mediate between the rappers and the cultural authorities, arguing that an authentic form of Cuban hip-hop, shorn of negative American influences, ultimately would serve the Cuban revolution by challenging it to address problems long ignored, such as renascent racism. She helped the angrier rappers edit their lyrics to walk the fine line between the daring and the imprisonable. She even organized a groundbreaking trip to New York for nine Cuban rappers, which gave Cuban hip-hop a presence in the holy Mecca where the culture was born. She couldn't go with them, of course. One of the rappers broke away from the group and defected, which was an embarrassment but only a minor one: these days, getting eight out of nine safely and willingly home to Cuba was a good average.

When I met her, she'd been in Cuba for twelve years. She hardly seemed the *desperada* described by the mutual friend who introduced us—"She's nice, I love her, man, but back in the real world she was *dangerous*," he'd said—but it was immediately apparent that she was a formidable woman. She was nearly six feet tall, with the confident stride and authoritative voice of a business executive, though she clearly didn't see herself that way. Both the dreadlocks and the jewelry she wore spoke of Africa. She had command presence; she was not a woman to be underestimated, and certainly not one to be ignored.

And like anyone who'd led the life she'd led, she was wary. We sat around a table in a little restaurant in Havana's faded Chinatown, enjoying a remarkably good hot-and-sour soup, and she grilled me for an hour before opening up. In the end she agreed to help me get inside the hip-hop scene, and to be quoted for publication about her involvement with the music—but not specifically about her status and life as an exile. At the time, the United States and Cuba were talking about embarking on a new round of talks about immigration and related issues. The exiles were worried that if such a conversation were to be held, it might get around to the subject of making an extradition treaty, which from their point of view would be about the worst thing that could ever happen. Over time the wariness faded, but the terms of our on-the-record conversations never did.

According to the FBI, she was indeed *dangerous*. The feds say she was part of a small, shadowy group of veterans from the revolutionary left—black liberation fighters, Weather Underground alumni, no more than a couple dozen in all—who called themselves The Family. They came together in the late 1970s, after most of their former comrades had retired to their organic communes, and went on a rampage through the bleak outskirts of the New York megalopolis, robbing armored cars at gunpoint to finance the violent social upheaval they had dedicated their lives to foment. I've been told—not by her—that she was a getaway driver in the robberies, not a shooter, but that distinction would be lost on the law, and also on the families of the security guard and the two police officers whom The Family shot dead. I know that she lived underground in the States for eight years with the FBI and the police on her tail, a period about which she will say nothing except that whenever she needed a place to spend the night, she was never turned away, not once. She finally fled to Cuba through a third country, and in Havana she was channeling all her fervor and activism into the hip-hop movement.

Anyone who pictures Nehanda reclining in luxury amid swaying palms and sun-kissed breezes is wrong. She was living something very close to an ordinary, rice-and-beans Cuban life. She had a small apartment in a distant, unlovely part of the city. She had a computer, thanks to connections back home, and since she wasn't a Cuban citizen she could buy Internet access, but only when she had the money, which wasn't as often as she'd like. She had to scramble for money, scramble for food to pick up where her ration card left off, scramble for every damn thing until the next windfall or the next remittance came through, same as every Cuban. She even made it tougher on herself by spending far more for transportation than she could afford. She didn't have a car, and she disliked riding the crowded buses because when she was on them she had no control of her immediate space—a holdover from her years on the run.

So she spent precious dollars on taxis, dollars that could have gone to buy food.

One evening shortly after I met her, I went to an outdoor hip-hop show at a recreation center where the whole gang was assembled: Pablo Herrera, Ariel Fernández, a few hundred dedicated fans, and most of the better-known rappers in Havana, including an up-and-coming MC who called himself Papo Record. Most of the Cuban rappers I'd met really did seem to care more about social activism than American-style bling-bling, but Papo was either the exception that proved the rule or the shape of things to come. He was dressed all in white, with a chunky gold cross on a thick chain around his neck, a big gold watch on his wrist, and six gold rings on his ten fingers. He was wearing his visor both upside-down and backwards, and he had his name tattooed in big Gothic letters down his arm. He didn't want to talk about racism or the need to further and improve the Cuban revolution. He wanted me to know about his upcoming concert at an impressively large auditorium, which he expected to be a sellout. His mission wasn't to bring about social change. He wanted to sign a big recording contract and become famous.

The headliners that night were supposed to be a husband-and-wife group called Obsesión. "This is probably the first time you'll see a five-months-pregnant rapper," Nehanda told me when I arrived, but sadly the sight remained unseen: Magia López, expecting the couple's first child, had miscarried earlier that day. Nehanda, the hardened fugitive, was crushed when she learned what had happened. She cried, she consoled, she cried some more. She spread the terrible news and then hugged everyone she told; she wept with them, and when no one was around she wept alone. Someone handed her a bottle of rum and she took long swigs and then poured a bit on the bare ground. "For the baby," she said softly. I didn't know if the ritual was Afro-Cuban, African, or maybe just an improvised remembrance. "For the baby."

Finally, in the middle of the show, she commandeered the stage and spoke to hundreds of her children in her heavily accented Spanish about their friends' sudden loss. And the children in their do-rags, their baggy jeans, their cornrows and their XXXL tees and their chunky footwear, Nehanda's children of rap, all joined her in a moment of silence for the unborn child and an outpouring of love for Alexey Rodríguez, Magia's husband and musical partner. The couple felt so much a part of the hip-hop movement, so much a part of what I now realized was a true community, that Magia had insisted Alexey leave her bedside and come to the show. Magia had wanted him to be with family.

Nehanda spent many evenings among these kids half her age, young Cubans brought together by their passion for a music that Nehanda understood and appreciated, that she admired for its power and its fierce engagement with the world, but that wasn't *her* music, wasn't the Philadelphia soul that she knew and loved and felt in her bones. She had a longtime Cuban boyfriend, a charmer known as a stylish and elegant dancer—he'd won a dance contest on a kitschy Cuban TV show—but they were currently on the outs; the rumor was that he had gone macho on her, maybe even tried to hit her, and she'd thrown him out. She had family in the States, and friends; she had neighbors in Cuba with whom she was close; she had her convictions. That was her life.

The first time I met Nehanda, she told me that unlikely as it might seem, she was sure that someday she'd go home again.

"She's right at the edge," another exile told me, a veteran. "She's right at the point where you realize you're not going anywhere. You realize that this is it. This is just it."

* * *

Bill Brent had passed that point years ago. He had the distinction of being the dean of Cuba's black revolutionary exiles, a resident since 1969. He also had the distinction of having been a Black Panther—for a brief time he was Eldridge Cleaver's bodyguard—and that made him revolutionary royalty. He acted like a king, haughty and superior, and courtiers came to visit him from afar. The other exiles thought him a pompous blowhard.

Brent was an ex-con when he joined the Panthers and almost

immediately became a discipline problem, with his continuing fondness for drink and drugs. On his own account he robbed a Bay Area gas station, then shot and wounded two police officers who were pursuing him. The Panthers disowned him, and vowing never to return to prison he jumped bail and singlehandedly hijacked a TWA flight from San Francisco to New York, giving the seventy-six passengers an unexpected layover in Havana. Cuban authorities promptly put him in jail and kept him there for twenty-two months, but when he got out he received treatment more in keeping with his Panther status. For a time he was installed in the Hotel Nacional, which even in steep decline still beat San Quentin any day. An auto-didact and self-proclaimed intellectual, Brent published an autobi-ography in 1995 titled *Long Time Gone,* in which he described his brief career as a revolutionary and his long one as a fugitive in no danger of capture. If any of the exiles could be called a success story, it was Bill Brent.

He opened the door to his apartment and I saw an old man past seventy, thin to the point of skin and bones, missing most of his teeth. He was dressed with an old man's formality in light wool trousers and a cotton shirt buttoned all the way to the neck. The clothes were faded and worn, and they were several sizes too big, hanging off his erector-set frame. Either they were secondhand or he had bought them years ago, when he had had the flesh and mus-cle to fill them out.

He lived in one of the city's better neighborhoods, much nicer than the homes of any of the other exiles I met. The apartment was in a small complex that had an almost California feel, with outdoor staircases that followed the contour of a lush green hillside. This was Cuba, though—the vegetation consisted more of weeds than plantings, and walls that should have gleamed white in the sun were dull with grime. The apartment was small, crowded with furniture and papers and books. He had no car, but he did have a bicycle, about which he had a story:

Bill Brent was a very dark-skinned man. One morning not long ago, he said, he had brought his bicycle downstairs and was about to ride away on an errand when a young boy playing on the side-walk—a young *white* boy—had yelled, "Stop! Thief! Everybody, the old man's stealing the bicycle!"

The story was to illustrate his latest literary effort, a history of black Cuba that would elucidate the racism that had been present in Cuba since the arrival of the first slave ships. As we sat drinking coffee in his cramped living room, he held forth on his subject, occasionally rising with some effort to rummage through stacks of papers or browse his bookshelves for evidence to buttress whatever historical point he was making. He showed me some of his notes, and they were a mess of scribbles and cross-outs and underlinings. It was clear that the book gave an old man a reason to get out of bed in the morning, but unclear whether it would ever actually be written.

His wife paid polite attention to the conversation but seemed distracted—she was probably thinking about *her* book, which was real enough to have a deadline. Brent was married to Jane McManus, a well-regarded writer of travel books about Cuba (which paid the rent), encomiums and apologias for the Cuban revolution (which didn't), and Cuban histories (which the Cuban state had honored with literary prizes). Thirty years ago, America's campuses were full of smart, idealistic, beautiful young women ablaze with radical ideas and brimming with solidarity for the Fidel Castro and his beautiful revolution. But few of them had the gumption to move to Cuba, and even fewer had the conviction and the tenacity to stay. On one level it was cliché, the rebellious little white girl who falls in love with the big bad Black Panther, but I couldn't dismiss Jane McManus's life as mere radical chic, not with the sacrifices she had made. She was a good deal younger than Brent, not yet out of her fifties, and here she was scratching out a living in a land of privation, her Black Panther now a shrunken old man dependent on her for sustenance and care. She was obviously both resilient and resourceful—at the moment, she was writing text for a coffee-table book being brought out by a European publisher. She wasn't a fugitive, she could go home anytime she wanted, but she stayed.

I hadn't been there more than twenty minutes before a couple of documentary filmmakers arrived, bringing pastries as a gift for the royal couple in exile. For some reason, I thought of social climbers coming to Paris to visit the aging Duke and Duchess of Windsor. The film people were more important to Bill Brent than I was, so he dismissed me with a vague promise of a longer interview "when the time is more propitious."

The problem, he said, was those immigration talks. At the moment, even exile royalty wanted to keep a low profile.

* * *

The exile I knew best, the one I considered a loyal friend, was a man named Charlie Hill. It is only fair to begin by telling what he did.

In 1971, after a mind-warping tour of duty in Vietnam, Charlie Hill was a soldier in the mostly imaginary army of a would-be country called the Republic of New Afrika, with a *k*. The group wanted to establish a separatist black nation in the American Southeast, and was willing to fight a war to do so. Along with two comrades, Michael Finney and Ralph Goodwin, Charlie was ordered to ferry a load of guns and explosives from San Francisco to Jackson, Mississippi. The first amazing thing about the story is that these three black men, with big Afros and bigger attitude, got as far as the outskirts of Albuquerque, New Mexico, before they attracted the professional notice of a state trooper. This is Charlie's account: "We were going the speed limit. He came past us, and he looked over, and then he slowed down, fell back, and just pulled in behind us. I said, 'Oh shit, here it comes.' So then he puts on the siren and pulls us over. Man." The trooper, a family man named Robert Rosenbloom, ordered them out of the car and demanded to search the trunk, where the weapons were hidden. "And then he got shot."

Charlie will not say not who pulled the trigger; his mother once told a reporter that he and Finney blamed the shooting on Goodwin, but that is impossible to evaluate because Goodwin is now dead. A few years ago, Rosenbloom's widow put up a Web site devoted to her murdered husband, in which she called Charlie and the others "cold-blooded cop-killing murderers" and "the scum of the earth." She also said that after three decades of torment she underwent a Christian rebirth, and that with the newfound understanding that the fate of her husband's killers was in God's hands, not Fidel Castro's, she had finally found some peace.

But on that New Mexico highway in 1971, there was no peace for anyone present and the fate of the Hill, Finney, and Goodwin was in their own hands. They decided to run for it. Charlie's mother was living in Albuquerque at the time and he knew the area well, which was a great advantage. They managed to hide out for nineteen days, mostly at the house of a friend who worked at the airport, while police frantically scoured the city. When the city became too hot they went out into the desert, camping in a culvert with an old mattress on top of them for camouflage. Charlie knew that eventually they would be found, so they came up with a plan. They used a pay phone to call for a tow truck. When the truck arrived they hijacked it, putting a pistol to the driver's head and directing him to the far side of the Albuquerque airport, away from the terminal. This was in the days before skyways, when passengers had to walk across the tarmac and up the stairs to the plane. They waited until a flight was boarding and then ordered the truck driver to crash through the fence. The three fugitives scrambled up the stairs after the last passenger and took control of TWA flight 106. "We knew we could go to either North Korea or Cuba," Charlie said; all in all, they made the better choice. In 1971, hijackings were common enough that there was a more-or-less standard protocol: if the hijackers agreed to free the passengers, the crew would fly them where they wanted to go. Flight 106 went first to Tampa, where it took on fuel, and then on to Havana. Charlie Hill has been in Cuba ever since.

He is now my friend.

The man I met nearly thirty years later was a survivor, a realist, a loving father, an aggrieved ex-spouse, a schemer with dreams and a dreamer with schemes, a student of history, a pauper, a true believer in the Afro-Cuban faith, a binge drinker, a man-about-Havana, and a living witness to three decades of socialist decline in the workers' paradise. I wasn't aware of it at the time but he was already something of a celebrity exile, having been written about in the *Boston Globe,* the *Miami Herald,* and other newspapers; he had even been featured in a starring role in an acclaimed Dutch documentary. The film was supposed to be a history of the Mafia years, centered on Meyer Lansky's Riviera Hotel, but the director had run into Charlie and obviously been taken by his untutored ability to dominate the screen.

For any English-speaking foreigner in Havana, especially any American, it was hard *not* to run into Charlie. For me, meeting him was an especially lucky break. He seemed to know everybody in town, seemed to know how everything worked, and the people and places he introduced me to over the years were simply invaluable.

Charlie made his living as a boulevardier, using his fluency in Spanish to guide visitors through Havana's obscure folkways and byways. His "office" was the Parque Central, with branch locations at the watering holes of Old Havana. He was able to scrape out a living because his native fluency in English and the American idiom gave him a leg up over the Cuban "Hello, my friend" *jineteros* working the same streets. He sold his clients contraband cigars, showed them the Havana nightlife, arranged their official or unofficial rental cars, took them to *babalawos* to have their futures divined, walked them through transactions with the ubiquitous Cuban bureaucracy, served them as simultaneous interpreter—he was like a full-service tourist agency. The clients bought him drinks and meals and gave him some money at the end, and that plus the profits from his cigar deals gave him almost enough to get by.

Almost, but not quite. He could never make enough to keep his telephone reliably turned on, and his dream of amassing enough capital to set up a real infrastructure with which he could earn some real money—buy himself a car, for example, or a downtown apartment that he could rent out to tourists—always remained far out of reach.

Part of his problem was his generosity. If he earned fifty dollars, forty-five would be gone by the next morning. Instead of going straight home he'd stop in Centro Habana at the home of his former wife—his "wife" in the modern Cuban sense, meaning that actual paperwork and an actual ceremony may or may not have been involved—and she'd demand money to help take care of their teenaged daughter, who lived with her. The ex-wife tended to fritter money away, so he'd give her just a few dollars and hand a few more directly to his daughter. He'd splurge on a two-dollar collective taxi-cab, and along the way he'd run into an old friend with a hard-luck story, or another old friend he owed money, and there would go another few dollars. He might stop at the market to buy some food, and then he might give some money to his current live-in girlfriend for household needs, and then he might go out for one quick beer that ended up being six or seven, and by the time he rolled home he'd be back at square one. The overdue phone bill would have to wait a bit longer.

Once he put together a substantial stake of a few hundred dollars, thanks to some carousing Shriners from the States, and I thought he'd at least be able to solve the telephone problem, but he ended up having to spend it on faith. He had progressed through the religion to the point where he was ready to become a *babalawo* himself, but that required an elaborate ceremony that cost a Cuban fortune. The presence of seven other senior *babalawos* was required, and they all had to be housed and fed for four days. Then there was the banquet he was expected to provide for all the offi-ciants and guests, and the cost of all the sacrificial animals, and the few dollars that had to be slipped to each of the *babalawos* at the end as a token of thanks and esteem. Charlie ended the week a wealthy man, in the spiritual sense; but in the real world, he was already back in debt.

When I met him, Charlie was living with a woman named Jacquelín and her adolescent son in a little three-room apartment in a dusty, forgotten, unattractive neighborhood on the outskirts of the city. The rooms were all in a row, like in a shotgun house in the rural South. The front door led directly into a little sitting room, which held a few chairs, an aging television set, and a shrine to

Eleggua in the corner. You walked through the living room into the bedroom, which was almost entirely filled by a queen-size bed; and past the bedroom was the kitchen. By Cuban standards, the place was adequate. Jacquelín was a country girl from the provinces, making her way in the big city; she was younger than Charlie by close to twenty years, and she was sweet and pretty but not excessively bright. Her mother lived around the corner, along with Jacquelín's brother and his family; their home was much humbler, more of a shack surrounded by a livestock yard, as if they had brought a little Dogpatch with them to the metropolis. Everyone knew the brother as Jabao, which wasn't a name but a description of his mahogany skin color; he was a salt-of-the-earth type without much to say. Charlie was definitely the high achiever of this extended family.

Another time when I came to town, however, Charlie told me that Jacquelín was gone. They had drifted apart, he explained; they really hadn't ever been on the same wavelength. His only regret was that the television set, which he had owned long before he met her, was gone as well.

"She found another place to live and I knew she was going to move out, and sure enough I came home this one evening and her things were gone, and she took the TV," Charlie told me, shaking his head. "The thing was, I would have *given* it to her. I knew her son liked to watch TV after school, it's one of the few luxuries the kid had, the only one, really. If she'd have asked, man, I would have given her the damn TV. I told her later, I said, 'Jackie, you didn't have to take it.' I was just disappointed, more than anything else." The bottom line, though, was that now he didn't have a television to watch.

He never spoke of the two comrades who came to Cuba with him unless pressed. Goodwin had drowned years earlier when he tried to rescue a swimmer in trouble at the beach. Finney was still alive and had a job with a radio station. He and Charlie didn't speak. They'd had a falling-out years ago, and Charlie would never tell me why. Finney would never consent to talk to me at all.

Charlie's time in Cuba had not been easy. He hadn't had the Bill Brent royal treatment, hadn't spent a comfortable sojourn at the Hotel Nacional or been given a cozy apartment in the fancy part of town. He hadn't been given anything. He had spent seasons cutting sugarcane. He had lived through the hunger and desperation of the worst of the Special Period. When he was younger he had gotten himself into trouble with marijuana and spent time in a Cuban prison, which instilled a powerful desire never to repeat the experience. He had learned fluent Spanish. He had gone to school to study Cuban history. He had immersed himself in a faith that gave him a measure of tranquility. He had become a father and then a grandfather. When his young daughter got pregnant and gave birth, he took the child into his own home for a time so the girl could finish her studies at a vocational high school, where she was preparing for a career in the tourist hotels and restaurants. He was proud of his daughter; she was after the most promising credential you could have in the new Cuba, the equivalent of a Harvard MBA.

None of that erased what he had done that night in New Mexico, and nothing he had endured in Cuba compared with the years of hard prison time he would have faced if he hadn't run away. But he knew those things better than I. He knew those things better than anyone could have known them. Of all the exiles, he seemed most keenly aware of how precious the second chance was that life had given him, whether he deserved it or not. He knew how foolish it would have been to waste it. Under the circumstances, day by day, he was trying his very best to lead a good life.

Someday, when Fidel is gone, the security that the exiles enjoy will go with him. Their stake in the shape of the coming revolution is incalculable. A new leader might decide to leave things as they are, extending Cuba's hospitality. A new government might just ship them all home, or tell them to leave and find other havens. Decisions might be made case by case; distinctions might be drawn. Or they might spend an extended period in excruciating limbo while governments talk of treaties and seconds tick away on the clock.

For the time being, though, nobody was bothering them. The hip-hop crowd, on the other hand, was getting a lot of unwanted attention. Cuban officialdom had heard quite enough from these impertinent, unruly kids for the time being.

11. "THAT SONG HAS BEEN SUSPENDED"

The legend goes that Clan 537 got its start at a discotheque on Havana's distant fringe, one of the happy two-dollar dives that Cubans can afford, if they save all week, and that tourists never see. One evening, to liven up the scene, two friends—a would-be deejay and a would-be rapper—got up and began riffing, improvising. They came back the next night and did it again. People liked what they were doing so much that they put together a group, an unusual one, adding keyboards, percussion, a singer versed in classic *son*. In a world of derivative rappers declaiming over recorded beats, the use of live instrumentation was a breath of fresh air, sort of a Cuban version of OutKast. Even more bracing was the group's easy gift for narrative and metaphor, its ability to swoop and soar where others plodded. A great hip-hop lyric hits just the right tone between the mundane and the fantastic, creating a heightened reality that somehow seems more valid and authentic than the real thing, and that's what Clan 537 did with its notorious anthem "¿Quién Tiró la Tiza?"

The title means "Who Threw the Chalk?"—the question an exasperated teacher asks when a piece of chalk comes flying from the back of the room. Performed live in no-name clubs and then circulated like a virus via bootleg cassettes, with no exposure in major venues and no boost from radio or television, "¿Quién Tiró la Tiza?" became the first hip-hop song to conquer all of Havana. In musical terms, it "crossed over"—it spread beyond the core group of hip-hop fanatics and into the larger public, displacing pop and *timba* and all the rest. *Everybody* was reciting the infectious lyrics, turning Clan 537's pithy lines into catchphrases.

For Fidel Castro and his government, this was a problem.

The song was about racism and inequality, two things that weren't supposed to exist in today's Cuba. "Who threw the chalk?" the lyric went. "It was that black kid . . . *Not* the doctor's son." It went on to cite the many differences between those two archetypal characters. The doctor's son wore Adidas and athletic socks and fancy cologne; he "deserved to be treated well." The black kid, son of a laborer, was presumed to be a criminal. The doctor's son lived the pampered life of someone whose father owned a car. The black kid's life was nothing but poverty and pain. The assumption was that the doctor's son would turn out to be a success, somehow. The black kid would surely amount to nothing. "¿Quién Tiró la Tiza?" became so popular that it finally made it onto the playlists of the Havana radio stations, and for the Cuban authorities a small problem grew into something big and urgent.

Other Cuban rappers had talked about racism in much tougher language, but Clan 537 had crossed the invisible line in two ways. First, the song had put its emphasis less on the discrimination the black kid faced than on the privileges the doctor's son enjoyed. For true believers in the Cuban revolution, economic inequality was in many ways an even touchier subject than racism. Everyone could see that the society was splitting into haves and have-nots, with the line drawn sharply between those who were in possession of dollars and those who were not. Fidel himself had made oblique references to the growing disparity, so the topic wasn't completely off limits. But Clan 537 seemed to be kicking sand in the government's face, insulting the Cuban revolution and its leader by blaring the fact that a system designed before anything else to guarantee economic and social equality was failing at even that basic, definitional task. It was like a playground taunt, one with an irresistible hook.

Second, and probably the more important factor, was simply

that the song had been such a huge hit. It was one thing to turn a blind eye while a few hundred kids got together once a week to vent their frustration. They could say what they wanted, and even if their harsh criticism was borderline counterrevolutionary, and even if it was uncomfortably out of control, at least it was safely contained. "¿Quién Tiró la Tiza?" was different by virtue of its wide diffusion. It was getting so much airplay that the whole city was singing and rapping along, saying things that in other contexts Cubans wouldn't have dared to say. It wasn't contained at all, it was rampant.

What happened next was priceless. The Cuban authorities, a bunch of "hepcats" if ever there was one, decided to fight fire with fire. They put together an "officialist" rap group, one that would support and defend the revolution in its lyrics, and issued an "answer" song called "Tiraste la Tiza, y Bien"—"You Threw the Chalk, and Good." It rebutted Clan 537's analysis: The doctor's son wasn't the problem, counterrevolutionary "speculators" and profiteers were. Racism wasn't the problem—nobody was denying the black kid a fulfilling life; the kid needed to take responsibility for his own actions. These patriotic sentiments were rapped in a husky, uninflected monotone by a lead MC who was rumored to be an overweight apparatchik in his forties. To say that the beat was pedestrian is to insult hacks the world over. Predictably, and with merciful swiftness, this ill-advised foray into officialist hip-hop quickly crashed and burned. People listened to it the way moviegoers watched *Ishtar* or *Gigli*, laughing in all the wrong places, and now the government looked not just weak but ridiculous.

What happened next was that "¿Quién Tiró la Tiza?" vanished from the airwaves.

The song lived on by taking the routes that Cuban dissidents had long taken—it went underground, surviving in Cuba via cassette, and it went to Miami, becoming the highlight of Clan 537's first album, which was released by a Florida-based record company. But in Havana the radio stations stopped playing it, the deejays in the clubs stopped playing it, every loudspeaker controlled by the state stopped playing it. A friend of mine who lives in Havana, a res-

ident correspondent for a U.S. news agency, called the Institute of
Music to ask what had happened.

The bureaucrat who answered gave the answer without irony:
"That song," my friend was told, "has been suspended."

* * *

Clan 537's suspension was just one of a series of moves the government made, beginning late in 2002, to rein in the hip-hop
movement. It wasn't sudden or drastic enough to be called a crackdown—the measures, taken individually, were little more than
annoyances—but when viewed from the distance of a few months,
it was clear that an expanding hip-hop universe was now being
forced to contract.

In truth, there were also other incidents, big and small, that the
government must have taken as baldly provocative. The most notorious had taken place in the birthplace of Cuban hip-hop, godforsaken Alamar.

That August, Alamar hosted its annual rap festival. The event
had begun in 1995 as a renegade celebration of alien music, but
since the declaration three years later that hip-hop was an authentic expression of Cuban culture, the festival had enjoyed official
support. The government helped promote it, helped arrange travel
and lodgings for performers coming from abroad, helped with
equipment, transportation, and the like. The Alamar rap fest had
become routine, just another date on the Cuban cultural calendar,
and in fact fewer big-name rappers from the States were scheduled
to appear than in some previous years. But starting in 2000 and
continuing through 2001, the international profile of Cuban rap
had risen impressively. Newspaper, magazine, and television correspondents from around the world had "discovered" the hip-hop
scene and almost unanimously had been stunned at its daring
vocabulary and its unmasked anger. Their stories were noticed by
other correspondents, and the result was that an unusually large
contingent from the foreign press was on hand for the 2002 festival.
Editors who didn't have the luxury of being able to send their own

reporters to Havana at least knew enough about the phenomenon to pay attention to the wire service reports from the Associated Press, Reuters, Agence France-Presse, and the other agencies; television viewers around the world could look forward to reports from CNN's resident correspondent. This year's Alamar festival would not go unnoticed.

The Cuban rappers were ready for their closeup. By then, quite a few of the groups had been profiled in glossy magazines and Sunday newspaper supplements—Explosión Suprema, 100% Original, Obsesión, Anónimo Consejo, quite a few others—and the exposure had made them even more confident, more full of themselves. They had the invincibility of young manhood, they had recognition, they had momentum, and they were going to say whatever they damn well wanted to say.

The reporters who had made the trek to Alamar's community amphitheater didn't have to wait long for their story. It came on the first night of the festival, August 15. The group called Alto Voltaje—"High Voltage"—went right up to the line, and arguably across it, when the rappers told the crowd that they had been stopped by police and forced to produce their documents *on the way to the concert.* Then, in their performance, they asked a delicate question: "I'm tired of the routine; how long is this going to last?" The reference to "this" might have meant police harassment and nothing more, but it also might have meant something else, something larger, the entire grand construct of dreams and philosophy and idealism and coercion and social concern and economic failure and shoddy construction that had produced such a place as Alamar and such a society as Cuba. It was ambiguous, no worse than what scores of rappers had said dozens of times in the mid-afternoon darkness of the tiny Cabaret Las Vegas. But that was a provocative ambiguity to leave hanging in the air at a moment when the world was watching.

That lyric was reported around the world. The bigger story at the festival, though, was provided by Papá Humbertico.

Humberto Cabrera was the slight, precocious, incandescent

young rapper I'd seen my first time at Las Vegas. He'd always been among the most radical and strident of all, with a tendency—unnerving to hip-hop elders like Nehanda and authority figures like Ariel—to make the dangerous leap from slamming the worst elements of the system to slamming the system itself. Pablo Herrera once told me that Humbertico was one of the most talented of all the Cuban MCs, "and a good kid, but really immature" in his daredevil flights of rhetoric. When he took the stage at the Alamar amphitheater that August night, he was still just eighteen years old.

"Police, police, you are not my friend; for Cuban youth you are the worst punishment," Humbertico rapped. The line was tame by his standards, but the activity behind him onstage was anything but: two young men hoisted a big banner that said "Denuncia Social."

A *denuncia* in legal terms is a formal complaint, such as an indictment. Humbertico was issuing a blanket indictment, and the only entity he could have been calling up on formal charges was the system itself, the revolutionary regime that Fidel Castro had established and still maintained.

This was far beyond the pale. It was, in effect, a suggestion that the state's police and juridical powers be turned back on the state itself. Blowing off steam was one thing, but Humbertico's banner seemed to suggest something more. It seemed to advocate a course of action, or at least posit that a course of action was available if Cubans chose to take it. And he hadn't just said these provocative words, he'd written them down and shown them to the world. In that one instant, Humbertico had written the universal headline that ran over coverage of the Eighth Annual Alamar Rap Festival: not the subtle "Cuban Youths Challenge Socialism to Live Up to Its Greatness," as Cuban officials might have unrealistically hoped, but simply "Cuban Youths Slam Government."

Several people who were in the crowd that night told me later that they were certain the authorities were going to move in and shut the festival down. In fact they did not; the evening's concert went on as scheduled. But the authorities did not show any of the festival on Cuban television, though they had announced they would; and the plan to stage the final night's concert downtown at the Piragua, instead of in distant Alamar, was summarily abandoned.

"The thing that must be avoided," an official was quoted as saying, "is that the enemy manipulates a happening of that kind."

A while later, the Casa de la Cultura in Alamar received an order from the Ministry of Culture: before any future hip-hop concert could begin, officials at the cultural center had to review—and approve—all the lyrics the rappers planned to recite.

If the rappers could find somewhere to recite them, that is. In Alamar and around the city, hip-hop culture found itself on the outs.

* * *

"That was *not* a good move."

Pablo Herrera was talking about Humbertico's "Denuncia Social" stunt, a couple of months after the fact. He was in his house, wandering groggily around his studio, looking for his cigarettes and trying to wake up. I hadn't been able to reach him by phone so I'd just dropped by, which was a perfectly normal thing to do in Cuba—any friend can drop by your house any time, any day, without prior notice; it's the price of friendship. I'd waited until noon, but Pablo keeps musician's hours, and my yelling his name from the sidewalk appeared to have been the first sound he'd heard that day, or at least the first he'd responded to. He finally found the cigarettes, but then launched an equally fogbound search for a glass of water.

"Humbertico was really talking about the police, and actually just about certain policemen, the real assholes," Pablo said, having settled for just the cigarette, no water. "But you know, that's not the way it was taken. It was taken as something against all policemen. And the thing was that all the media were there, CNN and everything."

I pointed out that he really hadn't said anything so radical, that I'd heard much more pointed criticism of the government at other hip-hop shows.

"Yeah, but it's not a good move to dis your brother in front of your enemy," Pablo said. "You're putting something out there that the enemy can use against you *and* your brother."

Pablo was still walking his fine line, spearheading a musical and cultural movement that had to criticize the government if it was to have any truth or purpose, but had to keep that criticism within the socialist framework if it was to survive. He and the rest of Cuban hip-hop's elders had taken Humbertico aside after the festival to let him know what time it was.

"All of us felt like we needed to say something to him," Pablo said. "You have to watch whether what you are saying is actually counterproductive. You have to know where you are. You have to pick the right time and the right place to say certain things. And you have to be specific. You have to make it clear that you're criticizing this one thing right here"—he held his thumb and index finger an inch apart—"and not the whole big thing." He illustrated the big thing by stretching his arms wide.

In the hours and days and weeks that followed, Pablo said, the Cuban hip-hop nation waited to see what repercussions would follow Humbertico's rash act. "People were suspicious, people were waiting. Especially after we saw how the media covered it, as if we were all against our own country. We didn't know what the reaction would be."

Now, he was beginning to feel as if the heat were off.

"I think we're getting past it, I hope so, and maybe we're growing out of that phase," he said. "As much as people remember that moment, they will forget it just as quickly. The thing to remember is that nothing really happened. That's what we wanted people here to realize, that nothing really happened. It was not real."

Pablo's message, delivered with obvious sincerity but also with the polish of a high-priced public relations consultant, was that the hip-hop movement in Cuba was maturing. "We're growing older and finding a way to make the movement a lot more cohesive," was the way he put it. Another way of describing what was happening is that the authorities had taken steps to bring hip-hop definitively into the fold, smothering it with bureaucracy and structure and oversight. The government had agreed to form a state-owned company to oversee the hip-hop industry, just like the existing companies that oversaw popular music and traditional music. There were plans to start a state-run recording label for hip-hop music, analogous to the EGREM label for *son* and salsa. There was even talk of a state-sponsored magazine devoted to the music. On paper and in theory, all this infrastructure could give Cuban hip-hop an important boost. In practice, it would bring the music and the movement under much tighter control.

One of the ways Fidel Castro presented himself to the Cuban nation was as a father figure, and over the years his government had raised paternalism to an art form. Its stewardship of culture, for example, was essentially paternalistic in nature. The state wasn't inserting itself into the private act of self-expression, it was fulfilling its responsibility to nurture all forms of "authentic" culture. The state wasn't meddling, it was helping. The state wasn't censoring, it was guiding.

And if artists under the state's umbrella strayed from the "authentic" revolutionary path, they would be encouraged to see the error of their ways. When Juan de Marcos had performed in Israel, the exit visas for his next tour somehow didn't come through in time. Similar coincidences certainly awaited any rapper who crossed the line.

I asked Pablo what his role would be in this new system.

"Actually, it's a little weight off my shoulders," he said. He would work for the new state enterprise as a producer, handling a few artists, mentoring, promoting, experimenting with instrumentation in the search for a fresh, distinctively Cuban sound. He wouldn't be torn in ten different directions the way he'd been for the past few years. He'd get more time to work on his own music, his still-in-progress symphony, which was coming along. His career as Cuban hip-hop's chief evangelist and field marshal was on hiatus, if not completely in the past.

The music was his focus now, the music itself.

"Tell me something," Pablo asked before I left. He'd heard about the avant-garde black rock-and-roll movement in the club scene in Brooklyn and Lower Manhattan. It was intriguing—black rockers, reclaiming the music of Chuck Berry and Little Richard—but he hadn't been able to actually hear any of the sounds. "What's the deal?" he asked. "Where do you think it's going?"

* * *

Later I got a less optimistic account of recent events from a hip-hop veteran who had watched sadly as the government moved in.

The "Denuncia Social" incident at the festival seemed to have tipped the balance within the government in favor of those who wanted to put these dangerous children into a safe, tight little box. Contrary to some reports in the foreign press, Humbertico hadn't been arrested or punished or anything like that. Instead, the authorities had sharply curtailed the whole hip-hop scene.

Aside from Café Cantante on Saturdays and one recreation center every other weekend, all the hip-hop venues had been closed. Maybe once a month there would be a special event at one of the big halls, but there was no regular schedule and no publicity. Even the clubs that just played recorded hip-hop had been told to change their entertainment. A club on the Malecón called La Pampa, which used to be a dense, smoky, bumpin' hip-hop hangout, had converted itself into a tourist dive that put on the saddest, cheesiest little cabaret show in all of Havana. Another place that used to be popular with the hip-hop crowd, a club in Centro Habana called Palermo, had been turned into some sort of cafeteria. Since the Alamar festival, there was nowhere for the hip-hop crowd to go. The squeeze was on.

Of the roughly two hundred hip-hop groups in metropolitan Havana, only three had been taken under the wing of the new state-run hip-hop enterprise. For the moment, only those three were receiving state support. One of the groups was fairly well known, another nobody had heard of, and the third was something of a joke because it played an embarrassing brand of "Communist Party hip-

hop" and was thought to have been organized, funded, and pro-
moted by the state from the start.

Pablo Herrera was indeed one of the producers at the new state
company, but none of his groups had been included. He had a job,
but no work to do. Which explained why he had so much time to
fiddle around with his own music.

* * *

One morning the word spread—there would be a hip-hop event
later that day at the Casa de la Música 2. Without cellphones or
Blackberries or instant messaging, the Cuban hip-hop nation still
managed to assemble a flash mob. By the time I got there at a quarter to four, there was a long line at the box office and another long
line at the door. This time there was enough room for everybody to
get in.

The Casa de la Música 2 (I came to think of it simply as "the
Dos") was brand new. It was an uncommonly shrewd, almost MBA-
like attempt by the state musical enterprise EGREM to extend the
Casa de la Música franchise by building a second one. The original
Casa de la Música had become the stuff of legend, a magnet for foreign tourists and a necessary venue for the city's great *orquestas*.
The club was so popular that whenever one of the top bands played,
it had to turn people away. Someone, thinking in capitalist terms,
must have recognized this as unsatisfied demand and realized that
this meant opportunity, for EGREM and the musicians alike.

The Casa de la Música had one real drawback, which was the
inconvenience of its location. It was a considerable distance from
the five-star hotels, or from any hotels for that matter; there were
never any taxis around; there were no restaurants or bars or bode-
gas or any other businesses within a half mile of the place. It stood
by itself in what was basically a residential neighborhood. It also
had any number of quirks; you could call them eccentricities if
you wanted to be kind, flaws if you didn't. It was so small that the
tables were on top of each other; the layout made every trip to the
bar or the restrooms an arduous adventure; the stage was too

high; the acoustics were harsh; the dance floor was so narrow that unpracticed Canadians or Germans sometimes sent their dance partners whirling into the front row of tables. Yet in all, the place was glorious.

The designers of the Dos sought to correct the flaws of the original. The location they got just right: a shuttered old theater in Centro Habana, on a main street called Galliano just blocks in from the Malecón and the sea. It was a four-block stroll from the hotels around the Parque Central, and also within walking distance of the big hotels in Vedado, like the Nacional and the Habana Libre, as well as the boutique hostelries that were opening in Old Havana. Inside the Dos, everything was better and less satisfying. It was spacious and well laid out, with tables on each side of a wide central aisle that led down to a commodious dance floor in front of a wide, deep stage. The acoustics were quite good. It was hard to tell, but it seemed there were adequate backstage accommodations for the musicians instead of the cramped little anteroom at the Casa de la Música. Everything was new and shiny, and the workmanship was quite good. There was nothing wrong with the place. The Dos was without obvious flaws, but also without obvious charms. Glorious it wasn't.

The hip-hop show was weird. It consisted of the usual cavalcade of groups, but a few of the regulars were conspicuously missing—Papá Humbertico among them. One of the first groups that did perform drew almost no reaction from the big, eager crowd, and I was confused until I realized this was the "Communist Party hip-hop" group. The lead rapper looked like the actor Michael Clarke Duncan and was probably as old. The groups that I knew and had enjoyed in the dank little Las Vegas—Explosión Suprema, for example, with Reynor and Isaac—had a hard time catching fire in this cavernous room. I recognized some of the kids in the crowd too, and they seemed to be enjoying themselves, but something was missing.

The gang was all there—Nehanda, Charlie Hill, a young Cuban photographer named Ifé who had become the semiofficial chronicler of the hip-hop scene, an American student doing research for a book. They weren't feeling it either, and no amount of three-year-old Havana Club rum seemed to light the flame. It was a pleasant way to pass the afternoon, but today it didn't feel like being a part of any movement. The rappers were saying the same things I'd heard before about the police, about racism, about justice for all, but they weren't breaking any new ground. A movement, by definition, has to move; this one seemed to be idling.

My friends—the Cubans, the exiles, the rappers—weren't in a mood to despair, though. I could see that hip-hop was being tamped down and muffled and tamed. I could also see that on a broad front, across the city and the country, the government was taking back the limited political and economic freedoms it had granted. But my friends had seen this movie before. They'd seen permissiveness and repression ebb and flow according to mysterious rhythms that no one quite understood, and they had to assume that sooner or later the tide would turn. Maybe the government's swings were no more mysterious than Fidel Castro's moods, or the vagaries of his health; maybe the whole thing turned on whether an old man was sleeping well at night or had developed chronic indigestion. Maybe it all depended on Fidel's heart, Fidel's prostate, Fidel's bunions. Whatever the ultimate cause, these things moved in cycles. The squeeze was on hip-hop now, following the provocation at the Alamar festival. Someday, the pressure would be released and the movement could resume its advance.

In the meantime, every Cuban had more immediate concerns. I was scanning the crowd when Ifé, the hip-hop court photographer, tapped my shoulder and asked if she could speak with me.

"I'm so sorry to ask you this, and I'm really embarrassed," she began, "but do you have a roll of film I could borrow? When I came here today I had five or six frames left on my last roll, and now I've used them up. I wouldn't ask but I thought you might have some."

I was sorry to have to tell her that I'd switched to digital. I would have given her the money to buy more film, but she'd have been mortified. Besides, if there was film anywhere to be found in

Havana, it would probably be in the hotel gift shops, which were for foreigners only.

I made a note to bring down a few rolls of film next time I came.

* * *

The "Dos" might have been antiseptic and soulless but it booked its share of the top acts, and because it was smack in the middle of Centro Habana, the most densely populated neighborhood in the city, the big-name shows often sold out. So it was without much hope of actually getting in that I went there one evening to try to catch the bad-boy heartthrob Carlos Manuel. It was one of the last nights I'd spend in Havana on that trip and I didn't want to spend it just sitting around the hotel, so I wandered over and got there at eleven fifteen. To my surprise I was plenty early. I had my choice of tables and picked one on the upper level with a good view of both the stage and the crowd.

I'd never really liked Carlos Manuel. He could be described as the Justin Timberlake of Cuban music, an ambitious young white kid who'd struck gold by appropriating music, attitude, and dance moves from black performers whom I considered more authentic. (All right, he was better than Justin Timberlake, just not my cup of tea.) Some of his music did, however, pay homage to hip-hop. He was enormously popular among the teenybopper crowd, and since Cuban teens rule the charts the way American teens do, he probably was the number-one act on the island. His biggest hit had been "Malo Cantidad," a merengue-like number in which he posed as an outlaw.

The show was late starting, and I spent a good hour nursing a *mojito* and watching the room fill with teenagers. But these weren't the hip-hop kids. These kids weren't on any kind of mission, didn't belong to any kind of movement. I saw something I'd never seen at a hip-hop event—girls who looked as young as sixteen or seventeen on the arms or in the laps of male European tourists. At first it was an interesting thing to observe and note, *jineteras* younger than any

I'd ever seen, but quickly the spectacle became simply grotesque. I could understand that this was partly a function of the economic situation, which was increasingly dire as dollarization expanded. I could understand that it was partly a reflection of the fact that these girls could see no future in following the traditional path of school and work and family, and in that sense were making a rational choice. But still, the sight of these babies draping themselves over leering, potbellied losers from Düsseldorf and Ravenna and Lyon was grotesque.

Carlos Manuel played "Malo Cantidad" and then a song from his new album. The room seemed to suck all the energy out of his music and also out of the crowd's response, or maybe it didn't have much energy to begin with. I don't know whether the concert ever did catch fire, because after fifteen minutes I just couldn't stand any more of this scene. As I walked out, the middle-aged tourists and their teenaged escorts were still walking in.

* * *

The hip-hop community of rappers, elders, producers, deejays, and loyal fans could only hope that the squeeze was just a turn of the wheel, a dip in the cycle, and that soon the pressure would relent. But they couldn't be sure, because the course of events depended, as usual, on a fundamentally unknowable factor. For more than forty years the nation had pondered the question the way a Zen novitiate ponders the koan his master gave him: What was Fidel Castro thinking?

A recent episode had given no one reason for optimism. In fact, it had been so bizarre that for the first time Cubans had to ask another, more unsettling question: Was the old man thinking clearly at all?

It was late April 2002. On a Sunday afternoon, the foreign editors of the major newspapers, newsmagazines, and broadcast networks of the United States, Europe, and Latin America all began receiving frantic phone calls from Cuban diplomats. Some of the editors were rousted at home or reached by cell phone at their children's soccer games. The message to each was the same: Can you get a correspondent to Havana by tomorrow evening? When the editors asked why, they were told only that President Castro planned to make a major announcement and wished to have the international press on hand. This was followed by another appeal to please, please send somebody to Havana by tomorrow.

Since the United States will not allow the Cuban news agency Prensa Latina to have a permanent U.S. office, Cuba traditionally did not allow U.S. news agencies to have permanent bureaus in Havana. In recent years the Cubans have relented in a few cases—the Associated Press, CNN, the *Chicago Tribune*, the *Dallas Morning News*—but for most American news organizations this summons meant the considerable expense and hassle of sending someone from the home office. Usually an editor wants to have some idea of what the story is before committing to cover it, but in this case no hint was forthcoming. What was strange, though, was the frenzied insistence of the Cuban diplomats, who in some cases resorted to personal appeals that verged on begging. Never, one of them confided, had he been under such pressure from Havana to get something done. Don't worry about applying for a journalist's visa, the Cuban diplomats said. Don't worry about any of the formalities. Stay as long as you want. Just come and we'll take care of the paperwork later.

So it was that more than one hundred correspondents from around the world sat in a Havana auditorium the following evening, tired and cranky from having scrambled through airports all day to get there. They might have been in a collective bad mood, but the room was buzzing with the electricity of a big story. Was he going to resign? Surely not, but maybe he would announce a new successor. Maybe he was planning to elevate himself to a ceremonial, head-of-state role and turn over the running of the government to someone else, like the canny Ricardo Alarcón or the clever Carlos Lage or the eager Felipe Pérez Roque. Maybe he was going to do what he obviously should have done years ago and call a free election. He would surely win, having spent the past forty years making sure that no one else in the whole country had a political following, and then all his many enemies would be effectively disarmed. But then again, what would he be without his enemies?

Finally Castro arrived. This is what happened next, according to a vivid account written the following day by *Washington Post* correspondent Kevin Sullivan: "Castro sat at a microphone. The room hushed. He took out a thick notebook. He began to read. About the Mexican foreign minister. About Mexican President Vicente Fox's bedtime. About how he does not like flying on a full stomach. About an escalator ride he took. About eating goat."

Castro had assembled the world's press so that he could settle an arcane grudge. A month earlier, he had abruptly left a United Nations development conference in Monterrey, Mexico, just before President George W. Bush was scheduled to arrive. A meeting between the two bitter adversaries would have been awkward for Fox, their Mexican host. It was speculated at the time that Fox had *asked* Castro to leave, but both the Mexicans and the Cubans had issued categorical denials that any such thing had taken place. The situation was particularly delicate for Fox: On the one hand, he was on the verge of winning sweeping new concessions on immigration and trade from a new U.S. president who spoke passable Spanish and whose idea of haute cuisine was Tex-Mex with cloth napkins. On the other, Mexico's long-standing friendship with Cuba was seen as an important element of its independence from the *yanqui* behemoth to the north, and any slight to Castro would be powerful ammunition that Fox's leftist domestic enemies could use against him.

That seemed to be the end of it. But some time later, at a UN conclave in Geneva, the Mexican delegation voted for the first time to support a resolution criticizing Cuba's record on human rights. Within days of this perfidy, the Cuban diplomats were making their frantic calls to correspondents and their editors.

Castro's major announcement was that Vicente Fox, the president of Mexico, was a liar. He played for the assembled press a tape recording of the private telephone conversation in which Fox asked

Castro to spend only one day at the Monterrey conference, leave before Bush arrived, and not "complicate" matters.

For what it was worth, Fidel certainly had Fox dead to rights. But it was extraordinary, and ultimately just plain odd, that he would commit such a flagrant breach of diplomatic etiquette. It was even more difficult to understand why he would alienate one of the few nations that had stood by his side all these years. Still, given his record of survival against the odds, Fidel probably deserved the benefit of the doubt. He had a history of making moves that at first looked disastrously counterproductive but in the end served to make his own position more secure than before.

No, the truly weird thing that evening was Fidel himself. As described by Sullivan and others who watched the event—it was televised live on Cuban television and radio, so lots of people saw or heard it—Fidel was florid and animated. As he recounted Fox's dastardly acts, he mugged and rolled his eyes for emphasis like some old vaudevillian. And when he played the tape of his conversation with Fox, he mouthed the words—both parts—as if he had spent long hours listening to them again and again and again. It was impossible to watch him and not see vainglory and obsession, impossible to see the lips moving and not see an old man who had lost touch with some inner lever of control. Cubans who saw the performance were deeply unsettled.

To his nation, Castro was both North Star and Southern Cross, a fixed point of reference amid the whirling chaos of modern life. He was all most Cubans had ever known. For the first time it looked as if he were coming unmoored, and this was disturbing even to those who truly hated him. There was the obvious question of what would come after him—liberation, anarchy, terror, jubilation, a new tomorrow, a civil war? Less obvious but more immediate was the question of what would come now, in his final years. What kind of dotage lay ahead for Fidel Castro? Would he be humbled by the approach of death? Would he soften into avuncularity and kindliness? Would he go senile, issuing orders and then quickly forgetting them, sending the country in one direction and then back the way it came until one of his courtiers, braver than the rest, had the courage to stop him? Or would he be a revolutionary Lear, raging against the manifold injustices visited upon him, raging against time itself, striking out at enemies seen and unseen, suspecting all, forgiving none?

And what on earth would become of Cuba?

Taking a taxicab late one night, I had a long conversation with the driver, a bright young man who took advantage of my presence, as many Cubans did, to practice his English. He had recently graduated from the University of Havana in engineering, but of course there were no jobs in his field so he was driving a cab instead. He considered himself lucky; even when you took into account the rent he had to pay for the cab and the gasoline he had to buy, and also the fact that fares were few and far between, he still was able to clear five or even ten dollars a night, which was vastly more than he could have made in an engineering job if one had been available to him. To earn this exalted income he had to work from sundown to dawn, but it was better than the alternative, which was the abyss. He seemed upbeat at first, but as we talked he became first reflective and then morose. He didn't want to leave Cuba. Even in moments when he did, he realized that he didn't have the stomach for a raft trip to Florida, which was the Cuban version of Russian roulette—he knew, personally, of people who had perished in the attempt. So he was stuck. But what did he have to look forward to? He was young, twenty-five years old. His life would be miserable under Fidel and worse under whatever came next.

After I got out, he turned up the radio and drove away. It was playing a number by a *timba* group called Manolito y su Trabuco, a rocking song called "Marcando la Distancia" about the end of a relationship. The narrator asserted that his lady love had done him wrong, and was banishing her from his sight. The white-hot, brilliant music echoed down the lonely street, and I realized once again how necessary the act of turning up the radio was in Fidel Castro's Cuba.

When I thought about Fidel's performance before the international press, I wondered one thing: Had his secretaries, his aides-de-camp, his loyal legislators, his Politburo colleagues, his brother, his secret wife, his secret children—had all of them been obliged to sit with him long into the night, or long into a string of endless nights, pretending to pay attention while he played the tape over and over, rewinding and fast-forwarding and pausing, again and again until he had committed every word to bitter memory?

12. THE OLD MAN, THE WHEELBARROW, AND THE BANANAS

In the winter of 2003, what at first seemed a gentle squeeze from the government, and then a not-so-gentle squeeze, tightened into real discomfort. The sustained pressure began to feel different from the usual now-you-can, now-you-can't oscillation that Cubans had become used to, and that no one took that seriously. This felt serious. It wasn't any one big thing, it was a thousand little things whose cumulative effect was to wring out of Cuba a large measure of its joy, and take from Cubans some of their few options.

* * *

One of my ironclad rules was never to miss a chance to see the great NG La Banda, especially if they were performing at the original Casa de la Música. I hadn't been to Cuba in a few months, and when a cabdriver told me he had heard that NG was giving a concert that night I made sure to get there at eleven, which I figured would be plenty early. I found a huge crowd in front of the gate, both tourists and locals, importuning to be let in. When the bouncer recognized me and immediately ushered me through the mob, I felt like a VIP. It turned out, though, that the place was empty—they just hadn't opened the doors yet; everyone would eventually get in. By now the management knew I was an American journalist who occasionally mentioned the place, so they brought NG's manager over to my table to meet me.

I told him how much I had always loved the band and how eagerly I was looking forward to the show.

"I hope you enjoy it," he said. "Tosco is trying to do something, well, a little different. We're trying something different, and I hope everyone likes it. In order to grow, everything has to change." I wondered why he seemed so nervous and why he wouldn't look me in the eye.

When the band came out I could see immediately that they were doing something radically different, not a little different. Where the hell was the band? The sixteen-piece *orquesta* had been diminished by half; the famed "Horns of Terror" were down to one trumpet and one saxophone, and the whole percussion section had gone AWOL. No congas, no bongos, nothing to make the band's trademark thunder. The musicians who did take their places were the wrong ones. Gone was Feliciano Arango, arguably the best bass player in Cuba. Gone was Tosco's longtime keyboard wizard. I recognized one of the four singers—Tony Calá, the band's signature voice for the past twenty years, one of the most acclaimed *soneros* in Cuba. The other three could have been Tony's children. They were teenagers, two girls and one boy; one of the girls had been with the band the last time I caught a show, about six months earlier, and the others were brand new.

The concert, to be blunt, was an unmitigated disaster.

To make up for the absence of a rhythm section, and to fill out the anemic sound, the band played over taped backing tracks. To go to see the hottest, tightest band in the whole of Cuba and witness them attempting to play their greatest hits with half the sound coming from a tape recording felt like more than a fiasco, it felt like a crime. It was like going to hear Renée Fleming give a recital and discovering after a few bars that she's lip-synching her arias. I wasn't alone in my dismay—or my feeling of betrayal. The crowd at the Casa de la Música is always primed to jump up and dance the minute NG La Banda begins to play, but tonight everyone just sat and stared.

The whole thing went downhill from there. Obviously the band had only a limited repertoire prepared—I gathered that either they didn't have taped rhythm tracks for many of their songs, or else the new band members hadn't learned them yet—so to pad out the evening, Tosco stretched his patter between songs to excruciating length. He asked whether there were any Italians in the audience and then spent way too long making stream-of-consciousness jokes about Italy. Then he did France, and then Spain, and on and on through the European Union before heading off to other regional blocs. If the performance had had any momentum these interruptions would have killed it, but as it was they just made a long night seem longer. None of the songs caught fire because there was no spontaneity, no dash and verve, no playfulness, none of the elements that make Cuban music so exciting to hear performed live. I pitied poor Tony Calá; at times he looked desperately bored, at other times acutely pained. He didn't even try to hit his high notes. What was the point?

During one number, the girl singer who was brand new to the band came in on the wrong measure, and Tosco fixed her with a devastating glare. He looked as if he might fire her on the spot, but he just stared and somehow she soldiered on. A few people finally came onto the dance floor, mostly tourists who didn't know what they were missing. Most of the Cubans in the audience sat on their hands throughout the evening, and from time to time there were even catcalls and whistles. The poor musicians on the stage must have been saying a mantra: "Just let it be over. Just let it be over. Just let it be over."

Twenty years is a long, long time to keep a band together, even a great one. All organizations have life cycles, and NG La Banda at last had succumbed to decay and centrifugal force. People get fed up, people move away, people get bored, people want change. Tosco was a great musician and a great spotter of talent. He'd be back. Just not tonight, unfortunately for me and the other paying guests.

It wasn't a wasted evening, though, because one number definitely caught my attention.

The song was new, and it was the equivalent of a public service announcement. Its subject was the evils of demon marijuana. The chorus went, "If they offer you a beer, tell them yes," and so forth, through other items that were all right to accept, until it got to the punch line: "If they offer you a joint, tell them no." The song was call-and-response, with the audience expected to join in on "tell them no."

This was weird and ironic: a band that had spent twenty years crafting and nurturing a renegade image, whose leader had probably not once been called abstemious in his whole life, suddenly and without apparent irony sounding all goody-two-shoes, performing a song whose chorus could have been written by Nancy Reagan. One look at the musicians' pained faces made it clear that this was not a choice, but an obligation.

In Cuba there were times when one had to do what was expected. And expectations had definitely changed.

* * *

Then there was the story of the old man, the wheelbarrow, and the bananas, a modern Cuban parable.

I called Charlie Hill, the genial fugitive, and he told me this story: Out in his neighborhood there lived an old man whom nobody liked. He was a faithful, dedicated, ideologically committed supporter of the revolution. That was fine with the neighbors; nobody objected to the fact that he believed so fervently in socialism, and even some people who long ago became cynical about the government found his loyalty honorable. But he was a snitch, and that was something people didn't like. He was always quick to report anyone who spoke about the government too critically, or who was illegally renting out a room to earn extra money, or whom he just suspected of lacking the proper enthusiasm for the revolutionary project. After he had retired, though, and the economy had collapsed, he found himself in the same boat as everyone else—with a state pension and a ration card that together didn't buy him enough food to get through half the month. He had no remittance income coming from Miami, and at his age he wasn't going to get a job in the tourist sector, so he did what he had to do to survive: he broke the law. He found a supplier who would sell him bananas, and he took them around the neighborhood in his wheelbarrow and resold them by the bunch for a modest profit. He had no license to operate his little business. This was "speculation" under Cuban law, and it was illegal, but this kind of lawbreaking was ubiquitous in Cuba since the economic collapse. Most of the neighbors just appreciated the bananas.

One recent day, Charlie recounted, the police came and hauled away the old man, the wheelbarrow, and the bananas. A couple of days later he was back home, but out of business. The police had kept the instrument—and the fruit—of his illegal labor.

Among a few of the neighbors there had been glee or at least schadenfreude at the old man's comeuppance, but mostly there had been sympathy. In this context the old man was a true Everyman: he was just trying to get by, the best way he knew how. Now, without his wheelbarrow, what would he do?

Similar interventions had been taking place all over the city, in a pattern that at first was hard to discern but gradually became visible, then clear, then inescapable. It literally seemed impossible to escape; it was hard to run across someone who *didn't* have a story.

One afternoon in the Vedado neighborhood, across the street from the Hotel Nacional, I stopped for a while to listen to a guitarist who was serenading tourists at a sidewalk cafe. He was awfully good and I was curious about his background, so after he finished and collected his tips I struck up a conversation. His name was Ramón, and he told me the same basic story I'd heard from dozens of other fantastically skilled musicians I'd found trying to eke out a living in cheap restaurants, crummy backwaters, and two-bit dives: He had spent six years studying classical guitar in the National Arts Schools. When he got out of school, there was no job to be had in his field. "*Everybody* in Cuba wants to make a living from music," he said with a sigh.

Then he told a story I hadn't heard before, one that requires a bit of background.

Hardly any leader in the world, and certainly no leader of such a poor country, was as masterful as Fidel Castro at making magnanimous internationalist gestures that presented him and his revolution in the best possible light. For years he had leveraged Cuba's huge surplus of doctors by dispatching them to poorer countries in Latin America and Africa, where they saved lives in remote towns and villages that might never have seen a medical professional before. The practice won Fidel an enormous amount of goodwill, which translated into third world support in international forums like the United Nations; it also gave him something to do with all those doctors, for whom there were neither enough facilities nor enough patients in Cuba. Now he went further: he vowed to establish in Havana an international medical school, which would offer free medical training to indigent students from throughout Latin America and other parts of the developing world, provided they agreed to go back to their home countries after they received their degrees and practice medicine among the poor. He based the school at an old beachside military campus west of the city, which he turned into a gleaming facility crammed with the latest equipment, and it soon filled with students.

(Clever Fidel even went a step further: during a visit to the United Nations, he spoke with members of the U.S. Congressional Black Caucus and extended his offer to students from the United States who vowed to go home and work in neglected minority communities in the rural South and the inner cities. Nonplussed U.S. officials could find nothing in the deal that violated the trade embargo—the students wouldn't be giving anything of value to Cuba, they'd be taking something away—and so the State Department had to watch as a few dozen American citizens learned the healing arts in the bosom of the enemy.)

The students at the international medical school were by definition foreigners—Guatemalans, Salvadorans, Nigerians, Venezuelans—and this meant they had the unquestioned right to purchase and own automobiles for private use. Most Cubans did not have that right. Within this discrepancy lay opportunity.

Ramón, the unemployed classical guitarist, called his two brothers in the United States—one lives in Brooklyn, the other in Miami; one of them had emigrated in the Mariel boat lift when he was five—and borrowed five thousand dollars. He then found a medical student at the international school who was happy to use Ramón's money to buy him a car, legally, in exchange for a commission. Hundreds of other Cubans had done the same thing; some of the fledgling doctors reportedly had three or four or five cars registered in their names. Ramón bought his car to use as a taxi, one of the few sure ways of generating income in today's mondo-bizarro Cuban economy.

But not long before I met Ramón, Fidel had made a rare visit to the medical school and given a speech. In it, he noted that some students had been offered money "to commit an illegality" involving cars, tempted by "idlers who receive all the services and who produce nothing." Then he explained his conclusion that automobiles were actually a serious, though previously unremarked, threat to the students' well-being.

"If we begin to see students with motorcycles, automobiles, et cetera, we are risking accidents," Castro said. "The saddest thing that could happen is a case of death in an accident. We have the duty to protect you as much as possible . . . Except for needs of a physical sort, or something similar . . . I don't see any benefit to being a scholarship student with an automobile here."

Within a few days the students' car-ownership permits were all revoked and the cars they had bought with them, including the hapless Ramón's, were summarily impounded. CNN did a story at the time and filmed the cars being locked away in police lots. That was where Ramón's was at the moment. Now he had no money and no car. "And why?" he asked. "What did that serve? They just don't want us to have anything. Anything at all."

According to the grapevine, there may have been an event that provoked Fidel's speech ending the medical-automotive gravy train. One of the deals may have gone bad, may have ended in a bitter argument; a student may have been beaten severely, or even killed.

Or maybe nothing like that had ever happened. No account of any such incident ever appeared in the Cuban press, but then again it wasn't the sort of thing that *Granma* ever reported anyway.

It really didn't matter. Deal gone bad or no deal gone bad, the edict against the car purchases fit the general pattern. Fidel and his lieutenants had taken stock of a situation and decided it was out of hand, and then had moved swiftly and comprehensively to shut it down. Their actions had nothing to do with automobiles, or with the rule of law, or even with the need for the Cuban people to maintain revolutionary discipline in the face of constant threat from the imperialist empire. There was no real attempt here to correct behavior in the sense of reforming it; there was no serious appeal to the higher values to which the revolution aspired. Fidel wasn't trying to make Cubans better, because that was unrealistic given the present circumstances. He had a more concrete and attainable goal: bringing them back under control.

* * *

That was the common theme these days, control. The most visible part of the Cuban government's control offensive in early 2003 took place in the streets. It wasn't necessary to do anything more than ride around in taxicabs to see that something was going on.

For one thing, the police were being more aggressive in their halting and questioning of pedestrians. Standard operating procedure had long been for the policemen stationed at busy intersections to spend most of their time just standing and strutting and flirting with pretty women, and every once in a while yank someone over and demand to see his or her papers. Usually the target of investigation was young, black, and male. Now, I noticed, the cops stayed busy. They hardly took a break, pulling people over one after another, and the profile had broadened to include a more representative sample of the metropolitan Havana population. You saw them hassling whites, women, people a little older than before. There also seemed to be a few more police on the streets than before. To tourists, this just meant there were more uniformed guides, unfailingly polite and respectful, to help them find their way around the city. To *habaneros,* it meant more harassment and more potential for trouble.

Also, where were the gays? On my first trip to Havana, I'd noticed that a huge crowd tended to gather late every night on the Malecón not far from the Hotel Nacional. I asked about it and was told that this was a gathering and cruising spot for Havana's gay community, which had become increasingly bold and visible since the "Strawberries and Chocolate" era. From then on, whenever I passed that spot in a cab at night I took note of whether the gay crowd was there or not, because it provided a fairly accurate gauge of how uncomfortable the streets were. On some trips I'd see a throng of people, on others I'd see just a few, a reflection of how the political temperature rose and fell. This time, there was no crowd at all.

The streets were a battleground precisely because they had become so relatively unruly. There was still no violent crime to speak of in Havana, compared with any city of comparable size. But the number of people loitering in the tourist zones, begging or hustling or selling their bodies, had increased markedly. Years earlier, at the bottom of the economic collapse, young women had flocked to Havana to earn money as prostitutes; for a time, streets around the major hotels, and even the Malecón itself, were literally lined with young, painted tarts from the sticks, trying to get over in the big city. Long before I started coming to Cuba the government rounded them all up and shipped them back where they came from. Now, for the first time in my experience, there were streets in Vedado where one had to walk past a gantlet of women murmuring from the shadows.

One night I stopped in a bar near the Habana Libre and the bartender and a friend were laughing. "Did you see what just happened?" he asked as he served my drink. "The police had a bus parked right over there, down that side street, out of sight. All night long they've been rounding up the *jineteras* and taking them to the bus. About fifteen minutes ago it finally got full, and they drove them all away. Man, can you imagine all the pissed-off women in that bus?"

"Some of them good looking, too," his friend said. "Jesus, Mary, and Joseph, I'd like to be on that bus."

Begging was also on the rise, a particularly acute embarrassment for a society that had eliminated inequality. It was mostly senior citizens who came up to you and asked for money, and they were a pitiful sight. For the most part, the police pretended not to see them. But younger people had begun to ask tourists for handouts too, and when they saw a policeman in the vicinity they scrammed.

All this stepped-up police activity in the tourist zones of Old Havana and Vedado could easily have been explained as a campaign to clean up the streets for the happy hordes of foreign visitors whose dollars were keeping the economy afloat. Why wouldn't the government want to clear the streets of prostitutes, beggars, and vagrants? But the struggle for control extended far beyond the few square miles any tourist was likely to see. I heard story after story like the one about the old man and the bananas, people trying to sell something or rent something else or otherwise earn a few dollars to get by, in ways that were proscribed by the law. An unlicensed *paladar* in Centro Habana was shut down. A family that had traded up to a bigger apartment without the necessary paperwork got in trouble.

And one by one, the discotheques were closed—not the deluxe venues with live music for tourists like the two Casas de la Música, not even the dives with a tourist clientele like Cabaret Las Vegas, but the two-bit discos out in the neighborhoods with recorded music and an occasional live band, places Cubans could go on a Saturday night. A lot of them were speakeasies, operating without license or sanction, but in the past they had been ignored. One week a happening joint out in Víbora or Cerro or Luyanó would be jumping, the next it would be dark and shuttered. No beer, no rum, no music, no dancing, no relief, no escape.

All this increased vigilance was explained, when officials bothered to explain at all, as an antidrug campaign. When I asked friends in the government about the closing of a couple of music spots, they said they didn't know about those specific cases but then went on to talk about the need to combat the scourge of illegal drugs. Fidel himself had mentioned the drug problem in recent speeches, giving the antidrug crusade the highest national priority.

This was not just a convenient fiction. Mostly because of Fidel Castro's puritanical and obsessive hatred of illegal drugs, and because of the harshness with which he dealt with drug offenders, Cuba had remained remarkably drug free since the revolution. It was not always thus: author Graham Greene wrote of visiting Havana in the Batista years and buying cocaine, or what he thought was cocaine, from a news vendor on the street. It turned out that the vendor was a cheat and sold him a worthless substitute— Greene described lying in his hotel room bed, waiting vainly for some effect from the white powder he'd put up his nose—but that's how easily obtainable even hard drugs were in the Sin City era. Fidel ended all that. He didn't eliminate marijuana, which grew readily on the island and was firmly engrained in Cuban culture, but he kept it under control with strict laws and swift punishment. His attitude toward hard drugs was zero tolerance, and attempts by critics to link him to the international drug trade never stuck.

The economy of Cuba was so moribund and Cubans were so poor that the high-life cocaine business as it is known in other countries simply could not exist. Nonetheless, Cuba lies within a tight triangle formed by the world's biggest drug-producing nation (Colombia), the world's biggest drug-trafficking nation (Mexico), and the world's biggest drug-consuming nation (the United States). This fact of geography meant that cocaine washed up in Cuba, literally: traffickers sometimes air-dropped bundles of cocaine into the sea at prearranged GPS locations for later pickup by speedboats, and sometimes the currents brought these packages to Cuba, where they washed up on the beaches. Enterprising Cubans sometimes found the drugs and sold them. It is also conceivable that military officers in command of fast planes or fast ships went into business for themselves and imported loads of cocaine. Castro executed several of them, including one of his top aides, in 1988 for doing just that (although some of his critics say that Castro himself was the ringleader, and others say he was just drumming up an excuse to eliminate a popular rival). But even with hard drugs reaching the island, few Cubans were willing to risk sure prison time for being caught with them. Experience throughout the world suggests that cocaine makes its own market, but it was hard to imagine how a substantial market could ever develop among Cubans.

One group on the island did have the money, and the recklessness, to create a market for cocaine, though: foreign tourists in search of fun in the sun, many of them coming from European countries where drug use was effectively decriminalized, fresh off the plane with a *mulata* on one arm, a *mojito* in the other hand, and pockets brimming with dollars. If they wanted illegal drugs, it was an unfortunate but inescapable fact that hard-pressed Cubans would find a way to supply them. That was basically the Cuban government's rationale for closing the discos, sweeping the streets, and taking away old men, wheelbarrows, and bananas—the whole thing was all about drugs, which was essentially a foreign problem anyway.

For fed-up *habaneros*, that explanation wasn't cutting it. There was a sourness in the air, a bitterness, a feeling that the government was failing to honor its part of the bargain. There were elements of the system that most Cubans, at least in my experience, genuinely seemed to cherish: free education and health care, both of high quality; the relative unimportance the society placed on material wealth; a certain genuine communitarian spirit that had been forged over four decades. There were also elements that hardly any Cubans liked: the lack of political options; the repression and censorship; and perhaps most urgently of all, the woeful economic management that made a hotel doorman a prince and a brain surgeon a pauper, that made life a time-wasting, soul-sapping, daily fight for survival that blotted out hope for a brighter future. That was the bargain, but to make it palatable, Cubans had to be allowed to have fun. There wasn't much to spend their money on, and they didn't have much money to spend anyway, but they could drink, they could laugh, they could flirt, they could make love, they could dance.

Now the government was taking away the only discotheques any normal person could afford, the long evenings on the Malecón, the fresh fruit sold by an old man to his neighbors, the occasional joint, the extra income from illegally renting out an extra room, the car bought with the help of a Nicaraguan medical student that was going to be used as a taxi to earn dollars, not just to buy food and clothing but also to go to the clubs and stay out late and drink too much rum and chase too many women. People saw this whole campaign as a move by Fidel to do away with fun, and they didn't like it one bit.

They especially didn't like it when they saw foreign tourists lapping up all the best of what Cuba had to offer.

"For the tourists it's a paradise," an artist named Zulema told me. "They can go anywhere they want. Into the Hotel Nacional? Into the Habana Libre? No problem, go in, spend money, have a good time. But can we go in there? No way. This country is for them, not for us."

* * *

In February Fidel went to Vietnam, a brother socialist nation. His arrival was the lead story on Cuban television's national newscast. He strode confidently down the steps of his Cubana jet and across the red-carpeted tarmac in a navy blue business suit, not the green fatigues; he walked slowly as he reviewed a spit-shined regiment of Vietnamese troops, but his old man's pace probably had less to do with his age than that of the Vietnamese officials who had come to the Hanoi airport to meet him. Of all these ancient Cold Warriors, Fidel looked the most vigorous, the most alive.

And by far the most animated: he paused to chat with old friends in the receiving line, grinning and mugging, patting comrades on the back. "It's been a long time," he said to one man as he shook his hand warmly.

This was the way it was supposed to be. Fidel Castro, at seventy-six, was supposed to be a revered elder statesman in a world that had finally awakened to embrace the socialist enterprise, thanks in no small part to his own clarion call. He was supposed to be greeted like this in nations big and small around the world, hailed as a legend, an exemplar, a visionary. He was supposed to march down red carpets lined with beautiful children bearing flowers in Brasília, in Santiago, in Luanda and Mexico City and Cairo and Rome, and of course in Beijing, Moscow, and the capitals of the eternal Eastern bloc.

He was supposed to be a hero, one of the founding fathers of a new world order. That didn't happen; his new world was now shrunken almost to oblivion, and his own time on earth was running out. He still had Vietnam, though.

While he was there he gave a speech at a university. He was almost wistful as he recalled his last visit and marveled at the pace of development, all the new buildings, the new highways. He didn't mention the fact that Vietnam, unlike Cuba, had begun to phase in a mixed economy, and that all the new high-rises and freeways and suburban office parks were a direct result of that transformation. He didn't mention the fact that China had embraced capitalism and grown into the second-greatest economic power on the globe. He didn't mention that all of Cuba's socialist brethren were adopting policies that amounted to an outright repudiation of what Fidel Castro had stood for all his life. And still stood for.

He noted in his speech that Vietnam had even joined the information age and now had factories that assembled computers. His hosts, he announced, had donated fifteen hundred personal computers to Cuba, for which he offered lavish thanks. He said he planned to use the computers to build a health-care network linking Cuba's hospitals and clinics—a much better way to harness this powerful technology, he said, than just allowing the computers to be sold to individuals.

He stuck out his jaw and said that the reigning free-market development model was failing three fourths of the world's people and that if a new model were not found, mankind would not survive. He spoke of "the new Empire," compared it to the declining years of the Roman Empire, and predicted it would not hold out as long as the Caesars did. The implication was that when the rotten edifice crumbled, Cuba—and its leader—would still be standing.

Almost fifty years earlier, in the speech that had launched his revolution, Fidel had electrified a courtroom and the world beyond with a simple statement of his freakish confidence in himself and his destiny: "History will absolve me." As far as he was concerned, absolution was already his, had always been his. No matter what anyone else might think.

"If they call me a dreamer," Fidel said in Vietnam, "I agree."

* * *

Amid the slow-moving government putsch against private initiative, amid Fidel's campaign for renewed control, there was still music.

One evening I went to hear Chucho Valdés play at the Hotel Nacional. At least that's what I thought I was going to hear, one of the world's greatest jazz pianists performing in a small room, but it turned out not to be a concert at all. I had stumbled into an odd event that was half press conference and half cocktail party. In the front of a big conference hall, workers had set up a long table with several microphones and a speaker's podium. Beside the podium was an electric keyboard. Rows of folding chairs faced the table, as in the normal setup for a press conference; a dozen or more photographers and several video crews were busily setting up their lights and cameras. Farther back in the room were big round tables surrounded by chairs, as if someone planned a banquet; the tables were bare, however, except for ashtrays. Hotel waiters were circulating throughout the room with trays laden with strong *mojitos* and greasy hors d'oeuvres.

I couldn't quite classify the crowd—there were people who looked like government functionaries, people who looked like musicians, people who looked like journalists, people who betrayed no affiliation at all—but right in the middle of it, towering over the others, was Chucho himself. I went over to say hello; he was warm but seemed distracted and not necessarily in the best of all possible moods. Whatever this scene was, it wasn't Chucho's.

Nothing happened for the longest time. Then all at once everything happened—the reporters and cameramen rushed to their stations and went on red alert, others took seats in the audience, and
the principals went up to sit behind the microphones at the head
table. Sitting next to Chucho, in what was clearly the seat of honor,
was a man who cut such a ridiculous figure that I wanted to laugh.
He was in his thirties or forties—it was hard to tell, since he was
wearing dark sunglasses—and he had long, unruly black hair that
was partially hidden by a Che Guevara beret. He was wearing Fidel-
style green fatigues that were a couple of sizes too small for his soft,
pudgy, dough-boy form. The line in my notebook reads: "Who is
this clown?"

He turned out to be an Italian pop star of some renown who
was in Cuba to perform. I missed his name, so I wrote it down as
Kid Milano. It seemed he was so taken with Cuba and the revolution that not only had he decided to dress up in this laughable cos-
tume, he had also agreed to lend his support to a big "concert for
peace" that was vaguely being planned for the Piragua. This was
during the run-up to the American invasion of Iraq, and it was clear
that this was the "peace" they were talking about, although everyone denied it. It was just for peace in general, Chucho said when his
brief turn at the microphone came. It was sad to see this towering
musician doing his patriotic duty and playing second fiddle to an
Italian buffoon, but that was a measure of Cuba's profound cultural
isolation. Whenever a big star came to town, whoever it might be,
the visit was automatically a much bigger deal than it should have
been. Cuban musicians were grateful to have contact with practically any of their foreign counterparts, even pop stars like Kid
Milano who were vastly their inferiors, who were unworthy even to
carry their drumsticks or adjust their piano stools. Actually Chucho
was too well known and well traveled to be in any sense grateful for
his participation in this farce. He looked as if he were here to do a
job, to fulfill an obligation, and then it would be over and he could
go home and take a shower.

The reporters in attendance were full of questions. Obviously every resident Havana correspondent for an Italian newspaper or television network had been ordered by his editors to file a story, because they were actually jostling to get in their probing questions for Kid Milano—how had he liked Cuba, what did he think of peace, how much did he hate the American administration. Finally the press conference petered out. Chucho went over to the keyboard, sat down, and began to play. I expected cool jazz, or maybe hot salsa, but what flowed from his fingers was a soulful blues. Chucho played toil and trouble, loss and redemption, pain and sex, joy and misery; Chucho played the blues and filled the room with sweet sadness.

Blue chords, blue mood, blue night, blue world. Blue Havana.

* * *

I ran across Ramón the guitarist one more time. He was at the same spot in Vedado where he liked to play for tourists, but this time he was packing up his guitar under the supervision of two policemen, who stood over him with their game faces on. "*Vamos,*" one of them said, hurrying him along. Ramón muttered curses as he walked away.

"Those sons of whores always chase me away now," he said when I caught up to him. "They know I'm just trying to make a living, and they used to show a little understanding, but now it's different, no questions asked. 'Move along, citizen. Let's go, *negro.*' Couple of stupid hicks, enjoying it. Assholes."

We were on the street, in the open, but his anger trumped all discretion.

"I hate the Old Man," he spat. "Look at what we've come to. I hate him, and I wish him health, because I'm frightened of what will happen when he's gone. There are so many scores to settle. It's going to be brother against brother. That old son of a whore, I wish him a very long life, because after he goes it's going to be much, much worse."

13. LAST DANCE IN HAVANA

ome events have a way of imposing themselves to divide the era into "before" and "after." A series of such knife-edge events swept Cuba in the spring of 2003. None of what happened had anything to do with music, except in the sense that Cuban musicians were witnesses along with their fellow citizens, and like other Cubans had no choice but to take away the appropriate lesson. It was a simple one: in the never-ending dance that is life in today's Cuba, guess who intends to lead?

It's not much of an exaggeration to say that on March 18, 2003, *nobody* was paying attention to Cuba, not even most Cubans. The world was riveted by the drama unfolding in Washington and Baghdad, as it became clear that the U.S.-led invasion of Iraq was imminent. March 18 was the day everyone realized there would be no last-minute reprieve. It was the day when Commander-in-Chief George W. Bush issued his ultimatum to Saddam Hussein and his sons Uday and Qusay, giving them forty-eight hours to get out of town; when the dogged but now disheartened United Nations weapons inspectors finally gave up and flew home to safety; when ordinary Iraqis, after months in denial, began stocking up on food and water for the impending siege. War was coming, it was a matter of days or hours, and the newspapers and talk shows could focus on nothing else.

In Havana, the crafty old dancer-in-chief rose to his feet and began to move.

While the world looked elsewhere, security agents began a series of raids from one end of Fidel Castro's island to the other. Over the next few days, as Bush's deadline expired and the Pentagon commenced its light-show bombardment of Baghdad, Cuban authorities conjured some "shock and awe" of their own, systematically arresting leaders and foot soldiers of the anti-Castro opposition. Nearly a hundred were taken into custody at least briefly; ultimately seventy-five were brought to trial and speedily convicted, most on charges of conspiring with the United States to overthrow the Cuban government. Fidel hadn't resorted to such heavy-handed use of his absolute police power in more than a decade.

To the few outside observers who were paying attention, it looked like a stunning reversal of the recent human-rights trend in Cuba, which had been toward emptying the jails of political prisoners and allowing the island's small community of dissidents to say and do pretty much what they wanted. But to Cubans—and Cubans knew about the arrests because they were reported in the official media, which was unusual and could only have been intended to make a point—this was no departure. It was the culmination of the Big Squeeze that had been tightening for many months.

Some of the accused traitors were people no one outside of Cuba had ever heard of—journalists who worked outside of the state media establishment, or ordinary citizens who had turned their homes into unauthorized "libraries" where Cubans could read books and magazines that were not shelved in the official libraries. Others arrested in the sweep were well-known dissidents, respected in the United States and Europe. Marta Beatriz Roque, an economist who had already served a prison term for criticizing the one-party system, was in the midst of a hunger strike in support of Cuba's two hundred or so existing political prisoners when she was hauled in. Raúl Rivero, the best known of Cuba's "independent" journalists who publish their critical dispatches overseas, was spirited off in the backseat of a Lada, along with garbage bags full of documents that agents seized from his home. The Associated Press reporter who rushed to the scene spoke with Rivero's wife, Blanca Reyes. "He is only a man who writes, he is not a politician," she said. "He knew they would come for him in this wave of repression. But until then he was informing the entire world what was happening here."

This was no clumsy, shoot-them-all purge from the Stalinist handbook. The roundup was highly selective, engineered for maximum effect. Like the best of the artists I'd seen on Cuban dance floors, Fidel had his steps planned out well in advance.

Proof of the raids' precision was that the two most prominent dissidents of all were not even visited, let alone arrested. One of them was Elizardo Sánchez, a disillusioned former professor of Marxism and longtime opponent of the regime who headed the Cuban Commission for Human Rights and National Reconciliation. Sánchez enjoyed great credibility inside and outside of Cuba because of his intelligence and manner—calm, reasoned, professorial—and because of his firm position against the U.S. trade embargo, which he argued was unfairly punitive and ultimately counterproductive. If the aim was to foster the growth of democratic ideas and values in Cuba, he argued, what sense did it make to keep the world's best ambassadors for those values—ordinary Americans—from any meaningful contact with Cubans? And if Fidel Castro had made Cubans poor, what was gained by making them poorer? This stance put him at odds with Miami's anti-Castro leadership but endeared him to Western liberals who also opposed the embargo. To many people outside of Cuba he looked like Castro's most impressive opponent, and it was odd that he hadn't been arrested.

Also left at large was the opposition figure of the moment, a man who had hit on an idea with the potential to cause Castro real problems. Oswaldo Payá was the leader of the Varela Project, a petition drive seeking to force Castro to allow opposition political parties, free elections, and a free press. Payá and his Christian Liberation Movement had scrupulously worked within the restrictions of Castro's own constitution to organize and conduct their petition campaign, which had drawn eleven thousand signatures, enough to force a public referendum on political change. Former president Jimmy Carter had given Payá's efforts a tremendous boost during his visit to Cuba in 2002, when he mentioned the Varela Project in a televised speech. Payá seemed to have caught Fidel flat-footed; the government quickly staged its own petition drive in favor of continued one-party socialism, which of course drew more than a million signatures, and then took the further step of passing new legislation that guaranteed the current one-party system in perpetuity. But the Varela petitions wouldn't go away—they satisfied all the legal requirements and the government didn't seem to know how to respond. It was hard to imagine Fidel's considering Payá anything but his current Public Enemy Number One. When the time came, though, he left the man alone.

Maybe Sánchez and Payá were too high profile. Maybe Fidel had decided they were untouchable. Or maybe this was another spin, another twirl—another move too subtle for slower dancers to understand.

A hint of Fidel's real purpose didn't dawn until several months later, when two officially sanctioned Cuban journalists—meaning that they were thoroughly vetted, politically sound, and working for the state—published a book alleging that Sánchez was in fact a double agent who worked for the government's security services. The book was full of names of alleged traitors, dates of alleged meetings, details of alleged conversations. It even included a photograph of Sánchez being awarded a decoration by a high-ranking Cuban intelligence officer, supposedly for information he had provided on dissidents and their contacts with shadowy paymasters in the United States.

Sánchez categorically denied being a spy, but admitted having met with security agents—at their instigation, he said—to try to open a channel for dialogue. The book was an obvious attempt to discredit him and his work, Sánchez said; if he were a spy, would he have spent four years in prison for opposing Fidel? Most of the dissidents who remained at large, including Payá, accepted his denial at face value. But the question had been raised, and the photograph was indeed troublesome. Perhaps Sánchez's longtime friends and associates could dismiss the whole thing as disinformation. But what about potential dissidents who might be looking for a figure to rally around? What were they supposed to think?

And even about Payá, what were people to think? Rumor had it that another state-sponsored book was soon to be published, with him as the subject. The Varela Project was fairly well known, thanks to Carter's intervention. It was a direct slap in the face of Fidel and the revolution. How could Fidel arrest so many others and let the most insolent of all remain free? Did this at least raise the possibility that Payá, too, might have had meetings and associations that no one knew about? Could he be trusted?

The truth was that *nobody* could be trusted. At the dissidents' slam-dunk trials, it was revealed that the whole anti-Castro movement was thoroughly infiltrated by government spies. Some were leaders of active organizations. Some had been in place for decades. Practically from the start, the dissidents hadn't made a move without Fidel's knowledge.

One example: In the days after the dissident arrests, American newspapers profiled Manuel David Orrio as a brave outsider who had somehow escaped the government's net. Orrio, president of the independent Federation of Cuban Journalists, was a former Marxist economist who had changed sides and now wrote stories for CubaNet.org, a Miami-based Web site funded by the U.S. government. Most of his work consisted of unflattering portraits of the Cuban government's economic failures; one vivid story, for example, told of a homeless man in Havana who rummaged for food in garbage cans. Orrio's was a stirring tale, and it was a lie: at Rivero's trial it was revealed that he was actually a government agent, code-named "Miguel." He testified for the prosecution.

Also testifying against Rivero was "Octavio," an eighty-two-year-old spy who boasted that he had been an undercover agent for an astounding forty years; not long before the arrests, U.S. officials in Havana had asked him to help lead a workshop on journalistic ethics. Agent "Tania" had been the leader of something called the Pro-Human Rights Party, apparently a shell organization meant to do little but confuse people looking for Sánchez's larger, well-established group. Another spy worked as the secretary for a dissident group, meaning that to gather her information all she had to do was answer the phone.

Mostly, the spies testified about money. Their main purpose appeared to be to bolster the government's contention that the dissidents were in fact "mercenaries" financed by the U.S. government in its never-ending campaign to destroy the Cuban revolution. There wasn't much money to testify about, mostly the small sums—as little as twenty dollars per article—that the journalists were paid by U.S.-based Web sites, some of which were indeed financed with U.S. government funds. "Tania" said U.S. groups paid her nearly five hundred dollars a month. And Cuban officials said that one of the arrested independent journalists was found with nearly fourteen thousand dollars hidden in the lining of a suit, and claimed—with at least partial justification, apparently—that the money could be traced to Uncle Sam.

U.S. officials were left sputtering. The Cuban government's stated rationale for the arrests—that James Cason, installed by the Bush administration as head of the U.S. Interests Section in Havana, had been unusually aggressive and open in his courting of the dissidents and undiplomatically bold in stating his aim of overthrowing the Castro regime—was objectively true. Cason's policies hadn't differed materially from those of his predecessors, but he was so public in meeting with the dissidents, and so strident in his attacks on the regime, that Cuban officials took it personally. Plus, there was the Bush factor. As far as the Cuban government was concerned, George W. Bush had been elected only because he took Florida, where his margin of victory came from the votes of the anti-Castro Miami exile community. Therefore Bush and his brother Jeb, the governor of Florida, were in hock to the "Miami mafia." Therefore there was no telling what reckless measures the administration might take toward Cuba, up to and including a possible invasion. There could even be a new Bay of Pigs invasion, sold to the American public as a necessary battle in the War on Terrorism! These people would stop at nothing!

There are those who believe Fidel rounded up the dissidents because he was genuinely worried about the impact they were having, particularly the Varela Project, though given the number of spies he had in place, one wonders if the movement could have done him much damage. There are those who believe he acted out of pique with the United States—though Cason's activities, while clumsy, didn't seem to pose any real threat. There are those who think he needed to magnify the enemy in order to justify his own iron-fisted rule—though on many occasions in the past, when U.S. sentiment had been turning toward improved relations, he had managed to raise the temperature without resorting to arrests and show trials that would also anger his European friends (which the Cuban economy could ill afford) and require unmasking a dozen of his more productive spies.

More likely, I think, was that the whole thing was strictly for internal consumption—to let Cubans know who was still in control, and how firmly. That seems to make even more sense in light of how Fidel handled the other big before-and-after event of the spring of 2003: the hijackings.

* * *

The months leading up to the crackdown on the dissident movement had seen an increase in attempted hijackings of Cuban passenger aircraft, with the aim of escaping to the United States. This was not the wisest choice of action by any standard. One thing the U.S. and Cuban governments had formally agreed on was that hijackings in either direction, whether by would-be Cuban exiles or latter-day Charlie Hills, were under no circumstances to be tolerated any longer; if the hijackers managed to reach their destination in either country, they would be punished to the full extent of the law. But in Cuba these were desperate times. In the seven months leading up to March there were four hijackings or full-blown attempts. Cuban officials say they uncovered and prevented two dozen other serious plots.

On March 19, while agents were still rounding up the dissidents, six hijackers commandeered a passenger plane and forced the pilot to fly them to Key West. On April 1, another passenger plane was forced to fly to Key West, this time by a Cuban man armed with fake hand grenades. In both cases, U.S. authorities arrested the hijackers and charged them with crimes that would bring them long prison terms. Passengers were given the choice of going home to Cuba or remaining in the United States. Most went back; a few stayed. The system worked the way it was supposed to work, but two hijackings in two weeks was rare and for the Cuban authorities must have been alarming.

Then on the morning of April 2, eleven men and women armed with knives and at least one pistol hijacked a ferryboat as it crossed Havana Bay and demanded to be taken to the United States. This made *three* hijackings in two weeks, and not only that: this last one, involving a ferry, was eerily like the 1994 ferry hijacking that had led to deaths on the high seas, a serious riot back home in Centro Habana, and ultimately concessions by the government. This time, Fidel was in no mood for concessions.

About thirty passengers were aboard the ferry *Baraguá,* along with two French tourists. The boat was slow and unsteady, certainly not a vessel to take out onto the high seas. The Cuban coast guard would have caught up quickly, even if the *Baraguá* hadn't run out of fuel. The hijackers threatened to start shooting passengers or throwing them overboard if they weren't somehow conveyed to Florida. Eventually coast guard officers persuaded them to let the ferry be towed back to Cuba for refueling. It landed at the port of Mariel about thirty miles west of Havana, the departure point for the infamous boat lift that two decades earlier had brought many thousands of Cubans to American shores.

Fidel reportedly went to Mariel to take charge of the negotiations personally. Despite lots of bluster and threats on both sides, not much progress was made until one of the French hostages suddenly jumped overboard. She explained later that she was afraid the hijackers were about to start shooting people, and she was almost right. The members of the gang who saw her go over the side scrambled fore and aft to try to find the man who was holding what may have been their one functional firearm, in order to have him shoot at the crazy Frenchwoman in the water.

But amid the confusion, before the gun could even be found, Cuban commandos stormed the *Baraguá* without loss of life. That was the end of the beginning of this short brutal story.

Within nine days, the hijackers had been tried and sentenced. Three women were given relatively short prison terms of less than five years; one man got thirty years; four men were condemned to life in prison; and three men, described as "the most active and brutal leaders" of the hijacking, were sentenced to death.

The government communiqué announcing the disposition of the cases noted that the death sentences had already been carried out by firing squad.

The idea that criminals, even hijackers, could be found guilty and executed barely a week after committing their crimes was hard to accept even in the United States, with its general support of the death penalty. For soft-on-Cuba liberals, it was impossible to swallow. And in Europe, where the death penalty is seen as sheer barbarism, the executions were a terrible blow to Cuba's image.

But none of that mattered. Fidel Castro was making a point to his fellow Cubans, and he wanted to be as clear as he could be: no more hijackings. There would be no riots, no concessions, no ceding of control. There would be none of *this*, not while he was still calling the tunes.

* * *

The hijackings ceased.

The dissidents struggled in disarray.

The issue of control was settled.

No one in Cuba had any doubt anymore about where things stood, at least for the time being. The reimposition of restrictions on private enterprise, on nightlife, on public gatherings, on displays of personal liberty in general had become not policy but fact.

This is not to say that Cuba, or Cubans, had regressed to the Soviet era. Nothing had fundamentally changed: the peso-based economy was still moribund, dollars were still necessary to make it to the end of the month, tourists and overseas relatives were still the sources of those dollars. But survival was even harder than before, because Cubans couldn't count on the government to look the other way while they stretched or broke the laws in order to take care of their needs. It was necessary to be more discreet, to take extra care. Necessarily, things would be much tougher, at least for a while.

Not everyone could take it. Escapes and defections seemed to pick up, although it was hard to tell—the summer months, before hurricane season, are often restless. One inventive family group tried to sail to Florida in a vintage pickup truck, which they had floated on improvised pontoons and rigged with a propeller. They didn't make it. U.S. authorities intercepted them in the Strait, and the wet-foot, dry-foot rule specifies that those Cubans who manage to reach dry land are allowed to stay while those encountered at sea are sent home. The pictures of a fifty-year-old truck motoring across the Florida Strait were priceless; in a just world, its crew would have received extra credit for creativity.

A couple of star baseball players escaped, apparently by boat. A couple of dancers defected while on tour. And then one high-profile defection overshadowed all the others.

At the beginning of June, the teen-idol singer Carlos Manuel— the one I'd seen at the soulless Casa de la Música "2"—was performing in Mexico City when he told his band that he didn't intend to return to Cuba.

The last time the singer had performed in Florida, two musicians and two technicians had defected, according to an Associated Press account. Carlos Manuel had returned to Cuba, however, and this may have inspired trust on the part of Cuban officials. That may explain why his mother, his sister, and the sister's boyfriend were all allowed to accompany the band to Mexico. They weren't planning to go home either.

Officials at the Cuban embassy were somehow alerted—they keep an eye on traveling celebrities as a matter of course—and made a predawn visit to the singer's hotel, according to the A.P.; they convinced the other band members to return to Cuba, but Carlos Manuel and his family avoided the Cubans by fleeing to another hotel. The next morning, they flew to Monterrey, took a cab to Matamoros, and crossed the border to Brownsville, Texas, where they turned themselves in to U.S. immigration authorities. Within days he had turned up in Miami.

Manuel said he had left Cuba because he was "tired of all the hypocrisy," and he mentioned the recent arrests of the dissidents. But he also mentioned his career frustrations as a reason for his departure—"I'm ambitious. I want to go all the way with my music"—and he sounded almost apologetic toward the Cuban nation he was leaving behind.

"I want to send a message to my people," he was quoted as saying. "One day, you will realize what the world is really like, and you will like me again."

* * *

In November 2003, I went back to Cuba to see what the crackdown had wrought. I found that everything had changed and nothing had changed.

The musicians I'd come to know were continuing to make their way, or at least most of them were.

Juan de Marcos was out of town, which was normal. He was still surfing the Buena Vista wave, which might have been waning but hadn't yet died. The albums put out by his assortment of groups were still selling well, concerts on his international tours were drawing good crowds and rave reviews, and meanwhile he was still searching for the Next Big Thing in Cuban music.

Bamboleo was still on fire, at least at home. The group was perhaps more popular than ever in Havana, its concerts having reached "event" status. There still was no new Bamboleo album for the international audience, though. Instead, Lazarito Valdés had released a solo album of jazz piano. It got enthusiastic reviews but made no impact in the American marketplace. Vannia Borges, the most recent Bamboleo singer to leave the group, had taken time off from her pursuit of a solo career to have her first child, a daughter; she was currently working herself, and her voice, back into shape. The *orisha* Yemanyá was still her protectress.

Ebano, the all-girl *timba* group, had completely disintegrated. The odds had been against Moraima, Daulema, and their friends from the beginning, and they never managed to accomplish the one thing all successful groups have to do: get noticed by somebody important. The government's Big Squeeze hadn't helped, because the closure of so many Havana nightspots limited the venues where an untested band might get a gig, but the die was probably cast much earlier. At last report, Ebano's singers were trying to constitute themselves as a new group, as yet unnamed.

And the Cuban hip-hop nation had gone underground. The weekly show had been moved out of Café Cantante and was reportedly going to resurface soon, somewhere. The ninth annual rap festival in Alamar had come and gone without incident: no "Denuncia Social," no lyrics that strayed dangerously across the line. The Cuban state, in fulfilling its solemn responsibility to promote Cuban culture, had exercised more control than ever before over who got to perform, and thus over what was said. Nothing to speak of had reached the record stores from the new state-run hip-hop music agency. The government's embrace of the rap movement had immobilized it—at least the small part the government could get its arms around.

But other groups, those without government sanction, were trying to emulate Clan 537's end-run around the state and nab their own overseas record contracts. And out of reach and mostly out of sight, hip-hop continued to grow. You had to pay attention to notice. You had to listen to what kids were playing on their boom boxes, pay attention to the young aspiring rappers practicing their flow on street corners; you had to notice how, when you got away from the tourist zones, the soundtrack switched from Buena Vista nostalgia to hard-edged rap. Hip-hop was gaining ground, and among its conquests was carnival.

Havana's annual carnival happened to be taking place while I was there, which in itself was unusual. Usually the festival is held in July, which coincides with the anniversary of the beginning of Fidel Castro's revolution. But in 2003 Cuba had staged a big fiftieth-anniversary commemoration of the revolution's birth—pegged at July 26, 1953, the date of Fidel's disastrous but glory-filled raid on the Moncada Barracks, the first act of armed rebellion—and since that had to be in July, carnival had been moved to November where it would also mark the anniversary of the founding of Havana. The city was 486 years old, and officials hoped to finish a massive restoration project in Old Havana and along the Malecón in time for five hundred.

For carnival the city erects grandstands on the Malecón from Old Havana to Vedado, and also blocks off some of the major streets in Centro Habana. Each day for two weeks, the Malecón is closed to automobile traffic from two in the afternoon until two in the morning so that it can be used for parades, dancing, and beer drinking on an epic scale. Beer stations are set up at one-block intervals, stalls where vendors dispense beer from industrial-size drums; revelers fill up their plastic two-liter soft drink bottles or their Big Gulp–size paper cups, and then guzzle and shimmy their way to the next dispensary. Near the beer stalls there was usually a Porta-Potty, but often only one, which made for long lines and a certain acrid tang in the air.

The crowds were claustrophobically thick, even when nothing special was going on. I saw a few falling-down drunks and a few belligerent drunks and a few manic drunks, and I'd been warned that carnival was the year's biggest payday for pickpockets, but I encountered no real trouble. In general the carnival goers were like other crowds I'd mixed with in Cuba—polite, unthreatening, good natured. For most of the afternoon and evening there was no actual entertainment being staged. At some point the parades would begin—floats built by proud work units from around the city, groups of drummers comprising a neighborhood's finest—but that didn't seem to be why people came to carnival. They came to drink, and to dance.

For most of the time, at various points along the Malecón loudspeakers blared loud recorded music and people danced. Most of the dancers were young people, and most of the music was hip-hop. It was a dislocating experience to walk down the Malecón, the boulevard by the sea, just ninety miles from the enemy, and hear Nelly boasting about his "Air Force Ones" or Missy urging the crowd to "Work It," as if the exhortation were needed.

In this gyrating, grinding, working-it multitude of young men and women along the seafront in Centro Habana, something new was being born.

Like it or not, the Cuban revolution had produced, and now would have to deal with, a hip-hop generation—a cohort of young people who had no memory of life before the Special Period, who knew all about the promises the Cuban revolution had broken and very little about the promises it had kept. Cubans in their teens and twenties knew only of the housing shortage that forced them to sleep on couches or in uncomfortable lofts, knew only of the scramble for dollars and the laughable inadequacy of salaries paid in pesos; for them, there was nothing young or experimental about Fidel's revolution, nothing bold or new. They were not organized into any kind of political force—in fact, they seemed notably apolitical—and they had shown no hint of desire to overthrow the only system they had ever known. But they were united by a single, universal wish: that the future somehow be strikingly different from the present, which offered them so little. Hip-hop was a part of that mind-set, with its defiance of authority and its evocation of community. Politically, that wasn't much to put your finger on. Culturally, it was a revolutionary mind-set.

There were no images like the ones of shipworkers on strike in Gdansk, no pictures of headband-wearing students in Tiananmen

Square. But no one said that the new Cuban revolution had to be televised.

* * *

Before I came home, there was one last chance to hear live music: Los Van Van were playing at the Habana Café.

The Habana Café was a local variation on the Hard Rock Cafe and Planet Hollywood concepts. The motif in this case was automotive; littered around the big room were the shiny shells of vintage American cars. I suppose it was the thought that counted, but all the cars really did was deprive the place of some much-needed seating space. Who needed to see old cars inside a bar when there were so many outside on the streets? The place had terrible acoustics too, but it was small enough to have an intimacy that no other venue in the city matched. It was also a decidedly upscale nightspot—it occupied a wing of the five-star Meliá Cohiba hotel complex, and it charged a hefty fifteen-dollar cover—which gave a spritz of glamour to the whole scene.

When I arrived, the velvet ropes were being guarded by one of the larger bouncers I've ever seen. Inside there was standing room only, with every table occupied and big crowds clustered alongside the two long bars.

The band cooked, as usual. Founder and bassist Juan Formell didn't show, but hardly anyone had expected him to; he was in his sixties and had been ill, and in recent months had served more as musical director than instrumentalist. His replacement, who played Formell's trademark white electric bass, was more than capable.

I did see someone I hadn't expected, though: Mario "Mayito" Rivera, one of the band's great singers, was in his usual spot. About a year earlier he had left the band to go out on his own, and the band had suffered. Now, suddenly, he was back—and not coincidentally, according to friends who knew the scene, had moved to a nice new house in Vedado. According to the rumor mill, Formell had asked for help from his friend Fidel in getting his star singer back. The story was that Fidel had offered the house as an incentive to return to the fold.

It turned out that Mayito was responsible for two indelible moments from that concert, two moments that for me encapsulated the contradictions of Cuba as the end of Fidel Castro's time approaches.

One moment was the opening song, which Mayito sang. Musically, it was classic Los Van Van—a churning, rocking *timba* groove that suddenly morphed into Weather Report's "Birdland." But the lyrics were hardly more than patriotic political sloganeer-ing. There were lines that celebrated Cuba but also lines that made unsubtle digs at the United States. The song reminded me of those embarrassing, opportunistic, bash-the-enemy country songs that always come out of Nashville whenever U.S. forces are sent to fight in a war.

But at least the Nashville tunes find a receptive audience; Mayito's flag waving was getting no rise out of the crowd at the Habana Café. It was his duty to sing the song and it was the duty of the audience to listen. That was the part of Cuba that hadn't changed, and that seemed unlikely to change: Fidel Castro was the leader, the one leader, and his leadership imposed inescapable duties.

The other moment came when Mayito sang "Soy Todo," the band's famous Afro-Cuban hymn. When the band is really on, as it was this evening, the song is transfixing to Cuban audiences. The dance floor fills and the dancers all fall into the song's hypnotic, al-most trancelike rhythms, while Mayito talks to the Yoruba oracle Orula and asks what is to become of him and what is to become of Cuba. Mayito professes faith in the *orishas* and demands to know his fate, Cuba's fate, and the whole crowd joins the backup singers in the chanted response, *"Ay Dios, ampárame!"*—"Oh God, protect me!"— and the rhythm and the tension build and build, without release.

Finally Mayito falls to his knees and asks the oracle one final question, on behalf of all Cubans. "Answer me, answer me!" he screams. *"¿Somos o no somos?"*

It was an innocent palindrome, a child's first word-game, but in context an accusation: Are we, or are we not?

The Habana Café erupted as everyone joined in, dancers and drinkers and hustlers and hookers and bartenders and bouncers and busboys, every single Cuban in the joint yelling "*¿Somos o no somos? ¿Somos o no somos? ¿Somos o no somos?*" Even in live performances, the song fades out. There is never a response. Over and over again the question rang out, and there was no answer. When the sun rose the next morning, Fidel Castro was one day older and his island was one day closer to the next revolution—the day when each Cuban will have to answer the question for himself.

APPENDIX: A LISTENER'S GUIDE TO CUBA

Contemporary Cuban music is not as easy to find in American record stores as it should be—that's one of the artists' greatest frustrations. Well-stocked outlets in big cities and college towns usually have at least a minimal selection. A more promising route is through the Internet, where Web sites specializing in Latin music offer a comprehensive selection of Cuban sounds.

Here are a few suggestions for getting a sense of what Cuba sounds like today:

Afro Cuban All Stars—Juan de Marcos, the savvy leader of this impeccable big band, takes music from the '40s and '50s and gives it a modern gloss with contemporary orchestrations and young, talented musicians. "Distinto, Diferente" is a good example.

Adalberto Álvarez y Su Son—a consistently popular Cuban band with a sound as smooth and refined as seven-year-old Cuban rum. Álvarez starts with traditional Cuban *son*, the basis of salsa, and gives it a modern twist. The result is either salsa with attitude or *timba* with manners. *Jugando con Candela* and *Suena Cubano* both show the band in top form.

Los Van Van—the unchallenged kings of the Havana scene. *Te Pone la Cabeza Mala* rocks from start to finish; *Llego . . . Van Van* is brilliant; and the live album *En el Malecón de la Habana* includes a great version of the Yoruba prayer "Soy Todo."

NG La Banda—an amazing band whose recordings, unfortunately, don't capture the energy and excitement of a live performance. A couple of exceptions: *En la Calle* is an early album that burns; *Échale Limon* shows the band in good form; and best of all is *En Directo Desde el Patio de Mi Casa*, recorded live before a Havana audience.

Bamboleo—this band's unique sound has overtones of 1970s American funk. *Ya No Hace Falta* is probably my favorite *timba* album, period; *Yo No Me Parezco a Nadie* gives an idea of what Bamboleo sounded like with its two original singers, Haila and Vannia; and there's a *Best Of . . .* compilation that includes some of the best of those two CDs.

La Charanga Habanera—the fastest, wildest, most inventive band on the Havana scene, the aural equivalent of a jolt of caffeine. *Soy Cubano, Soy Popular* is a good choice; *Chan Chan Charanga* includes an incendiary update of an old song from the Buena Vista Social Club days; and *Charanguero Mayor* is pure Cuban party music.

Orishas—the first, and so far only, group to come out of the Cuban hip-hop scene and make a dent in the international market. It's a sign of Cuba's isolation that the group had to leave the island to make its mark; the four rappers are now based in Paris, where their breakthrough album, *A Lo Cubano*, was recorded.

Cuban Hip Hop All Stars, Vol. 1—a sampler CD featuring tracks from several of Cuba's most popular home-grown hip-hop groups. The production values are uneven, but Spanish speakers will be fascinated by the lyrics—angry denunciations of racism and police brutality, and bleak portraits of daily life in Havana's forgotten neighborhoods.

Clan 537—the main attraction of the group's eponymous first album is the controversial song the Cuban government "suspended" from the airwaves, "¿Quién Tiró la Tiza?" But the rest of the album is worth a listen too.

For those who want to explore further, the direction to go is back toward Cuban music's roots:

Los Muñequitos de Matanzas—an acclaimed ensemble whose

music is stripped to the bare Afro-Cuban essentials—drums, more drums, fine voices, total commitment, abiding faith. The group's *Live in New York* album gives a sense of how rhythms brought across the Atlantic by slaves evolved into the salsa, *timba* and hip-hop of today.

Beny Moré—a seminal figure in Cuban music of the '40s and '50s. He was a prolific genius of rhythm, and his improvisational singing style has influenced every Cuban vocalist since. It's hard to choose among the many compilations on the market, but the good news is that Beny Moré is one of the few artists whose work is easy to find in U.S. record stores.

Celia Cruz—not much remains to be said about one of the greatest singers of the twentieth century, in any genre. Her voice was a gift from the *orishas*. When she left her beloved island for the United States, Fidel Castro's radio stations stopped playing her music. But when she died, after forty years in exile, all of Cuba mourned.

ACKNOWLEDGMENTS

This book would not exist but for the support, encouragement and forbearance of my wife, Avis, and our sons Lowell and Aaron, and to them I offer my most profound gratitude and love. Many others were instrumental in making it a better book than it otherwise could have been. My friend and colleague, the photographer Dudley M. Brooks, was a full partner in exploring the many riddles of contemporary Cuba; without his help, many doors would have gone unopened and questions unanswered. Charles Hill was the best possible guide to Havana and the rest of the island, and also a loyal friend. The Cuban musicians who welcomed me so warmly, and so cheered my soul with their fearsome excellence, all deserve my thanks; a few among them—Juan de Marcos, Lázaro Valdés, Giraldo Piloto, Pablo Herrera, Reynor Hernández, Moraima Marín, Vannia Borges—were so patient with me that I must mention them by name. The greatest amateur boxer in history, Teófilo Stevenson, is not mentioned in this book but was instrumental in helping me understand what it means to be Cuban (and how to throw a left jab). Nehanda Abiodun was my entrée to the Cuban hip-hop world.

My agent, Rafe Sagalyn, discerned the outlines of a book where others did not. My editor at Free Press, Bruce Nichols, applied his sharp eye for structural weakness and unerring ear for facile cant, and helped me replace this cardboard with sterner stuff. The lapses that remain are mine alone.

I thank my colleagues at the *Washington Post*, both the great journalists I work for and the great journalists who work for me, for tolerating the absences the reporting of this book necessitated. I thank the Cuban officials who welcomed me back again and again, whether my newspaper articles had been to their liking or not.

And finally, I open my heart in gratitude to the people of Cuba, who taught me what it means to dance.

INDEX

Erik B. and Rakim, 112
escapes, increase in, 251–252
executions, in Cuba, 250
exiles, American, in Cuba, 189–204
Explosión Suprema, 106, 107, 114,
    123, 216

Familia Cubana, at Cabaret Las
    Vegas, 123
The Family, 193
fashion, in Cuba, 5
Fernández, Alina, 49
Fernández, Ariel, 116–120, 189, 194
Ferrer, Ibrahim, in Buena Vista
    Social Club, 28–29, 30, 175
film (camera), availability of,
    217–218
Finney, Michael, 198–199, 202
"The Fisherman," in Elián story, 60
Florida, refugees to, 35, 155–156,
    157, 247
Formell, Juan (Los Van Van), 43,
    45, 46, 256
Fox, Vicente, Castro's grudge
    against, 221–222
freestyling contest, 106
Fuentevilla, Daulema (Ebano), 90,
    93–94, 181–185, 253
fun, importance of, 236–237
funk, Bamboleo's use of, 87
future, uncertainty of, 18–19

Garzón, Leocadia "Chicha," 109
gay community, 233
Gold, Nick, 28
González, Ana María, 97–98
González, Elián, 22–23
    billboards of, 55, 57
    house of, 80–81
    media coverage of, 59–60
    public opinion on, 63, 66, 75, 78
    story of, 60–61
González, Juan Miguel, 61, 79
González, Rubén, 30
Goodwin, Ralph, 198–199, 202
government. See also Castro Ruz,
    Fidel
    Afro-Cuban faith and, 139
    age and, 53–54
    black Cubans in, 156
    control of
        over hip-hop, 212–213,
            214–215
        over media, 67
        reassertion of, 217,

        228–229, 232–241, 243
    control over, 158
    as father figure, 213
    freedoms granted by, 117, 156,
        217
    hip-hop supported by, 114,
        115–116, 208, 214–215
    people's "bargain" with, 236–237
    racism and, 156–157
Granma (yacht), 108, 116
Great Man scheme of history,
    61–62
Guerrillero Heróico (Korda), 95
Guevara, Che, 53–54, 95–96, 146,
    161, 187–188

Habana Café, 256–258
Habana Libre, 1
Haila. See Mompié, Haila
Hancock, Herbie, 15
hardship, virtue and, 54–55
Havana, 23–24, 155
Hemingway, Ernest, 109–110
Hernández, Reynor (Explosión
    Suprema), 105–106, 107,
    112–113, 188–189
Herrera, Pablo, 106, 108, 120–123,
    194, 211–213, 215
hijackings, 248–250
Hill, Charlie, 198–203, 216,
    228–229
hip-hop (Cuban), 253
    birth of, 111–112
    at carnival, 255
    at Casa de la Música 2, 215–219
    Communist, 214–215, 216
    criticism in, vs. dissent, 119–120
    Cuban music sampled in, 122
    future of, 115
    government and
        controlled by, 212–213,
            214–215
        interference of, 206–208
        position on, 119, 187
        supported by, 114,
            115–116, 119–120, 208
    issues addressed in, 106–107,
        113, 121
    Juan de Marcos and, 178
    lyrics in, 106–107, 122–123
    maturation of, 212–213
    in modern music, xi
    Nehanda Abiodun and, 191–192,
        194–195
    officialist, 207

ABOUT THE AUTHOR

Eugene Robinson is assistant managing editor of the *Washington Post*, where he edits the award-winning Style section. His prior positions at the *Post* include foreign editor, London bureau chief, and South American correspondent. He was born in Orangeburg, South Carolina, and is an alumnus of the University of Michigan and Harvard University's Nieman Fellowship program. He is the author of *Coal to Cream: A Black Man's Journey Beyond Color to an Affirmation of Race* (Free Press, 1999). He lives with his wife, Avis, and their two sons in Arlington, Virginia.